SALT WATER
FISHING TACTICS

LEARN FROM
THE EXPERTS AT

Salt Water
SPORTSMAN
MAGAZINE

CREATIVE
PUBLISHING
international

MINNETONKA, MINNESOTA

Salt Water Sportsman
Salt Water Fishing Tactics

Introduction by Barry Gibson, Editor, SALT WATER SPORTSMAN

President: Iain Macfarlane
Group Director, Book Development: Zoe Graul
Director, Creative Development: Lisa Rosenthal
Executive Managing Editor: Elaine Perry

Executive Editor, Outdoor Group: Don Oster
Project Leader and Article Editor: David L. Tieszen
Managing Editor: Denise Bornhausen
Associate Creative Director: Brad Springer
Photo Researcher: Angie Spann
Copy Editor: Janice Cauley
Mac Production: Joe Fahey
Desktop Publishing Specialist: Laurie Kristensen
Publishing Production Manager: Kim Gerber
Cover Credits: John Carroll Doyle: sailfish painting, Andy Anderson: background,
    Bill Lindner: bottom left, Al Ristori: bottom center, Gary Kramer: bottom right
Endpaper Illustrations: by Peter Goadby from *Saltwater Gamefishing; Offshore and Onshore,*
reproduced with permission by HarperCollins Publishers

Special thanks to: Richard S. Alfano, President, *Salt Water Sportsman*; Barry Gibson, Rip
Cunningham, Scott Boyan, Chris Powers, and the staff of *Salt Water Sportsman* magazine

Contributing Photographers: Andy Anderson, Joel Arrington, Tony Arruza/Bruce
Coleman, Inc., Chip Bates, Scott Boyan, William Boyce, Dick Brown, Hanson Carroll,
Pete Cooper, Jr., S. L. Craig, Jr./Bruce Coleman, Inc., Angelo Cuanang, Ray Dittenhoefer,
Richard Gibson, Jim Hendricks, Kenneth J. Howard, Scott Kerrigan, Gary Kramer, Lefty
Kreh, Bill Lindner, David Linkiewicz, Bob McNally, Ron McPeak, Brian O'Keefe, Bob
O'Shaughnessy, C. Boyd Pfeiffer, John E. Phillips, George Poveromo, Tom Richardson,
Al Ristori, Michael A. Rivlin, Jim Rizzuto, David J. Sams/Texas Inprint, Robert Sloan,
Sam Talarico, Earl & Deborah Waters

Contributing Illustrators: Chris Armstrong, Dan Daly, John Dyess, Steve T. Goione, David
McHose, *Salt Water Sportsman*, Dave Shepherd

Printed on American Paper by: R. R. Donnelley & Sons Co.

03 02 01 00 99 / 5 4 3 2 1

Library of Congress Cataloging–in–Publication Data

Salt water fishing tactics : learn from the experts at Salt water
  sportsman magazine
     p. cm.
  Includes index
  ISBN 0-86573-085-7 (hardcover)
  1. Salt water fishing.   I. Salt water sportsman.
SH457.S324 1999
799. 1'6--dc21   98-49172

Table of Contents

Introduction

I t wasn't too long ago that salt water anglers were perceived to be divided into two distinct groups – the well-heeled "sports" who worked blue water aboard flashy cruisers in pursuit of marlin and other big-game species, and the everyday folks with baited hand-lines who crowded piers, jetties, and party boats in quest of a fresh seafood dinner. There didn't seem to be a whole lot of fishermen in between.

That's all changed today, of course. A dizzying selection of quality tackle along with a vast array of affordable boats, motors, and marine electronics has opened up the sport of salt water fishing to some ten million Americans from all walks of life. From the beaches of New Jersey to the Gulf's offshore oil rigs and up to the salmon-rich waters of the Northwest, more and more anglers are plying shorelines, bays, and open ocean in search of their favorite gamesters. Indeed, salt water fishing has become the number-one recreational activity in nearly half our coastal states today and ranks within the top five in many others. It's here to stay, and it's growing.

Fishing has become more user-friendly, too. A modern spinning outfit and a half hour of instruction can transform a novice into a competent surf caster, and today's high-tech artificial lures feature lifelike actions that go head-to-head with live bait in tempting game fish into striking. Compact, state-of-the-art navigation equipment provides even the most casual boat angler with the ability to find productive wrecks, reefs, and other hot spots, and sophisticated fishfinders help us zero-in on our quarry when we get there. Clearly we have the means to make some pretty impressive catches.

But as the new millennium dawns, many of us find that we can't seem to carve out as much fishing time from our busy schedules as we'd like. Family and career demands plus a host of other leisure-time interests compete for our attention, so days on the water are often at a premium. And when we do get out, we don't want to spend a lot of time behind the learning curve. We want to get right into the action.

That's where *Salt Water Fishing Tactics* comes in. This is a book that cuts to the chase. You won't find any long, involved history of the sport, boring backgrounders, or space wasted by some Izaak Walton wannabe philosophizing about the true meaning of fishing. What you will find is 175 pages of solid, proven how-to guidance from some of the most distinguished anglers/writers in the business. Each chapter author in this compendium is a recognized expert in at least one particular facet of the sport, and each contributes to *Salt Water Sports-*

man, a monthly magazine established in 1939 that continues to enjoy a sterling reputation for providing the most factual, useful, and timely marine sport fishing information found anywhere on the globe. Each writer is a hands-on fisherman first – many are long-standing guides and charterboat captains – and draws from years of experience on the water. And none hold back on providing inside information – even "trade secrets" and their own hard-earned personal discoveries – that will quickly help you put your fair share of fish on the beach or in the boat. That's the deal we have with them. And they certainly keep their end of the bargain.

Subjects covered in *Salt Water Fishing Tactics* range from the most basic to the advanced and are divided into four categories – general techniques and helpful information; fishing from shore; inshore boat fishing, and offshore fishing. If you're just getting started in the sport there are chapters on rigging terminal tackle, bottom-fishing fundamentals, surf- and fly-casting techniques, and pier fishing. If you've got a little experience under your belt yet want to catch more or bigger striped bass, halibut or seatrout, or scout out productive new grounds for red drum or yellowtail, you'll find plenty of helpful advice to jump-start you on your way. And if you're an offshore buff who enjoys the challenge of chasing billfish, tuna, sharks, kingfish, and other top-rated big game and want to fine-tune your tactics, there are plenty of up-to-the-minute tricks to help you win that big tournament. It's the kind of detailed information and guidance that'll help you get the most enjoyment out of those precious hours spent on the water pursuing your favorite species.

Many of the chapters consist of updated and refined versions of some of the most valuable and acclaimed how-to articles that have appeared in *Salt Water Sportsman,* and others are brand-new, commissioned exclusively for this book. And because there's such a variety of contributors, you'll find a wide range of readable, enjoyable writing and presentation styles, including first-person accounts of successful fishing trips when special techniques or a bit of extra insight really paid off. And, of course, you'll find the conservation and catch-and-release ethic woven into many of the articles to highlight the importance of sound conservation, so that we'll have plenty of fish to catch in the future.

It's all here, to be shared, and we hope it will help you become a more competent, successful, and enlightened salt water angler.

Barry Gibson, Editor
SALT WATER SPORTSMAN

Bottom-Fishing Basics • Pro's Tips for Success •

How to Lose 'Em • Ten Tips for Beginning Fly Fishermen •

Salt Water
BASICS

SALT WATER BASICS

LESSONS FOR LIVIES

By Bob McNally

To get finicky game fish to strike, you've got to teach your live baits a few new moves.

May on the flats of Florida's southwest coast is a choice time to fish. Tarpon are beginning to enter the scene, redfish are in good supply, seatrout are lurking over the grass beds, and snook are so abundant that 100-fish days are possible.

Those facts didn't escape fellow writer Bill Sargent and me as we left the posh marina at South Seas Plantation on Captiva Island in charter captain Larry Mendez's skiff. We ran a short distance into Pine Island Sound and stopped at a shallow grass flat just as the sun became a thumbnail of red in the east. Mendez was serious about gathering lots of live baits before beginning the day. "It's nothing to go through several hundred live baits in a morning, at least if you're fishing *right*," said the renowned inshore guide as he threw a ten-foot castnet over a secret spot.

The cast resulted in nearly 100 three- to four-inch shimmering pilchards, which were quickly deposited in a large, specialized live well (right) in Mendez's custom-rigged Hydra-Sports skiff. A few more well-placed casts and we had enough baits to at least "get started," according to Mendez.

We ran northeast through a maze of mangrove islands and across shallows that would have stymied less experienced anglers. After shutting down in front of a large island we began a slow, calculated drift that brought us over broad, fishy-looking grass beds and kept us within casting range of the mangroves. As the

To "work" a live bait properly it must be hooked in the head, as it would be for trolling. For small fish, run the hook through the nostrils or lips (bottom up). A loop of rigging twine can also be sewn through the nose, then the hook can be attached to the loop. When fishing grass beds or floating sargasso weed, a weedless hook can be helpful.

While live baits can be hooked through the eyes, it's better if they can see an approaching game fish. This causes it to panic, sending out distress signals that often trigger a strike.

Many veteran anglers prefer spinning tackle for working live baits, since it's easier to make gentle lob casts with light baits. A long rod in the seven- to eight-foot range helps facilitate long casts without tearing the bait off the hook.

quiet of the morning settled around us, loud popping sounds could be heard emanating from the mangroves, proving that Mendez had found the snook.

"Hook a pilchard through the nose and cast toward the mangroves, then bring it out over the grass," he instructed, dipping bait from the well. Sargent and I tossed out our pilchards, anticipating a strike the moment they hit the water.

Nothing happened. We retrieved slowly and cast again, then again. Still nothing.

We were careful not to move our baits when they became excited, for we didn't want to spook a stalking predator. However, this would allow the baits to burrow into the grass or become tangled in the mangrove roots. In 30 minutes, Sargent and I lost at least a dozen baits and caught nothing. In that same time Mendez lost four baits to four fish: a ten-pound snook, a chunky redfish, and a pair of seatrout.

Don't Let It Sit

"Sometimes you gotta move a live bait like a lure to get the most outta it," Mendez said as he made a long, slow lob cast. "Retrieving a live bait allows you to cover a lot of water, and you still have the advantage of the bait's odor, color, and excited movements when it sees a bigger fish. If you just let a bait swim around it'll bury itself in the grass or hide in the mangroves, where it's not likely to attract many predators. Even if a game fish takes the bait, it's likely to foul the line or hook on the strike and you won't land it anyway."

Imparting action to a live bait is about as foreign to me as not imparting action to an artificial lure. It goes against logic. After all, a live bait is supposed to act as natural as possible, which means letting it do its own thing, right? But not all the time, as Mendez was proving by outfishing us four to one. So we decided to give his "bait-retrieve" technique a try.

Sargent was first to score. He made a lob cast to a mangrove point and started a smart retrieve with his rod held high, like he was working a swimming plug. Halfway to the boat, as his bait was being pulled across a grass patch, the surface boiled. A few minutes later, Sargent landed a five-pound snook.

It took a number of casts and several baits for me to get the hang of it. Some baits I worked too hard or too fast, pulling the hook out of their noses or killing them before a fish could home in on it, but eventually I learned how to twitch my rod tip just enough to make the bait dart left or right when I wanted.

"It's important to use only the friskiest baits," Mendez said as he set up on yet another big trout. "When you kill or injure a bait after a cast or two, replace it and throw it down-current of where you're fishing. Sometimes having a few wounded baits around acts like chum, drawing fish to your hooked baits. You can go through hundreds of baits a day with this technique, but often it's the only thing that works, especially on big fish or when they're very spooky due to fishing pressure or clear water."

Offshore Applications

Mendez and fellow guide Scott Moore believe that moving or retrieving a live bait is particularly effective when the fish are scattered. "A moving bait can be worked through a broad area and presented to many more fish than a stationary one," said Moore. "This is why slow-trolling live baits works so well for many species, especially offshore. It's also why casting and retrieving live baits can be effective for fish like barracuda, dolphin, cobia, sailfish, and African pompano. Baits cast into floating weed lines often hide from predators in the grass. But if you pull 'em out and give 'em action with the rod tip, it's almost sure to draw a strike if game fish are nearby. It's an especially good technique for dolphin that have been fished hard by other anglers, or a school that begins to cool down, or when bigger, wiser fish are encountered."

There was no question that imparting extra action to our baits was the key to our banner day of snook and seatrout fishing in Pine Island Sound. The next day was even more noteworthy, as we caught over two dozen snook up to 15 pounds and many more seatrout using the bait-retrieve technique. Meanwhile some friends who were fishing nearby caught almost nothing.

Since I learned to fish live baits like lures, the technique has paid off more times than I originally thought possible. While we were slow-trolling live menhaden (pogies) over a wreck recently, two barracuda in the 30-pound range appeared behind our baits. One of them made a pass and then hung back, eyeing the bait cautiously. I grabbed a rod and threw the reel in free-spool, dropping the bait back. The 'cudas dropped back too, maintaining the same distance behind the frantic bait. In desperation I cranked the bait rapidly toward the boat. The response was instantaneous. Both 'cudas charged, and one of them crashed the bait.

Another time, while fishing at night near Charleston, South Carolina, with friend Gordon Townsend, we were surrounded by bluefish that repeatedly rushed our free-lined shrimp, yet wouldn't strike. Few fish are as aggressive as bluefish, so I couldn't believe they wouldn't hit the live shrimp. Eventually we found that the finicky fish could be coaxed into striking by twitching the shrimp.

Whenever possible, try to discern the reactions of the game fish you are trying to tempt with a live bait, then modify your retrieve to make them strike. Last April, for example, while fishing for cobia with charter captain Ben Fairey out of Orange Beach, Alabama, I watched veteran angler Herb Malone "work" a cobia off the bow of Fairey's boat *Necessity* with a live eel.

A live eel dropped anywhere near a cobia is usually gobbled without hesitation, but this 50-pounder repeatedly turned up its nose at the offering until Malone began working his bait like an artificial lure. At first he cast ahead of and beyond the fish, retrieving the nose-hooked eel on a collision course with the cobia. When the bait was two feet from the fish he stopped the retrieve, which made the eel drop like a stone. The cobia turned toward the bait, but when the eel dove it continued on its original course. Malone tried this three times and met with the same disappointing result. On the fourth cast he reeled the eel to within inches of the cobia's nose. This time when he stopped his retrieve, the cobia simply opened its mouth and sucked in the bait.

Now *that's* the way to work a baitfish!

Tactics & Tackle:
PRO'S TIPS FOR SUCCESS

By Mark Sosin

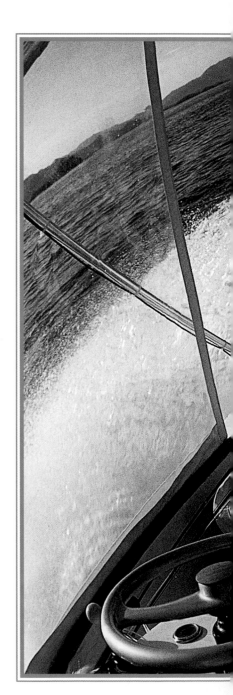

Professional skippers and guides share a common trait. They ooze confidence every morning when they leave the dock, knowing that they will put their clients on fish. Meanwhile, most other anglers take a fingers-crossed approach that this will be the day. Hope and anticipation outweigh confidence.

One learns early in the game that "magic" spots don't exist and that there are no lures guaranteed to catch fish. The key to consistent success centers on attention to detail and making minor, systematic variations in your tackle and technique. In fact, if you want to improve your fishing skills, concentrate on the subtleties rather than the obvious. Here's a list of nine critical areas worth focusing on.

Pick the Right Bait

Fish can be fussy feeders or as gluttonous as starved hogs at a trough of slop. However, you should always assume that every fish has just gorged on delicacies and that your job is to tempt it into taking one more bite. If you're fishing dead bait, it should be the freshest you can find and be sure to change it frequently so it continues to give off a strong scent. Take along a variety of different baits if they are available.

With live bait, make sure it's frisky and is hooked to give off the maximum distress vibrations. Use small hooks so it can swim unencumbered. When a live bait shows signs of getting tired, change it. Fish generally ignore all but the most natural-looking baits.

Think Small

Most of us use hooks too large for the task, fearing that they will bend during the battle. Actually, you'll bury the barb and land more fish if you opt for small, light-wire hooks. This becomes increasingly important with lighter line. Crushing the barb with a pair of pliers will also make it easier for the hook to penetrate the fish's mouth.

Choosing Artificials

Picking an effective lure focuses on size, shape, color, and sink rate. Your lure should approximate the size and shape of the natural bait in the area, or come close to matching the primary food source of the species you seek.

Sink rate is also important. The lure should work the portion of the water column where the fish are most likely to be. When choosing color, think in terms of light or dark first. Predators look for movement and contrast to isolate their prey. Make certain the artificial you choose provides the right silhouette based on water clarity and prevailing light conditions. If a fish has trouble seeing your offering, you won't get many strikes.

BEFORE YOU START FISHING, make sure your tackle and terminal rigs are 100-percent and are suited to the species and the conditions. Consider using the lightest sinkers and leaders you can get away with and still do the job, and remember that barbless, light-wire hooks penetrate easier.

Go Light

The lighter the tackle you use (within reason), the more natural the presentation. Opt for fine-diameter line when possible and use the lightest leader that's practical. A minor adjustment here sometimes makes a major difference. For leaders, single-strand wire is better than cable or coated wire, and mono ranks above single-strand. Use the lightest sinker and/or leadhead that will reach bottom. Eliminate as much hardware as possible in the terminal tackle, such as swivels and snaps. You want the lightest, least-visible rig that's consistent with what you intend to catch and the conditions under which you are fishing.

A Natural Presentation

Fish are creatures of habit. They learn early in life to live in a specific environment and to be wary of anything that looks different. Your bait or lure must fool fish into thinking it's the real thing. Fish generally expect their food to be carried by the current. That's the first clue to presenting a bait or lure effectively. You want the fish to "discover" your offering and then, whether it's a live bait or an artificial, think that the goodie is trying to escape. Once you satisfy those two requirements, the strike should be imminent.

Silence Is Golden

Once a fish suspects your presence or senses that an unknown entity has entered its realm, it becomes increasingly difficult to catch. Even in deep water, a stealthy approach pays big dividends, and it is paramount in shallow water and along shorelines. Don't run over areas you intend to fish and don't let your wake crash into a shoreline you are about to cast to. Loud sounds created in the boat are transmitted through the hull and into the water. Try to avoid moving anything that will make noise. Use a pushpole or electric motor to enter shallow zones and don't drop a bait or lure precisely on top of the spot you expect your quarry to be holding.

The Perfect Question

If you could only ask one question aimed at helping you find fish, it should focus on depth. You want to know how deep the fish were that somebody else caught, because chances are that other fish will be at that same depth in the spots you choose. The stage of the tide is also critical. You have to learn where to be and when to be there. For many species, only a small portion of the tide will produce results. Be prepared to work the entire water column, and don't forget to concentrate on some form of structure. You are trying to uncover a pattern that will produce results. Do it calmly, consistently, and through careful experimentation.

Trolling Tactics

Inshore or in blue water, trolling tactics follow similar guidelines. Work a patch of water systematically and move in relation to water movement (with it, against it, across it). Vary your speed depending on species and conditions. Try dragging one line very, very long if the standard pattern isn't working. You might want to troll another line close to the transom in the middle of the wake. Even in white water, a dark bait or lure is easy to spot from below. Check baits or lures frequently and keep making adjustments until you find the combination that works.

Don't Miss 'Em

The reel rather than the rod should be your primary hook-setting tool. All of us have the tendency to yank back on the rod the instant we feel a bite or witness a strike. Far too often, this results in missed fish. Rod holders boast a higher hook-up rate than most anglers, and they don't even move. The best technique is to simply crank the reel handle as fast as you can until the line comes absolutely tight. Don't move the rod! This only alerts the fish that something is wrong. Just keep on cranking until the drag starts slipping. Then you can set the hook any way you see fit. However, at that point it shouldn't make much difference.

Bottom-Fishing Basics

By Mark Sosin

Successful bottom fishing goes beyond simply tying on a sinker and soaking a bait. Like any form of fishing, you have to work to make things happen. You need to probe the area thoroughly.

Call it impatience if you must, but targeting those critters that make their homes in the lower ten percent of the water column is an aggressive exercise for me. I'm not about to sit around idly, waiting for a fish to happen along. Rather, I like to work my bait continuously, you can bet that my rig will be one in which I have complete confidence. Those are critical factors in catching fish.

Developing the Touch

If there is a secret to probing the bottom effectively, it centers on developing what my father used to call "the touch." That's nothing more than the feel it takes to know when the sinker is on the bottom and the line is tight. A mental image went along with the touch: you had to be able to picture what was happening down there and how you wanted the bait to perform. Suffice it to say that developing the touch requires lots of practice and some serious concentration. However, I use the same system today.

Bottom dwellers seldom rise very high in the water column to chase food. They expect to find their meals on or near the bottom, which is where you must keep your bait. It sounds pretty basic, but it's not always easy to do. My experience has shown me that I catch more fish by using the lightest sinker that will still keep my bait on the bottom. That's where the sense of touch comes in. If you use a window-sash weight to get your rig down, you won't have to worry about keeping it on the bottom; however, you won't be able to feel when a fish picks up the bait, either.

In addition to sinker size, I have found that my success improves if I move my offering frequently. If the boat is drifting, this movement may only be a lift and a drop-back. When anchored in a current, I may lift the bait and let the current carry it back just a tad. Sometimes the situation warrants casting and then dragging the sinker across the bottom very slowly with brief pauses in between. Not long ago, a friend learned that lesson the hard way. He held steady while I moved my rig. Until I convinced him to do the same, he couldn't get a bite, and there were plenty of fish down there.

Understand that there are no firm rules in bottom fishing. Good fishermen practice an experimental approach, constantly making minor modifications in their rigs and techniques until they find the combination that works on a given day or on a particular stage of the tide.

Strikes occur in a variety of ways. Sometimes you may feel a pronounced tapping at your bait, while at other times the pick-up may be barely perceptible. If you are moving the bait, it will often feel as if you have hung bottom. One response to this is to lift very slowly and try to feel movement on the end of your line. I believe that most bottom fish are missed because anglers insist on jerking the rod upward the moment they feel the least little tap. You'll catch more fish consistently if you simply start to reel. If the rod doubles over and you feel movement, then you can set the hook. Most of the time I simply continue to reel, relying on a sharp hook to do the work for me.

If you follow the practice of reeling first before moving the rod and you happen to miss the fish, the bait will remain in the vicinity and there is a good chance of another strike. Wait a few moments. If nothing happens, drop back to the bottom for a very short time and then reel in to check your bait.

Bait should be checked and replaced frequently. Fresh bait can make a big difference, and you should always use the best you can find. Be sure to hook your baits carefully and trim cut bait neatly: fish can be fussy feeders.

I eliminate swivels and crimps whenever possible, since this hardware can often turn the fish off. It's equally important to use the lightest, thinnest leader that will do the job. Pick monofilament over wire, except when targeting sharp-toothed fish. If you do use wire, make it a short piece near the hook and then attach mono for abrasion.

Three Basic Rigs

Almost all of my bottom fishing is done with three basic rigs. The guppy or *dropper-loop rig* is my first choice for fishing in deep water. It is particularly good when drifting, because the sinker can be used to find the bottom without the risk of getting hung up. With two hooks, there is also an extra bait down there if one gets stolen. A bank sinker is usually best for this rig, and it should be attached about a foot below the first dropper loop. Depending on the species you seek, the dropper loops should be spaced 12 to 18 inches apart.

If I'm using heavy line, I may tie the rig directly into the line. However, most of the time I'll want a slightly heavier leader. That means tying a Bimini twist in my fishing line and a No-Name Knot to connect the Bimini and the leader. You can also use a swivel between the two.

My second favorite rig is the standard *fishfinder*. In the Northeast, I'll generally use a slide (also called a fishfinder) and a pyramid sinker. A swivel usually acts as the stop for the slide. If you rig without a swivel, a tiny split-shot sinker can be clamped on the leader for a stop. The advantage of the fishfinder is that

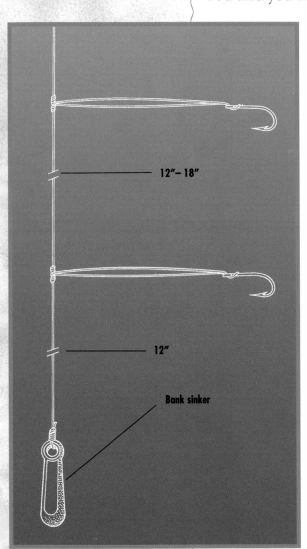

12"–18"

12"

Bank sinker

THE DROPPER-LOOP RIG, also known as the "guppy" rig, is the author's first choice for fishing deep water.

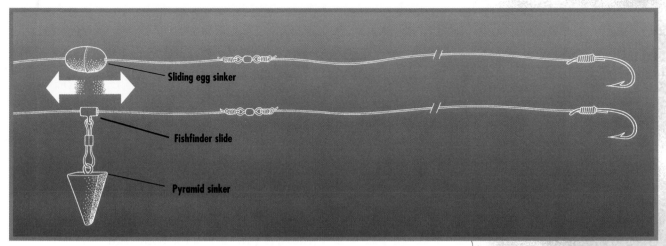

Sliding egg sinker

Fishfinder slide

Pyramid sinker

it allows the fish to take the bait without feeling resistance from the sinker. In the south, the fishfinder is made with an egg sinker. If you want to limit the slide, place the egg sinker between two swivels.

If I want to cast and probe the bottom, particularly in shallow water, I use a *dipsey rig*. It's my favorite for flounder, striped bass, and other critters that inhabit relatively shallow water. The advantage of this rig is that the dipsey sinker rolls around the bottom without hanging up, allowing me to retrieve it or simply troll it slowly. To make the rig, tie your fishing line to one eye of a three-way swivel and attach a dipsey sinker to a second eye with about six to eight inches of monofilament. Tie a three- or four-foot leader with a small hook to the third eye of the swivel. That keeps the bait slightly off the bottom and about a yard away from the sinker.

Bottom fishing is definitely a developed skill. It demands constant work, and one must continuously analyze all of the variable factors. Those who put in their time and use an intelligent and systematic approach are going to score more consistently than those who simply sit back and work on their suntan.

THE FISHFINDER RIG, whether used with an egg sinker or a slide, is useful for fishing over a sand or mud bottom. It allows the fish to pick up the bait without feeling any resistance from the sinker.

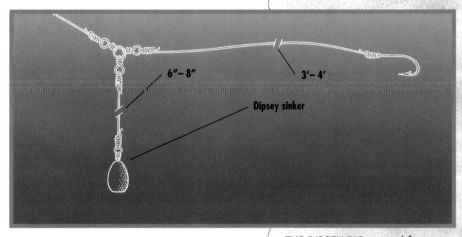

6"– 8"   3'– 4'

Dipsey sinker

THE DIPSEY RIG is good for casting or trolling a bait in shallow water. The sinker bumps along the bottom while the bait follows behind.

Get the LEADHEAD OUT!

By Al Ristori

The leadhead jig is the most basic and versatile of lures. From casting to bonefish in a few inches of water to deep-dropping on an offshore hump for snapper and grouper, no other lure can be used to catch so many different types of fish. But while nearly every fisherman has a leadhead somewhere in his tackle box, very few take full advantage of them.

Unlike most other lures, which come as a single unit, the leadhead jig has interchangeable parts. Even if you buy a brand-name model, the original dressing can often be removed and easily replaced with another type or color. You can even spice it up with a strip of bait or pork rind.

For years I referred to leadhead jigs as "bucktails" because that's what they were originally dressed with – deer-tail hair. Southern anglers tend to use less-expensive nylon-tailed jigs due to routine losses caused by sharp-toothed predators, but even those jigs are often referred to as "bucktails" in the generic sense. In terms of action, it's hard to beat real deer hair, especially for slow retrieves, although some of the new synthetic materials are almost as good and a lot tougher to boot. And it probably doesn't make a bit of difference what type of hair is used when the the jig is retrieved fast for speedsters like mackerel, tuna, bonito, and bluefish.

With most leadheads, the hook is molded into the head. There are a few exceptions where the hook swings free, but the major difference in jigs involves the head shape and the dressing. The variety of head shapes available is amazing, and some are more effective than others depending on the situation. Most heads don't provide a particular action by themselves, but a few do "work" a bit in a current or while trolling.

Smilin' Bills & Tiger Tails

One example is the so-called lima bean jig, also known as the Upperman, named after a famous striped bass fisherman who popularized the design. The jig's flat sides caused it to shimmy on the drop and the retrieve. Another example is the notched-face or "hot lips" design. When I first started fishing off

The ubiquitous leadhead jig has long been a mainstay of fishermen throughout the world, and can be used to take almost every game species imaginable.

Massachusetts' Nantucket Island in the mid-1960s, the late Capt. Bud Henderson trolled nothing but Smilin' Bill bucktail jigs. The Smilin' Bill had an indentation in the head that provided some action, and when combined with a strip of Uncle Josh pork rind the jigs were absolutely deadly on bass.

The more common oval, bullet, and ball head shapes provide no action by themselves, but that's usually not important because the fisherman can give the jig a variety of moves by working the rod tip. While a fast retrieve is essential for tuna and mackerel, a slow retrieve works better for bonefish. A pronounced up-and-down jigging motion is best for most species; however, that's not always the case. For instance, weakfish often hit best when little or no action is imparted to the jig. During the years of weakfish abundance in Peconic Bay on New York's Long Island during the 1970s, we used to cast out a jig tipped with a nine-inch plastic worm and stick the rod in a holder. While we drifted the jig would bump across the bottom. I hate to admit it, but that "dead stick" caught more fish than I did by casting and retrieving the jigs. Striped bass are another species that sometimes prefers a slow retrieve without a lot of heavy jigging, and they too will frequently hit dead-sticked jigs fished on the bottom.

One of the most effective jigs ever devised was created by Brooklyn angler Don Bingler, who simply attached a plastic tube to a long jig head. The original short-tubed version was dubbed the Tiger Tail and proved to be deadly on stripers and weaks, even though it was fished along the bottom with little or no jigging. Figuring that those fish thought the jig was a sand eel, Bingler came up with an even more realistic version with a long, slim tube tail, which he called the Nordic Eel.

Both of those lures worked well when simply dragged over the bottom or on a very slow retrieve a few feet off the bottom. Although the sand eel decline has compromised the effectiveness of these lures along the Mid-Atlantic and the Northeast coasts, they're surprisingly attractive to tarpon and snook in the Florida Keys.

Jig anglers in the tropics do very well with a "whipping" technique, which is particularly effective when deep-jigging over the reefs. If that gets to be too much work and you're not a purist, try adding a strip of bait to the jig and working it slower. That technique is particularly effective over reefs that have been worked hard and have a more discerning fish population, but a drawback is the number of short hits you'll get from small species, such as triggerfish and red hind.

A plain jig head with bait as a dressing is a standard offering used by guides fishing the reefs and Gulf wrecks off Key West. They buy the tiny "beanie" jigs by the hundreds in a couple of sizes to provide just enough weight to send small baits such as fry, crabs, and pieces of squid or fish slowly toward bottom. This technique is effective on a variety of species, ranging from yellowtail snapper to permit.

Naturally, any discussion of leadheads wouldn't be complete without mention of soft-plastic tails and dressings. These come in many shapes, styles, and colors. Most of the earlier plastic baits for salt water, such as the old-style shrimp tail, had little or no action, but all that has changed and "action tails" now dominate the market. It's hard to beat the lifelike action of modern soft-plastics, although losses can be heavy when toothy species are around. Gulf anglers are particularly fond of soft-plastics, which are especially effective when fished in shallow water for snook, redfish, and seatrout. Most of today's plastics are made from very soft material in order to provide maximum action.

Success in the West

Along the West Coast, leadhead fishing has its roots in Southern California, where fishermen discovered in the late '60s that salt water calico and sand bass responded to many of the same techniques used for fresh water black bass. Today, leadheads rigged with soft-plastic tails are the rage among California anglers, and their influence has spread from Baja to Alaska. So far they've proven effective on halibut, lingcod, surfperch, yellowtail barracuda, cabezon, bonito, dorado, and a

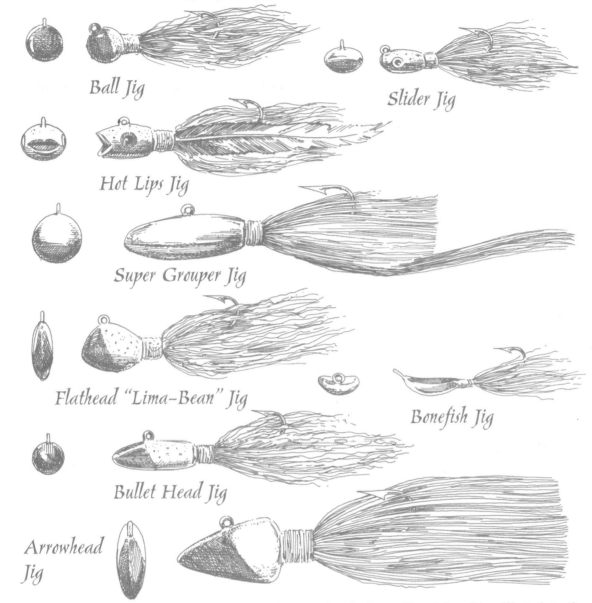

Ball Jig

Slider Jig

Hot Lips Jig

Super Grouper Jig

Flathead "Lima–Bean" Jig

Bonefish Jig

Bullet Head Jig

Arrowhead Jig

BALL JIG: Primarily used inshore. Good for working inlets, passes, and shallow rips influenced by strong currents. The ball jig packs more weight into a small profile. It sinks fast and tracks straight on the retrieve.

SLIDER JIG: Flat on top with an oval belly, the hook on this popular inshore jig rides up. It's designed to be hopped or skimmed over shallow grass beds, oyster bars, rocky troughs, and flats.

HOT LIPS JIG: Similar to the ball jig, but with an indentation or pocket molded into it. This design sinks quickly while producing a slightly erratic action. When retrieved or jigged, it emits a unique vibration caused by the pocket. Performs well in shallow, swift-moving waters.

SUPER GROUPER JIG: A new type of deep jig, the Super Grouper is really an oversized bullet head. Weighing up to a pound, these jigs are ideal for presenting natural baits over structure as deep as 300 feet. Although it can be jigged, most anglers prefer to let it bounce or hover just off the bottom. For use with heavy gear.

FLATHEAD JIG: Also dubbed the lima-bean or Upperman design, this relatively flat-sided jig has a wide profile. Because of this, it also sinks slower than other designs while producing a slight wobble. Used primarily inshore and sometimes offshore on schooling fish. The flatty's action and shape make it appear like an injured baitfish or sinking piece of chum. It can be difficult to work in fast-moving water.

BULLET HEAD JIG: This elongated, semi-oval design is the traditional favorite among offshore anglers. Available in a variety of weights, the bullet head sinks straight and rapidly, cutting through the water with a minimum of resistance. Often tipped with bait or a plastic worm for more appeal, it can be hopped off the bottom for bottom species, or jigged through the entire water column for other fish.

BONEFISH JIG: This tapered, flat-headed design is balanced so the hook rides upright. When twitched across a flat, this virtually snag-free lure has a fluttering, burrowing-type action similar to a crab.

ARROWHEAD JIG: A popular choice for those targeting both bottom species and open-ocean game fish. Its streamlined design is similar to an arrowhead and sinks nose-first, enabling it to cut through water and sink rapidly, even in a swift current. When jigged, the head produces a sharp up-and-down action.

variety of rockfish species. Anglers commonly jig them near rock piles, wrecks, and kelp paddies for structure-oriented species, or hop them along sandy bottoms for fish such as sand bass and halibut. And when fish have been chummed up into a frenzy behind the boat, jigs can be deadly.

Interestingly, it was the Salty Dog Shrimp that served as the original model for West Coast leadhead manufacturers. To this day, a majority of leadheads found in coastal tackle shops feature the Salty Dog's classic bullet-shaped head. One such leadhead is the Scampi, which also features a double curl-tail design. Today, it's probably the most widely known jig of its kind on the West Coast. The soft-plastic curl-tails were actually a spin-off of the original Mister Twister, which became a favorite among San Francisco Bay striped bass anglers in the '70s.

In the '70s and '80s, Northwest anglers found soft-plastics to be effective on lingcod, halibut, and rockfish, although leadheads now take a back seat to the lead-minnow jigging lures like the Point Wilson Dart.

Size Considerations

Head profile and overall body size are probably the most important considerations when selecting a jig. First consider what the fish are feeding on. If the bait is long and slim you'll want to use something similar, perhaps adding pork rind to provide both action and additional length. However, if the natural forage is small, you should select a jig with very little dressing. Small jigs aren't normally considered "big fish" lures, but, when fish are feeding on small bait they'll often work wonders. In fact, I was once surprised by a 32-pound striped bass while fishing tiny leadheads for school stripers along New York's Montauk Point.

Some species can be more of a challenge

Matching size and style to the prevailing baitfish in the area is always my first consideration when selecting a jig.

to catch when they're feeding on tiny bait. I used to catch little tunny (false albacore) consistently off Montauk by casting a quarter-ounce or half-ounce jig in front of the breaking fish and retrieving it as fast as I could. The trick is to get them to hit the jig instinctively since, as small as it is, it's still larger than the bait they're chasing.

Small isn't always the way to go, however. Big jigs work great on big fish, and sometimes you need a big, heavy jig to get down deep in a fast current. On the West Coast, deep-water rockcod enthusiasts often drop one- and two-pound leadheads rigged with huge plastic tails to entice big rockfish and lingcod lurking hundreds of feet below. The same technique is used on the Gulf Coast to target big snapper and grouper over offshore structure and around deep-water oil rigs. Many anglers often use the jigs to take their natural baits to the proper depth. And in the Florida Keys, a select group of fishermen use big jigs to send down lobsters for cubera snapper!

Matching size and style to the prevailing baitfish in the area is always my first consideration when selecting a jig. Color is only secondary. White has always been the favorite bucktail color in the Northeast, while southern anglers tend to favor yellow. How often color actually makes a difference to colorblind fish is debatable, but you can also try varying the color of the dressing.

Basic Rules

Since jigs work everywhere, on so many different species, in such a variety of conditions, there aren't too many absolutes in choosing and using them. However, one rule that applies to all jigs is to keep the hook sharp, especially when using light tackle or when deep-jigging. In most jig-fishing situations, the lure isn't moving at high speed and may even be free-falling when the strike occurs. This means that the

over, but shallow water requires the lightest of heads.

The standard quarter-ounce bonefish jig works well most of the time, and the weight is needed for long casts from a boat. However, when trying to get very close to the bonefish, a jig that size will spook the fish when it hits the water. In that situation, I prefer to use a $\frac{1}{16}$-ounce head with a tiny plastic-grub body, which can be flipped to a fish 25 feet away without disturbing it. Unfortunately, such jigs often carry light fresh water hooks, which may bend open if too much drag is applied.

angler must react instantly to the slightest tap, removing all the stretch of the mono in order to set the hook.

Another absolute is that you'll get more hits with a light mono leader as opposed to heavy mono or wire. If the fish arcn't too fussy, you can get away with wire leaders for such species as king mackerel, since those fish will hit a high-speed retrieve. On the other hand, I use mono for bluefish, even though it means losing a few jigs. Heavy mono will present the lure in decent fashion while taking some abuse before being cut through. For species such as stripers and weakfish, I drop down to 30-pound test or lighter, and often tie the jig directly to the main line. When using light line for bonefish and permit on the flats, some guides use a 12- to 20-pound leader or just double the line with an Albright or a Spider hitch.

Selecting the right size jig head for various situations is critical. A head that's too heavy may drag on the bottom and hang up in rough areas, while a jig that's too light won't reach the strike zone. Carry lots of heads so adjustments can be made as you move into different depths or as the current changes. When deep-jigging, you'll need heavy heads to get down quickly before the important structure is drifted

Leadhead jigs are among the deadliest of trolling lures. They can be trolled at any depth, but are particularly effective in the same areas they're usually worked while casting. For decades, Montauk trollers have fished leadheads on wire line for stripers and blues. For a while, those old stand-bys took a back seat to the newer umbrella rig, but since sand eels have become scarce again there has been a return to jig trolling as the preferred method, especially in the fall. A jig-and-pork-rind combo worked in the rips imitates young snapper blues, sea robins, blowfish, porgies, and other small fish heading out to sea, but to be effective they must be jigged hard. Today, most wire-line trollers use a parachute jig with a reverse skirt that has a billowing action as it's jigged. It's normally tipped with pork rind of various colors.

Volumes could be written on the subject of jigs and how to fish them, but hopefully the tips provided in this article will get you to spend more time using them. Who knows? These old stand-bys could turn out to be the most effective lures in your tackle box.

How to Lose 'Em

By Barry Gibson

There are plenty of ways to lose big fish, and over the years I've found most of them. Here are ten of my favorites, all based on personal experience.

It happened on the last day of a small East Coast tuna tournament back in late July of 1977. We were drifting live pogies from my 34-foot *Shark II* on a bright, flat sea some six miles off Boothbay Harbor, Maine, and at 11:04 A.M. the orange balloon went down. Glenn Hodgdon of nearby Southport scrambled into the chair as my cockpit chief, 19-year-old Jon Williams, hastily cranked in the other lines. I jumped to the bridge, hit the starter, and the big Buick roared to life. We were on.

Jon struggled to buckle Glenn into the canvas kidney harness as the fish raced westward, peeling line from the 12/0 Senator. The newly rewrapped Harnell rod crackled audibly under the strain, its varnished wooden butt gleaming in the sun. Glenn grinned and gave me the thumbs-up. "This one's going home with us!" he hollered over his shoulder, then turned and bent to the task.

Flat calm turned to a light chop as noon approached. Glenn pumped and reeled, only to end up losing much of the line he managed to gain. But by 1:15 the line was within an inch of the bars, and minutes later 800 pounds of bluefin tuna surfaced, dorsal and tail high in excitement, flashing that spectacular iridescent blue-green belly. But the fish kept its distance for nearly an hour, resisting Glenn's efforts to turn its head, no matter what I did with the boat.

This was a good fish, I knew. Not a great fish, but one that would probably take the rod-and-reel division, maybe even smoke the guys in the harpoon and handline classes, too. Just maybe, because high eights and low nines were the fish to beat in '77. But we were running out of time, and I knew that with each minute that passed late in a long fight like this, the odds of something going wrong increased.

There weren't many rules as to how a tuna could be landed

in the tournament, so I made a decision. I pulled the engine into neutral, descended the ladder, and grabbed a pair of cotton gloves. I took a wrap on the 130-pound Dacron, and Jon backed me up with another. Working as a team and coaxing the fish in a foot at a time, we got to the Bimini, then worked the double line a little harder. Glenn, nearly exhausted, wound the slack in carefully. I finally got my glove around the swivel. The fish stopped, never even flinched, and simply settled several feet deeper as the boat drifted over its massive bulk.

Suddenly I felt the sickening finality of the leader caught on something – *hard*. I let it go slack, then pulled. Nothing. I tried again. Jon and I peered over the side, only to watch the spent giant hang momentarily by the steel leader that was caught on the rudder post, then break free and disappear into the depths. Visions of the $300 prize check and desk-set barometer trophy vanished with it.

I lost him, and I say "I" because Glenn and Jon performed their jobs flawlessly. The blame was clearly mine and I've had to live with it. The fact is, I've lost a lot of nice fish over the years, and I've watched plenty of other people lose fish as well. But every lost fish is a lesson, and lessons, they say, should be shared, so here are my ten best tips for losing 'em – all based on personal experience.

1. Try to Land a Big Fish on the Downwind Side of a Dead Boat.

The above episode clearly illustrates this one. It just about guarantees failure. Instead, keep the boat moving slowly ahead, and try not to let the fish get forward of the corner of the transom. The wireman needs to be able to keep the fish's head up and coming at him. Some skippers like to "pinwheel," putting the engine farthest away from the fish in forward gear and turning the steering wheel against the engine, so that the boat makes a slow turn and the fish stays on the outside corner. The angler should remain in the chair (or harnessed to the stand-up outfit) with the drag slightly backed off until the fish is either released or secured.

2. Always Use Small, Light Hooks.

The idea of using the smallest, lightest-wire hooks possible has been pounded into our brains by well-meaning fishing writers for years. In general, it's a pretty good credo, but there's a limit. While fishing for snook in Belize's Sibun River back in 1988, I decided to try a small, yellow mullet-imitating darting plug more suited for spotted seatrout. I chucked it into a clump of thick mangroves on a 20-pound outfit and a snook the length of my leg charged out from beneath the bank and grabbed it.

Not wanting him to retreat to safety in the barnacle-covered roots, I clamped both thumbs down on the spool. Several seconds of some truly frightening thrashing ensued in the bushes, and then my plug returned to me as if fired from a slingshot. The line had held. The hooks hadn't. It would have been the fish of the trip.

Lesson learned? If you're fishing an area where there's a reasonable chance you'll hook a big fish, make sure your hook or hooks are beefy enough for the job.

3. Forget to Take the Plastic Hook Protector Off a New Trolling Lure.

I've made this embarrassing little screw-up twice, once with a marlin lure during a trip to the west coast of Costa Rica, and again with a giant tuna spreader rig off New England. Although in both instances the oversight was rectified before a fish actually hit, just thinking about the possible consequences sends shivers down my spine. I can also tell you that having one of your buddies discover what you've done provides plenty of merriment for others on the boat, but a long and rather tiresome day for you.

4. Set Your Rod, with the Reel in Free-Spool, in the Rod Holder for Just a Second.

We were live-lining tinker mackerel for striped bass from my 24-foot outboard, and I was having trouble getting my bait to swim away from the safety of the boat. So when my client in the bow said he thought he was tangled in the anchor, I set my outfit in free-spool and placed it in a rod holder, in hopes that my mackerel might cooperate and take out another foot of line in my absence.

As I bent over the bow to investigate, there was a watery explosion off the stern. I turned just in time to see a 25-pound striper do a barrel roll behind the motor and disappear, leaving a desktop-sized boil. Line hissed for an instant from my reel, then mushroomed into a world-class backlash. The rod tip bucked violently downwards, only to spring upwards when the 20-pound mono parted with a *sssssnap!* The outfit rattled momentarily in the holder, then deafening silence.

Moral? Never take your thumb off a reel in free-spool when you have a bait out. And putting just the clicker on won't always save you, either. Put the reel in full strike drag, or just a touch below it, if you need to leave it unattended. You'll be amazed at how many fish you'll hook this way, and you'll never get a backlash.

5. Use the Same Leader Loop in Your Jig or Plug Day After Day.

I learned this lesson in front of a disgruntled charter group. Inshore trolling had been very slow for several days due to a raw northeaster, but finally we got a sizzling hook-up on a Rapala Magnum, and it appeared to be the big striped bass that would save the trip. The guy was doing a nice job of working the fish in, but after about ten minutes the rod snapped straight and the fish was gone. Close inspection revealed that 30 hours of trolling had allowed the lure's fixed eye to wear completely through the perfection loop I had tied in the 50-pound mono leader.

Solution? Simple. Use a stainless split ring instead of a loop knot on swimming and topwater plugs, or else retie your loops every few hours or after each fish or two you catch.

6. Tie Your Knot in a Hurry So You Can Get Back to Fishing.

Nothing is more frustrating – or embarrassing – than discovering that little curlicue at the end of your line or leader where the knot pulled loose while you were fighting a good fish. This usually happens to me after I've tied on a hook or lure with trembling fingers when fish were busting and smashing all around the boat. Although I can't prove exactly why these knots fail, I suspect it's because (A) I didn't make enough wraps with knots such as a clinch knot or Duncan loop; (B) I didn't tighten down the tag end enough; (C) I didn't lubricate the knot before snugging it up; (D) I just plain tied it wrong in all the excitement, or (E) all of the above.

7. Ignore the Advice of Your Travel Agent When Packing for a Fishing Trip.

Several years ago I made a trip to Venezuela to do a story on marlin fishing, with a day trip to Guri Lake to catch peacock bass. I was all set with the marlin gear, but since I'd never caught a peacock I asked my agent, Doug Schlink at Anglers Adventures, to send a recommended tackle list. He did, and it said to bring several stout outfits loaded with 30-pound line, along with some eight-inch topwater lures with extra-strong hooks.

For some sort of trumped-up *fresh water* bass? Hey, I thought, I didn't just fall off the turnip truck when it comes to fishing, and besides, I'm a real sport. I packed an eight-pound outfit.

After hours of casting a crankbait in the intense heat, a ten-pound peacock charged out from a submerged tree and swallowed my little plug whole. In a heartbeat it turned and bolted back into the branches, leaving me wide-eyed – and with a broken line. It was my only peacock strike of the trip. The guide just shook his head sadly and stared at his toes.

8. Don't Check the Snap on Your Snap Swivel Before You Set Your Bait or Lure Out.

There are two ways you might unwittingly fish with an open snap. The first is that you, or someone, forgot to close it when attaching the lure or leader. The second is that the strike from a fish can spring it open if the lure eye or leader loop cocks around just right. During a trip to Chub Cay in the Bahamas, Bob Stearns and I watched a tiny 10-pound sailfish open a No. 6 snap this way and get off.

Either way, an open snap is an invitation for disaster. Although you don't have much control over the second scenario (except to tie or wire the snap shut, as Bob once suggested) you should check it every time you bring the lure or bait back to the boat, and after each strike or fish caught.

Some styles of snaps, such as Bcrklcy's Cross-Lok, may be tougher for fish to open, and the corkscrew-type popular in Europe is immune to the problem.

9. When Putting New Line on Your Reel in the Middle of the Season, Just Strip Off Half of the Old Stuff and Tie On a Fresh Section.

I did exactly that this past summer on a 20-pound-class Baitrunner spinning reel, figuring that most of the abuse had been taken by just the first 100 yards anyway. A few weeks later I took the reel on an offshore catch-and-release shark trip with my 10-year-old son, Michael, and his 9-year-old friend, J. J. Shields, aboard Capt. Ken Sullivan's *Hopscotch II*. A big blue shark soon picked up the bait. J. J. grabbed the outfit, let the fish run for a five-count, then engaged the drag. The shark took off, peeling line. We all cheered. Suddenly the spool stopped turning and J. J. was yanked up against the gunwale. It was all he could do to hang on as the rod tip arced toward the surface. Then the line parted and he almost fell over backwards. Good-bye shark.

What had happened? The line on the reel's spool had jammed underneath the back-to-back uni-knot I had used to tie on the new section. J. J. took it like a man (it sure wasn't his fault), but I could have kicked myself. Next time I'll replace *all* the line, even if it's only midseason.

10. Forget Your Pantyhose.

This one happened over Panama's Hannibal Bank, famous for its black marlin, but also where enormous schools of brick-red "mullet" snapper in the 10- to 20-pound class will ascend from the depths and churn the surface for a few minutes each day. I desperately wanted to catch one on six-pound test and be a hero.

On the last day I was at the right place at the right time. A school came up 20 yards off the bow. I grabbed my little spinning outfit and cast out a bucktail jig. It was engulfed immediately. I carefully feathered the spool as the snapper sounded, but seconds later the fish and I mysteriously partcd ways.

I wound in what remained of the line, and noticed that it was virtually in tatters. Further inspection revealed a fractured ceramic ring in the rod's damaged tiptop. The line had buried itself in the break when the fish took off, and the ceramic's sharp edges were akin to a pair of vegetable peelers.

Over-zealous baggage handling or a careless foot in the bottom of the boat was probably responsible. There's no sure-fire preventative for breaks or chips, but you can easily check for them by simply running a foot-long piece of nylon stocking through the ring. The nylon will hang up and alert you if there's any imperfection. Best bet is to "hose" test your rod guides before you pack for a trip, and again when you unpack at your destination. And always carry a couple of spare guides and tips.

SALT WATER BASICS

Ten Tips for
BEGINNING FLY FISHERMEN

By Dick Brown

Ironically, what prevents many light-tackle anglers from learning to fly fish in salt water is that they are already such accomplished fishermen. They are so adept at throwing jigs, plugs, and bait with spinning and casting rigs that when they pick up a fly rod, they expect to just flick their wrists and watch the line shoot out through the guides. When it doesn't, they quit.

That's too bad, because they're missing out on what most veteran anglers regard as the ultimate fishing method – in terms of both enjoyment and effectiveness. And contrary to its reputation, fly fishing is not that difficult to learn. It's no more demanding than any other compound-skill sport, such as golf or bowling.

Like other challenging pastimes, however, fly fishing does require that you master several individual skills, which takes a bit of practice. But if you proceed one step at a time and seek out help on the hand-eye-body coordination needed to produce a good casting technique, you should be able to pick up the sport in no time.

The following are ten tips that will get you started on the right foot, including advice on avoiding the worst pitfalls. Give them a try and you'll increase your chances of hooking fish, as well as your enjoyment of this great sport.

1. Cast Short

If you were just learning to play baseball, you wouldn't try to belt a home run on your first turn at bat – you'd be happy just to hit the ball. Why then does every novice feel he or she has to throw a 90-foot cast from the start? Instead, begin by casting what you can handle. Start out with 20 or 30 feet, then add a few feet at a time. Incidentally, you seldom have to cast as far with a fly rod as you do with other light tackle. Since flies land more quietly than heavy lures, they let you approach fish more closely. Most fish caught on a fly in salt water are hooked between 20 and 40 feet from the angler. Take advantage of it.

Ten simple yet important tips that will improve your salt water fly fishing technique.

A second reason for casting short is to avoid "lining" the fish. The fat profile of a fly line spooks fish when it lands over them. Better to throw a lesser distance, exposing only your leader and your fly to the fish. You can always recast if you are too short of the target.

2. Retrieve with Your Stripping Hand

Fly fishing requires you to use both hands. While your casting hand gives action to the rod, you use your stripping, or non-casting, hand (below) to retrieve line and make the fly move. Learn to apply different action to your fly for different kinds of fish – and remember, do this by hand, not with the rod tip.

With blues, stripers, and other species that chase baitfish, repetitive long strips will "swim" your fly realistically. Bottom feeders, however, such as bonefish or permit, require a brisk strip-strip-strip-and-stop that jigs the fly and drops it abruptly. This imitates the natural action of shrimp and crabs that dive to the bottom for cover when attacked.

3. Point Your Rod at the Fly

When you retrieve the fly, keep your rod low and pointed in the same direction as your line. You must create a direct path between you and the fly, because only then will the fly move when your hand moves. A tight, immediate connection also allows you to set the hook more effectively.

4. Strike with Your Stripping Hand

It is possible to strike a fish by lifting your rod tip (just as you do on a spinning rig), but it's much more effective to keep your rod tip pointed at the fish and strike by using your stripping hand – a maneuver called the "strip strike." When the fish takes your fly, make a firm strip, which drives the hook into the fish's mouth. When you feel the fish on the end of the line, lift your rod to complete the strike.

The strip strike's biggest advantage is that if the fish has not taken your fly, you won't have moved the end of your line more than a foot or two. This leaves the fly near the fish or its buddies, which may come after the fly again.

5. Get the Fish on the Reel

Failing to clear your line and get the fish on the reel causes more break-offs than any other problem in fly fishing – especially with fast salt water fish. Unlike all other fishing methods, fly fishing does not automatically put the fish directly on your reel when you hook up. Instead, you must manually guide (and clear) the loose line on the casting deck or in your stripping basket so it shoots through the rod guides before you can play the fish from the reel.

If you fail to clear your line properly, you can be sure that a knot will jam in the rod guides as the fish begins to streak away. Or a loop of line can catch around a deck cleat

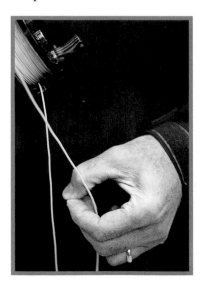

or get caught under your own foot! Any of these situations will result in a break-off.

You can avoid these problems by forming an "O" around the line with the thumb and forefinger of your stripping hand, which helps

clear the line of knots and twists as it's being pulled out. This also lets you guide the line away from hazards. Watch out, too, for line wrapping around your rod butt, hook keeper, or reel handle.

6. Eliminate Snags

Boats have plenty of hazards for fly fishermen, things that grab your line, trip you up, and interfere with your casting.

If you are fishing on a flats skiff, make sure the forward cleats and pole clamps are covered. On open hulls and center-console boats, watch out for steering gear, shift

levers, antennas, and seat fittings – all notorious snaggers. Get rid of these hazards by covering them with a wet towel or netting, or change your position so that your loose line is clear and your casting path is safe.

7. Use the Rod to Control the Fish

Fly rods do not control fish as efficiently as short rods, but they will put a surprising amount of pressure on a fish when needed. When you're trying to turn a fast-running bonito or subdue a big striper, angle your rod to the side opposite the direction the fish is swimming and apply full pressure. Then change the angle often to keep it off balance.

When fighting fish in very shallow water, such as on a coastal mud flat or tropical sand flat, you may have to hold the rod overhead to lift your line clear of jagged bottom hazards, such as sea fans and coral.

8. Get Low to Cast Against the Wind

Wind is the fly fisherman's enemy. Try to stand so that it blows at your back or at least to the side. If you have to cast into it, keep your backcast high and your forward cast low and drive the line down onto the water. Also, be sure to press your casting thumb hard into the rod grip on the forward stroke. This creates tight loops that slice through the wind, and also keeps the fly from nailing the back of your shoulder. Stepping down off the casting platform and getting lower in the boat helps you cast into the wind, too.

9. Seek Expert Advice

There is no faster way to learn salt water fly fishing – especially the casting skills – than by getting some personal training. An experienced teacher can teach you the basic skills in a few hours. More importantly, he or she can correct your mistakes as you make them.

10. Leave the Spinning Outfit at Home!

Of all the tips on learning to fly fish, the most important is this: leave the spinning rod at home. Don't say, "I'll take both the spinning and the fly rod along in case it gets windy." It's always windy out there! As long as you go fishing with the attitude that a fly rod is secondary, you will never use it.

FREEZER-
FRIENDLY FISH

By Ray Rychnovsky

Here's how to properly prepare and freeze your catch so you can enjoy fresh-tasting fish dinners whenever you like.

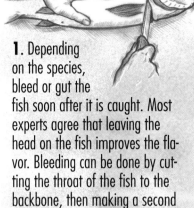

1. Depending on the species, bleed or gut the fish soon after it is caught. Most experts agree that leaving the head on the fish improves the flavor. Bleeding can be done by cutting the throat of the fish to the backbone, then making a second slice at the base of the tail.

I love fresh seafood, and there's nothing better than eating a fish I caught that same day. However, I also like to keep some fish on hand for those days when I'm, er, not so lucky. While many people view frozen fish with a scant eye, proper preparation will assure that it will taste fresh months after it was caught. My experience has been that well-packaged fish stored at a constant temperature of zero degrees Fahrenheit or colder will taste very good up to about six months with fatty fish like salmon, and up to a year with lean fish like halibut.

I found out how much difference good preparation can make when I brought some fish home from Cross Sound Lodge in Elfin Cove, Alaska, two years ago. The lodge staff had meticulously prepared, packaged, and frozen the fish, and it was the best-tasting salmon and halibut I have ever eaten. It tasted fresh and flavorful even after spending several months in my freezer. Here is how they processed the fish to preserve it so well.

As soon as a salmon or halibut was caught, the skipper bled the fish by putting it in a large plastic tank on the deck of the boat and cutting its throat. Whenever we had a lull in fishing, he filleted the fish and washed the meat in cold salt water. Back at the lodge, the fillets were vacuum-sealed in heavy plastic to remove all air, and quickly frozen in a large commercial freezer.

2. Immediately place the fish on a bed of crushed ice after the bleeding or gutting process. Do not pack the fish under a layer of heavy ice, which can damage the flesh.

When a fish is removed from the water, several processes begin that will eventually spoil the fish. First, the process of rigor mortis tightens the fish's muscles. Then bacteria on the surface and in the gut of the fish invade the flesh and begin to multiply. Enzymes begin to break down the flesh and change its composition and texture.

But this process isn't all bad. Studies have shown that fish doesn't reach its peak flavor and texture until several hours to a few days after it has been killed. I am usually the cook on our fishing trips, and I want the fish filleted and kept on ice overnight before I cook it. That time to chill enhances the flavor, and the fillets don't curl up in the cooking process.

The chemical reactions that rob fish of its flavor or create an unpleasant taste begin on the exposed flesh surfaces. To avoid this, package any fish for freezing so as to avoid exposure of the flesh to air. This prevents oxidation at the surface and prevents fluids from sublimating out of the fish (sublimation is

3. After returning to the dock, or after the fish has stiffened, fillet or steak-out the fish. Leaving the skin on the fish will better protect it during the freezing process.

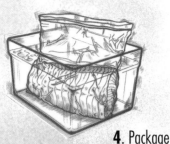

4. Package the fish so as to minimize exposure of flesh to air. This can be done with a vacuum-sealer or by dipping or dunking the bagged fish in a bucket of water, which forces out the air. Another way to protect the fish is to freeze it in a heavy plastic bag or small container filled with water.

5. Freeze quickly by placing the fish directly on the freezing surface of your freezer. Store the fillets or steaks at a constant temperature of zero degrees Fahrenheit or colder. Bypassing some of these rules won't ruin the fish, but it will shorten its shelf life.

a process in which a solid, such as dry ice, changes directly to a gas without passing through a liquid state).

Cut your fish in a shape that minimizes the amount of exposed flesh. Skin is a good protector, so leave it on for freezing; you can cut it off just before cooking. Fillets have a poor configuration for freezing, since they have a high surface area, but freezing them in water helps preserve them and works well for fish that won't be stored too long. Use plastic containers or cut the tops off half-gallon milk cartons and place your fillets in the bottom. Cover them with water and freeze the whole block. Or pack the fillets in freezer-weight plastic bags and fill with enough water to cover the fish. Some people freeze their tuna whole and saw off serving-size chunks from the end of a frozen fish. Of course, the new cut is exposed to air, but only until it's time for another tuna meal, not long enough to affect the taste.

Try the following procedures to protect the surface of the fish from air. Double-wrap the fish with freezer paper or heavy plastic, pressing as much air out of the package as possible.

Freeze the bagged or plastic-wrapped fillet in water, glaze it with ice after it is frozen, or vacuum-seal it to remove most of the air from the package before sealing. If you don't have a vacuum sealer, you can remove the air from a bagged fillet by dipping the bag in a bucket of water, which forces out any air from the bag.

Fast Freezing

Fish will taste fresher and stay flavorful longer if it is frozen very quickly, so commercial processors go to great lengths to minimize freezing time. Some use blast freezers that blow super-cold air across the fish, or they may immerse the fish in a very cold fluid to freeze it quickly. For valuable fish, such as bluefin tuna, they may pack the fish in dry ice at minus 109 degrees Fahrenheit, or spray it with liquid nitrogen at minus 321 degrees Fahrenheit to freeze it very quickly. However, home freezers aren't going to freeze fish that fast, thereby shortening the acceptable storage time.

When you have a lot of fish to freeze at one time, you need to plan ahead. To minimize freezing time, place the packaged fish directly on the freezing surface of your freezer (check the freezer manual if you don't know where the freezing surface is located). Use only enough water to cover the fish when freezing it in water; excess water just adds more mass that must be frozen and slows the freezing process.

Maintaining a constant temperature is also important. A fish is composed of about 75 percent water, which freezes at 32 degrees Fahrenheit. However, some of the fluids in a fish freeze at lower temperatures. Most, but not all, is frozen at zero degrees Fahrenheit, the temperature of most home freezers. If the freezer is warmer than that, or cycles up and down in temperature, the fish won't last as long.

Keeping Fish Tasting Fresh

Frozen fish deteriorates as it ages, but there are ways to improve the flavor. Always remove the skin and trim off any dry or off-color meat. Some of the strong flavor can be removed by soaking the trimmed meat in salt water, dilute vinegar water, marinade, or milk. Smoking the fish using a dry or wet process also improves its flavor. Fish that's smoked even after spending several months in the freezer will taste almost as good as fresh-smoked fish.

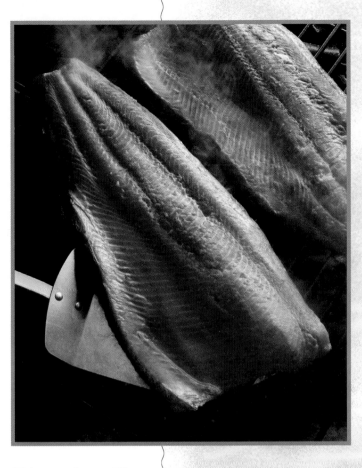

Fish should be thawed slowly and placed in a refrigerator before it is completely thawed. If it has been frozen in ice, it should be left on a counter at room temperature until most of the ice has thawed (the ice will keep the fish cool), then put in the refrigerator. Thawing in water will rob some flavor, while thawing it in a microwave may slightly cook the surface. Use a microwave as a last resort if you need to thaw the fish quickly.

As an example of how to prepare a frozen-fish dinner, here is how I go about preparing a salmon fillet. I first place the fillet on a flat cutting board, skin side down. Using a sharp fillet knife, I carefully trim off any dry or discolored flesh. Next I trim a thin layer off the end of the fillet. I carefully cut the skin away, then turn the fillet over and trim off all of the dark meat.

I like to marinate any fish that has been frozen for a long time (see recipe at right). Marinade can be used before cooking or prior to smoking, and restores moisture to the surface of the fish while adding flavor. I marinate the fish in the refrigerator for 30 minutes, turning it once in the middle of the process. With the skin removed, the fish may stick to the grill and fall apart easily, so I arrange the fish in a rectangular wire barbecue basket, the kind with a long handle that's made for fillets, and place it on a preheated grill. I drizzle extra marinade over the fish, immediately turn the basket of fish, and apply a generous portion to the other side. Remember that bacteria from raw fish are transferred to the used marinade and may make the fish unsafe to eat if it is used late in the cooking process.

As your frozen fish approaches the end of its shelf life, you can alter your preparation methods to produce a very appealing meal. However, the best way to always have good, fresh-tasting fish is to bleed and cool it soon after it is caught, package it properly, and freeze it quickly. Take care of your fish from the start and you'll have great-tasting fish dinners long after the season is over.

Marinade Recipe for Frozen Fish

A simple but delicious marinade can be made by combining the following ingredients:

3 tablespoons lemon juice

1 tablespoon soy sauce

½ tablespoon Worcestershire sauce

1 tablespoon olive oil (or cooking oil)

1 clove of garlic smashed once to release flavor

1 teaspoon dill

Ground black pepper

Mark Sosin's
GUIDE TO
RELEASING FISH

By Mark Sosin

*The reason why you practice
catch and release isn't as
important as how to do it.*

The jury reached its verdict a long time ago. Repeated tagging studies on a multitude of species from sharks to striped bass, redfish to billfish, demonstrate convincingly that the majority of fish can survive being caught if they are released correctly. Take snook, for example. Florida state biologist Jim Whittington reports that there is only about a three-percent mortality rate in his state's catch-and-release snook fishery during the off-season. Similar results have been found with striped bass in the Northeast and redfish in the Gulf. Catch and release used to be virtually unheard of, but now it's common practice, even in cases where the fish may be legally retained. Furthermore, today's size, seasons, and catch restrictions make the release of many species mandatory, so it's important to

THE PROPER WAY to release an exhausted billfish is to have a crew member hold the fish upright while the helmsman idles forward to force water through its gills. Do not let go of the fish until it is able to swim off on its own.

make sure that every fish has the best chance of survival.

Set It Quick

If you're really serious about catch and release, there are steps you can take to increase a fish's chance of survival even *before* you hook it. For example, if you're using, natural bait or scented lures, set the hook quickly when you feel a strike. Most predators can inhale a bait in less than a second. The idea that a fish must swim off with the bait, mash it, and then turn it around for swallowing is more speculation than reality. Setting the hook as soon as you feel a strike will help prevent the fish from taking the hook deep in its throat, where it may be hard or impossible to remove.

Another way you can help reduce the amount of injury is to limit the number of hooks you use. On lures with multiple treble hooks, remove one set of trebles or cut one hook off each treble. Crushing the barbs on your hooks also makes them easier to remove. Some anglers equip their casting or trolling plugs with single, barbless hooks, which lets them return the fish to the water quickly and with a minimum of handling. In some Northwest salmon fisheries, this is even required.

On the other hand, some studies have shown that small single hooks can actually cause more damage than trebles when used with drifted or still-fished natural bait, since they're easier to swallow. Again, setting the hook quickly should reduce this problem. Another answer may be the use of circle hooks, which have generated a lot of interest in recent years among bait fishermen, especially in the bluefin tuna chunk fishery. These hooks lodge in the corner of the fish's mouth a high percentage of the time, causing minimal damage. Similar results have been reported by anglers who use circle hooks to catch striped bass, grouper and snapper.

Once the fish is hooked, try to land it quickly. Studies show that the longer a fish is fought, the less likely it is to survive after release. The chances of survival decrease even more if the fish is already stressed because of disease, malnutrition, or extreme water temperatures.

Sometimes the fish may appear to swim off just fine, only to succumb later to the stress of the fight. Also, an exhausted or severely stressed fish is more vulnerable to attack from predators, and is less able to ward off infection. The only time the fight should be prolonged is when pulling a fish out of deep water. In this case, slow down so the fish can adjust to the change in pressure and its swim bladder won't expand as dramatically.

Removing the Hook

No matter what material they are made of, hooks do not rust out in a couple of days. Rust requires oxygen, and there isn't a lot of oxygen underwater. While it's true that fish are often able to work a hook loose after a while, and can even feed normally with a hook in their mouth, it's always best to remove the hook whenever possible.

There are lots of tools that can help you remove a hook that's imbedded deep in

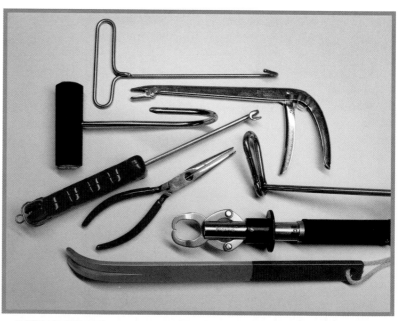

MANY FISHERMEN USE DEVICES like the Boga Grip (second from bottom) and various hook-removal tools designed to minimize handling.

MANY GAME FISH can be safely controlled by grasping the lower jaw between your thumb and forefinger, a method known as "lipping." To minimize stress and handling, try to keep the fish in the water during the hook-removal process.

the fish's throat, such as needlenose pliers, hemostats, Hookouts, even homemade vee-notched devices. However, if it appears that you may cause greater harm to the fish by attempting to remove the hook, simply cut the leader as close to the hook as possible. Never jerk or "pop" the leader to break a fish off, which is sometimes practiced in release tournaments. If the hook is lodged in the throat, gills, or stomach, this can cause severe damage to the fish.

Reduce Handling

The main rule of release is to leave the fish in the water with its body just under the surface. Try to handle the fish as little as possible. Use a tool to remove the hook or, if the fish is hooked deeply, cut the leader as close to the hook as practical. A small gaff hook or J-shaped release tool makes a great hook remover. Grab the bend of the hook with the curved end of the tool and lift upwards while pulling down on the leader. The weight of the fish should pull the barb free.

Whether the fish is alongside the boat or in the surf, you want to keep it from thrashing around and injuring itself. If necessary, use a net, but remember that the mesh will remove the mucous coating that protects the fish against infection. Try to use a net with a mesh made of soft, non-abrasive material.

With larger fish, a short release gaff slipped through the lower jaw can be used to hold the fish while you remove the hook. However, do not lift the fish clear of the water with the gaff, which places its entire body weight on the jaw. A tool called The Lipper can be used to hold the jaws of smaller fish without applying excessive pressure and handling. Some kinds of fish can be safely handled with a tailer. This device features a loop that is slipped over the tail of the fish and cinched tight. The fish can then be lifted from the water to remove the hook.

If you must handle the fish, use a wet glove or towel to touch its body, and avoid sticking your fingers in the eyes or gills. If you bring the fish onboard, lay it on a soft, wetted surface (some charter captains use a towel or piece of carpet) and cover its eyes with a wet towel or rag, which often has a calming effect. Turning the fish upside down may also keep it from thrashing around. Above all, get the fish back in the water as soon as possible.

Be Careful!

Teeth are not the only danger in handling a fish. Many species have sharp spines and razor-edged gill plates that can cause nasty wounds. Sharks are among the species you definitely don't want to bring in the boat! If you can't remove the hook easily with a tool while the shark is in the water, cut the leader as close to the mouth as possible. Sharks have a cartilaginous skeleton instead of a bony one, which means they can just about bite their own tail. If you hold a shark improperly, its jaws may find your wrist. Accurate Fishing Products makes a long-handled release tool for releasing sharks and other big fish. It features a carabiner clip welded to a long, metal pole. The carabiner is clipped around the leader, which guides it to the hook. Once the clip reaches the bend of the hook, the pole can

be used to push the barb free from a safe distance.

Other species, such as dolphin or cobia, tend to thrash around violently in a boat, causing injury to themselves or possibly a crew member. If possible, deal with them in the water or use a tailer and a glove for more control.

Releasing Billfish

Sailfish and marlin rank as the offshore glamour species, and most anglers choose to release them. Releasing billfish is even more important when you consider that stocks of blue and white marlin in the Atlantic are at less than 25 percent of maximum sustainable yield. They're in serious trouble.

Follow the same procedure as you would with any other species. Try to control the fish at boatside and remove the hook if at all possible. With sailfish, white marlin, and smaller blue marlin, you can grab the bill and hold the fish's head underwater (it remains calmer this way) while the hook is being removed by another crew member. When grabbing the bill, make sure your thumbs face each other, so you can push the fish away from the boat if it tries to jump. There is a relatively new tool called a "snooter" that can be slipped over the bill of a billfish, allowing you to control the fish and hold its head underwater during the hook-removal process. As of this writing it wasn't available commercially.

If you plan to tag your billfish, first get it alongside the boat. Attempting to stab the fish with a long tag stick while it's airborne defeats the purpose. The tag must be planted in the shoulder of the fish, well back from the head and gills. Those anglers who jab at the fish often miss the target area and wind up puncturing the body cavity, which may eventually kill the fish.

Revival Technique

Once the hook is removed, it's time to revive the fish. This is the critical moment. You don't want the fish to turn belly-up, sink to the bottom, or swim off without enough strength to avoid a predator. The easiest method is to simply place the fish in the water, facing into the current or direction of the seas, while you support its belly and hold its tail gently. If the fish needs resuscitation, work it back and forth gently, forcing water through its gills. Do not let go of the fish until it is able to swim strongly out of your hands.

With a billfish, hold it by the bill and keep its head underwater. Have someone kick the boat in gear and move forward very slowly. This pushes oxygen through the gills and the fish will eventually swim off under its own power. If the fish turns belly-up or doesn't swim off, don't give up. Grab the fish again and keep trying to resuscitate it until it is able to swim on its own.

Fish taken from deep water pose a different sort of problem. The air bladders of many bottom fish expand as they are brought up rapidly from deep water, which prevents them from returning to their homes until the air is vented. The easiest way to "deflate" a bottom fish is to use a 12-gauge hypodermic needle or a thin ice pick (do not use the tip of a filet knife). Puncture the air bladder, massage the air out gently, and release the fish. With large fish, try to do this without bringing the fish onboard, which can cause damage to internal organs. (Note: Make sure you know where the air bladder is located before attempting to deflate the fish, otherwise you could end up puncturing other organs.)

ALTHOUGH A GENTLE RELEASE is generally recommended, dropping a game fish, especially deep-water species like this amberjack, into the water head-first helps drive it deep while forcing water through its gills.

Although a gentle release is generally recommended, there are times when a more forceful approach can be effective. With tunas, little tunny (false albacore), and bonito, it's often best to drop the fish into the water head-first, driving it as deep as you can. The same approach often works with species that are taken from deep water, such as amberjack.

If you take the time to handle and release your catch quickly and carefully, it stands an excellent chance of survival. To me, there's no greater sight on the water than watching a game fish swim off with nothing hurt other than its pride. Try it. Releasing fish becomes habit-forming, and makes you feel good in the process.

Shore FISHING

◆

30 Do's & Don'ts for Fly Fishing the Flats

• *Top Ten Shoreline Fishing Spots* • *How to Surf Cast*

TOP 10 SHORELINE FISHING SPOTS

By Bob McNally

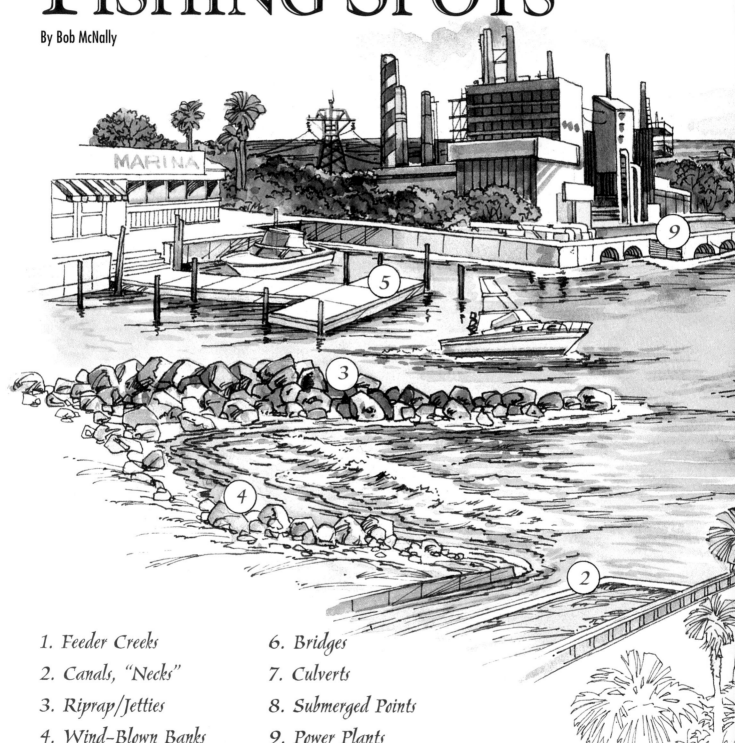

1. Feeder Creeks
2. Canals, "Necks"
3. Riprap/Jetties
4. Wind-Blown Banks
5. Docks, Piers & Pilings
6. Bridges
7. Culverts
8. Submerged Points
9. Power Plants
10. Surf

You don't need a boat to catch marine fish if you concentrate your efforts in these proven places.

A boat capable of running far offshore isn't necessary to enjoy some of the best fishing salt water has to offer. Indeed, every year IGFA records are caught by anglers who cast lures and baits from bulkheads, bridges, and banks. But like the man working distant offshore waters in his custom Hatteras yacht, not every fishing spot along a shoreline will yield hefty catches. However, there are some select places that consistently offer the bank-bound

angler better opportunities of finding and catching fish. The following ten spots are among them.

1. Feeder Creeks

An area where a feeder creek flows into a larger body of water like a river, bay or estuary should always be carefully fished from shore. There will normally be a slight drop-off at the mouth of the feeder where water from it has gouged out a hole in the larger body of water. Even a minor drop-off of only a few inches is important, and offers many inshore marine fish (redfish, striped bass, flounder, etc.) a place to hold and wait in ambush for food washed out of the feeder creek.

Creek mouths can also have swirling currents and back-eddies that inshore fish love because they're first-class dining rooms, loaded with such choice foods as minnows, shrimp, crabs, and other goodies.

Creek mouths can offer especially good fishing during falling tides. Water flushed out of the creek contains abundant food, so sport fish hold at feeder mouths to dine on the smorgasbord. Often feeder creek water is discolored or muddy. The "line" or rip where clear water meets discolored water of a creek is a prime spot, and often easily fished from shore.

2. Canals, "Necks"

Narrow canals or "necks" connecting creeks and bays with larger rivers, estuaries, and sounds frequently are among the best places for shoreline fishermen to find fast action. When bluefish, jacks, or striped bass herd bait into the tight confines of a canal or "neck," it can create wild, fast action, and big catches can be made in short order. Fish often use "necks" as inshore highways to move about with the tide flow to feed. They usually move along the high sides or edges of canals, pausing at places that are distinguished differently from the rest of the canal edge.

Some of the very best "neck" fishing is found near small inshore river locks or even mini-dams that create barriers to bait schools, which form "end-of-the-line" feeding stations for marine predators. Anglers should take special note of seagulls, terns, pelicans, herons, ospreys, and eagles. Often such birds lead to outstanding fishing. If birds are found diving into the water or are stationed along a canal bank or rock wall, it's a good bet baitfish schools – and game fish – are nearby.

3. Riprap/Jetties

Riprap or jetties – the large rocks used to reinforce roadways, causeways, railroad rights-of-ways, and inlets – are easy-to-find, simple-to-fish shoreline structures. But riprap can be confusing to fish for average anglers because it's not uncommon to find riprap along several miles of shoreline. With so much water that seemingly appears all the same, it's no wonder many anglers opt for fishing more eye-appealing spots. This is a mistake, however, because riprap is invariably jammed with food (minnows, barnacles, crabs, shrimp, etc.) and therefore is attractive to all manner of fish.

The difficult part of fishing a jetty is usually the visible shoreline is long and straight, with no points or turns anglers easily can recognize that draw fish. But on any riprap shore there will be places where – underwater – the rocks extend farther into the water than the rest of the bank. Also, there will be places along riprap where the water is deeper than most other areas. Find underwater riprap points extending farthest to deep water, and it's likely you've discovered a classic sport fish lair.

Another key to good jetty fishing is working places where tidewater flows through the rocks. The current and "flushing" action where water drains through rocks to open water in an adjacent creek or bay is a key spot to find feeding fish, and well worth working carefully with lures and baits.

4. Wind-Blown Banks

Most anglers despise strong wind because it makes fishing difficult. And while fishing in whitecap water and three-foot swells is no one's idea of fun, the truth is that wind can sometimes concentrate baitfish, and that draws sport fish in large schools. It doesn't take much wind to do this. Often just a gentle breeze blowing into a shoreline is all that's needed to ripple the water and create current that "pushes" hapless baitfish where they're vulnerable to feeding game fish.

Naturally, not every place where the wind plows water into a bank is good for fishing. Usually the area must have some cover such as rocks, weeds, timber, or brush, and deep water nearby. An ideal spot would be an area where wind is blowing across a broad expanse of deep, open water, forcing waves and fish into a band of weeds, brush, or rocks along a well-defined "wall."

Rocky banks have especially good fishing in wind, particularly where a creek or river channel forms a bluff wall. Such "walls" normally have holes and pockets attractive to bait. When a mile or more of open water "pushes" into a bank, with tidal current surging, too, the stage is set for a fish feeding binge.

5. Docks, Piers & Pilings

Few places draw more attention from shoreline anglers than boat docks, piers, and pilings. There's just something "fishy" about such cover, and plenty of game fish are caught from it every year.

While almost any dock can occasionally give up a snook, striper or sheepshead, there are some that consistently hold tremendous numbers of fish. Docks that extend the farthest to deep water, or are close to a creek or river channel, are likely to be best. A dock with a lift or deep-draft boat usually has deeper-than-usual water where the boat engine has "washed" out the bottom. Sailboat docks can be excellent because they're deep to prevent damaging keels.

Anytime you're working piers and docks, take careful note near the shoreline and look for old pilings from piers that have rotted away. Often such pilings harbor schools of fish, particularly flounder, and

they're seldom tapped by average anglers. A floating raft used by swimmers is a good clue to deep water, and any piers or docks in the area should be fished meticulously.

6. Bridges

I never met a bridge I didn't like – at least for fishing. Few places offer more consistently good fishing than bridges. Although bridges of any size, shape, or material can provide some of the fastest fishing any angler could ever hope for, I like low-to-the-water wooden ones, 100 to 200 yards long. Shorter bridges usually don't offer enough pilings to harbor lots of fish. Longer bridges have so many pilings they can be impossible to fish properly in a week's time.

Low bridges offer lots of shade, and that's a major plus, especially during summer's broiling heat. I don't know why, but it's been my experience that wooden bridges attract more forage fish, and I've consequently had better fishing around them. Older wooden span bridges also seem to have more support cross beams, which makes for additional cover, and so is more appealing to cover-conscious predators.

Most bridges span some type of river or creek channel, and it's around these channels where the best bridge fishing is had. Support pilings on the edge of the channel are prime spots. Pilings in the channel are likely to harbor lots of suspended fish. Vertical fishing with spoons, diamond jigs, grubs, and natural baits are death on bridge-living fish. Work lures and baits carefully from just under the surface all the way to bottom.

7. Culverts

Some of the best, easiest-to-find, and simplest-to-fish inshore water is found around culverts – those large open drains leading under road beds and earthen barriers from one tidewater spot to another. Many culverts are off the beaten track, and are seldom fished. Other culverts are huge, open chasms that anyone within half a mile of the place can easily recognize.

While easily accessible large culverts receive heavy fishing pressure, they can still attract a wide variety of game fish species throughout the year and during various tide phases. The draw to culverts is swift current pushing through a confined area that funnels and disorients baitfish, crabs, shrimp, etc.

Often the best fishing around a culvert is on the edges of the swiftest water. Fish hold in the slack water to ambush food as it's swept by in fast current. Any backwater eddies or current swirls should be probed with lures and baits.

While fish can be caught from culverts almost any time, dawn, dark, and dusk are choice because fishing pressure is low, and wary game fish like snook, tarpon, and striped bass may be on the prowl.

8. Submerged Points

One of the easily identifiable fish havens for shore-bound anglers is a submerged bar, which usually extends from a point of land. Good bars can be quickly located simply by observing shoreline terrain. Frequently, a point that tapers to the water on shore continues out into a bay or river as a bar – sometimes for hundreds of yards. Bars can also be discovered by carefully studying inshore charts.

The best bars taper slowly from very shallow water to very deep water – preferably 20 or 30 feet. An ideal bar has a hard bottom of sand, clay, or rock with an extensive, broad, shallow flat and lots of weeds, or best of all, hard shell. Irregularly shaped bars are most appealing to sport fish, and often sharp turns, "fingers," and cuts on, around, and into a bar will harbor the most and largest fish. Sharp, "inside" turns of deep bars seem to be especially appealing to active fish. Many times, schools of fish are not on the tip of a tapering bar as many people would expect, but rather off to the sides of the bar or feeding on top, which attracts diving birds.

Fan-casting with jigs, sinking and swimming plugs, and spoons is a good technique for fishing bars. Such systematic fishing also enables anglers to thoroughly probe the nooks and crannies that appeal to bar sport fish.

9. Power Plants

Power plants are like heaven-sent pockets of summer warmth to winter-weary shoreline fishermen. Further, warm-water discharges from power plants attract fish from long distances. So, hot-water discharges can hold an unusually large number of active, feeding fish of several different species. Another important part of hot-water discharge fishing is that many such places offer easily accessible shoreline fishing spots, including handicap access sites in some areas.

It's common for anglers fishing a hot-water discharge to catch seatrout, stripers, flounder, and redfish in a single outing. In some regions, in even the coldest temperatures, snook, tarpon, and mangrove snapper can be caught around the same discharge zone.

Virtually all types of power plants discharge warm water. Nuclear, coal, and oil-fired generating plants use cold water from tidal rivers, sounds, and bays to cool plant equipment. Cold water piped into a plant dissipates machinery heat by warming the water. This hot water is then returned back into the sound or river. The "used" water is invariably hotter than when it started its power plant cycle, and this rare discharge of summer-like water is a magnet to all manner of inshore fish and marine bait living in an otherwise deep freeze of fall-winter-spring water temperatures.

10. Surf

The most important part of surf fishing is choosing the right place to cast a lure or bait. An endless beach to your eye may all look the same. But to fish swimming parallel to it, the surf floor is a different place indeed.

It's best to look for prime surf fishing areas at low tide so you can see sandbars and places where it will be deep during high tide. It's also possible at low tide to find spots where slots or "run-outs" form during high, falling water. You want to fish

the slots because they are highways or passes into deep beach sloughs for feeding sport fish. It's smart to concentrate on beaches littered with shells, because shell usually indicates there is good, deep water in the surf. There is also plenty of food along a shell beach, and that, of course, attracts fish.

Some beach areas with large rocks or different bottom makeup than the surrounding region can offer superb surf fishing. Often such places have subtle differences, but to fish they are important. Any difference in water color along the surf is worthy of attention. The color change

is caused by tide, current flow, sandbars, and weeds, which may hold game fish. Likewise, watch for unusual tide rips or indications of abnormal currents along a beach. These things don't happen by accident, and they can attract feeding fish. Watch for baitfish pods as they move along a beach, because, simply, where there is food there are often game fish.

Beach areas around inlets, sounds, and river mouths can offer terrific fishing, too. The mix of tides, currents, and wave action, and the fresh water-salt water exchange, are all attractive to many marine game fish species.

BASIC RIGS
for the Shore Fisherman
By Al Ristori

Fishing a basic rig in the right place will increase your success.

KEEP IT SIMPLE! That's the watchword when it comes to rigging for fishing from shore. Not only does casting involve some losses through break-offs, but streamlined rigs are also easier to cast as there's less wind resistence.

The handiest rig for a variety of shore fishing uses is the fishfinder. I was introduced to that rig when my next door neighbor in Merrick, Long Island, Mr. Kern, took me surfcasting at Jones Beach for the first time almost a half-century ago. In those days, a piece of leather was used to prevent the sliding sinker clip from riding down all the way to the hook.

Fishfinder Rig

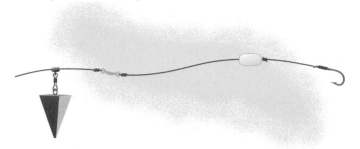

The modern fishfinder rig consists of a plastic piece called a slide that your line goes through, plus a sinker snap attached to the bottom of the slide. A swivel at the end of the leader acts as a stop for the pull slide. When a fish picks up the bait, it can line through the slide before feeling any resistance. Indeed, you can fish with an open bail or in free-spool when using large baits and give the fish a chance to move off with the bait without ever moving the sinker before you set the hook. This is the most popular rig for use with seaworms and chunks of baitfish such as menhaden (bunkers, pogies, fatbacks) and mackerel, and works just as well with clams.

Rigs such as the fishfinder that lie on the bottom can be somewhat protected from crabs by the addition of a cork on the leader. Most surf tackle shops carry corks of various sizes with a hole through the middle and a stopper. These are placed on the leader, with the proximity to your hook determining how far the bait will be raised. Bluefish anglers favor a fluorescent cork, which is pushed onto a short wire leader next to the bait, in order to provide more attraction. On the other hand, many striper fishermen feel the cork is a drawback, as bass seem to prefer stationary baits. In any case, the cork is a very definite liability when casting and should be eliminated if maximum distance is an objective. As a general rule, corks aren't necessary early and late in the season or any time surf water temperatures drop and crabs become inactive.

Long leaders make casting difficult, but they really aren't necessary with fishfinders because you can drop back as much line

as desired from the sinker in the current – and your line is probably lighter than the leader material. The fact that the sinker is sliding on the line must also be accounted for in casting, as failure to make smooth casts will result in the sinker falling back from the rig and greatly shortening the distance achieved.

Stationary Rig

Of course, that problem can be eliminated by simply using a stationary rig consisting of a long leader tied to a three-way swivel with a clip or loop for the sinker and your line tied to it. Fish will feel the sinker when they try to run with the bait, but that's no problem with species that can be hooked immediately.

Basic Two-Hook Dropper Rig

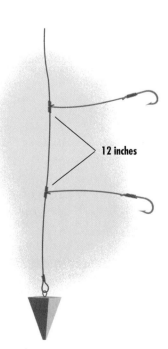

12 inches

The other basic casting rig is more suitable for smaller baits and fish that tend to hit hard while not spooking from terminal tackle. Actually, that includes most species – even the regal striped bass. The basic two-hook dropper rig is similar to that used by bottom fishermen for a variety of species. It basically consists of a piece of leader material (about two feet) into which two dropper loops are tied about a foot apart along with a loop or clip at the end for a sinker.

The dropper loop can be slipped through the eye of the hook if it's large enough. If the hook eye is too small, clip one end of the dropper loop near the knot and you'll have a short leader on which to tie the hook. This is probably the most common rig for fishing clams in the surf for stripers. Fresh clams will stay on the hook well, but if you're forced to use frozen clams (which are much softer) try wrapping a few turns of sewing thread around the bait to hold it on during the cast and to provide some protection against bait stealers. As the waters warm and crabs get more active, the bottom hook is cleaned off quickly but you may get a little longer soak time with the top hook.

While the rigs described above are standard for most species caught from shore, sharp-toothed fish require a piece of wire ahead of the hook. Finger mullet are a very popular bait for bluefish, especially during early fall when both fish migrate south along the surf. A very specific rig has been developed for use with mullet. It involves a double hook in either a very long-shanked model or with a piece of wire attached. The rig is attached with a clip so the hook can be removed to be inserted through the mullet's vent and pushed through to the mouth before being re-rigged. This provides solid hooking results and also keeps the chopper's teeth away from the main line.

Surfcasters who fish sand bottoms almost invariably use pyramid sinkers or the even better-holding Hatteras sinker, which tends to dig in with its slim foot and flat top. Conventional bank sinkers, even in large sizes, tend to roll around rather than hold bottom. However, they're a better choice in a cast-and-retrieve situation, such as when working baits in the surf or off jetties for summer flounder (fluke), which much prefer moving targets.

Pyramids are exactly the opposite of what you want when fishing on rough bottom. Bank sinkers are less likely to get snagged in such circumstances, but losses

may still be severe. If strong currents and long casts aren't a problem, it's often possible to substitute other materials that can be sacrificed for use as sinkers. They're getting harder to come by than in the old days, but discarded spark plugs make ideal sinkers. Tautog (blackfish) anglers discovered them a long time ago. Tied on with a piece of line lighter than your main line, they can be left in the bottom while your rig is pulled free. Light cloth bags filled with sand have also been used as sinkers in rugged bottom areas.

Egg sinkers, which are favored by Florida anglers on the reefs, provide another good means of avoiding constant break-offs in rough bottom. They can be fished just like the fishfinder rig, with a swivel at the end of the leader, though the loops of heavy-leadered hooks may not be sufficient to keep them from sliding down (especially when distance casting is required) unless the diameter of the egg sinker's hole is very small. A swivel may have to be used in this case, or a very small pinch-on sinker.

Teaser Rig

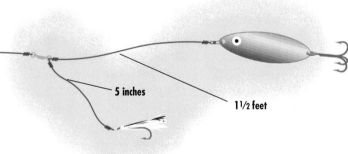

5 inches

1½ feet

Rigs for casting lures are generally very basic, simply involving a lure tied to the leader or a snap at the end of the line. However, there are many occasions when teasers will make a big difference. That's particularly the case when stripers are feeding on very small bait. Teasers also provide an opportunity to hook other species, such as weakfish, summer flounder, and hickory shad, which may not hit the main lure being cast for larger quarry.

Most of the time I fish a teaser about 1½

feet ahead of my main lure. Simply take a length of leader material (I prefer 30-pound fluorocarbon) and tie a snap to one end for the lure, plus a small swivel to the other end. A dropper loop can be tied into the leader for the teaser, but I cut a few inches of fluorocarbon for the teaser and tie the other end to the swivel. If you're using mono, find the stiffest available, since you don't want it wrapping around your line.

Teasers should be small and light. Streamer flies are very effective, as are 3- to 5-inch Felmlee plastic eels, and any other nearly weightless lure that imitates a small baitfish being chased by the larger plug. Doubleheaders of school stripers are common with these rigs, but don't use them if a lot of blues are around. Not only will they destroy your teasers, but they'll also probably cut your line – most likely when you're hooked into a big striper!

The only disadvantage of using a teaser rig is in casting. That tiny teaser doesn't look like much, but it will cut down on distance. That's especially true when casting into a wind, and you may have to eliminate the teaser if distance is critical – such as when trying to throw plugs into a northeaster.

Most species aren't particularly leader-shy, but striper pros usually feel they fool more bass by using light leaders (20-pound monofilament and under). Fluorocarbon enables the angler to have the best of both worlds by using a heavier and more abrasion-resistent leader while also greatly reducing visibility, as fluorocarbon is practically invisible in the water. The only drawback is the price, which is many times that of mono. However, if you're willing to spend a few dollars more, fluorocarbon is hard to beat.

While most shore fishing with bait involves casting to a spot and leaving the rig there, whether holding the rod or placing it in a sand spike, there are many occasions when results can be improved by using a cast-and-retrieve technique, such as with lures – though at a fairly slow pace. That's especially the case with summer flounder (fluke), which prefer a moving bait. The standard three-way rig is fine for this fishing, and attracting hardware can be added if desired. I don't like metal spinners, but beads won't hurt and the Worden's Spin-n-Glow can provide lots of attraction while not interfering too much with the cast.

Another alternative for fluke is the use of a bucktail leadhead jig or a leadhead jig rigged with a soft-plastic bait, such as the Fin-S Fish or Kalin's Super Floozy, simply tied to the end of your line or a short leader. Bucktails should be enhanced with a strip of squid or fish belly. Just hook it through once at the tip, as it must lay out straight. The length of the strip isn't critical since fluke have large mouths and tend to hit at the head of the lure in any case, but too long a strip will cut down on casting distance.

I've caught quite a few fluke in the surf on the plastic jigs without any added attraction while fishing them for stripers and weakfish, but your catch will be enhanced by adding just a small strip to provide some scent. The key to success involves slow movement on, or just over, bottom.

Utilizing the proper rig for the task at hand will improve your success while shore fishing, but always keep in mind the thought I started this article with – KEEP IT SIMPLE!

PIER-FISHING BASICS

By Bob McNally

Where, when, and how you fish a pier are the determining factors in the size, type, and number of fish you'll catch.

Fishing piers get no respect. They're kind of the Rodney Dangerfield of salt water angling. Ask the man sitting at the helm of a Bertram when was the last time he fished the local pier and you'll likely get a blank, disbelieving stare. Even the guy launching a little 14-foot skiff for a day of bay seatrout action likely has never fished the pier just around the corner from his house. And rare is the topic of conversation at the local marina, salt water fishing club, or tackle store about fishing "the rail" at the pier.

Quite simply, there is little glamour in pier fishing, no pizzazz, no fanfare. The guy peacefully soaking a shrimp off a pier doesn't bubble with excitement from the drone of powerful diesels under his feet. He isn't likely to get into discussions with his fellow anglers about how the billfishing was last season at Cozumel, nor is his biggest

concern whether to buy a new GPS unit or a sophisticated color scope depth recorder.

The general impression of many anglers is that people who fish from piers are very young, elderly, or do not own or have access to fishing boats. While that may generally be true, there are some savvy salt water anglers who know that under the right conditions, the best place to catch fish is from a good pier.

"I got a boat, and I fish from it a lot, but there are times when I can't get offshore, so I hit the piers," says Jeff Wilson, of Palm Beach, Florida. "Spring can be a tough time to fish offshore in Florida, but it's also one of the best times to fish from a pier, especially for bluefish. When the blues are in it's no trouble to fish one of the South Florida piers during a good nor'easter blow and pull in a dozen blues to four pounds. In that kind of weather you couldn't fish the

schools from a boat, and surf fishing is impossible because you couldn't cast out far enough to reach fish, nor would a sinker hold the bait right in the sloughs. You can only get 'em good from a pier."

Every spring, cobia migrate in mass along the Upper Gulf Coast. From about April through June the whole region of Panhandle Florida and parts of Alabama and Mississippi have "ling fever." While boaters cruise the coast and usually land plenty of the migratory cobia, pier fishermen have their innings, too, and at times more and bigger cobia are taken by "board walkers" than by anglers bobbing in boats. At places like Panama City, Florida, and Orange Beach, Alabama, cobia can sometimes cruise so tight to the beach that boaters can't get within casting range of them because it's dangerous to navigate so close to breakers.

"I've seen cobia comin' down the beach inside the surf line that boats just 50 yards away couldn't see nor get a cast to because of the breakers," says Mel Thomas, of Panama City. "In years when the fish are tight to the coast, I'll spend my time with the crowds on a pier looking for ling, 'cause at least I'll get to cast at some and catch a few instead of jus' goin' for a boat ride."

Important fish species, big ones, are caught annually from piers. Heavyweight tarpon, kingfish, snook, seatrout, and even sailfish have been landed from piers. A number of world-record catches have been made from piers over the years. Certainly the most amazing pier-fishing record ever established was the one Walter Maxwell set in June, 1964, at the Cherry Grove pier near Myrtle Beach, South Carolina. With 130-pound-class tackle and a 16/0 reel, Maxwell fought a massive tiger shark for nearly five hours that set an IGFA record for the species. The shark measured almost 14 feet long, with an 8½-foot girth, and weighed an astonishing 1,780 pounds!

Elvin Hooper caught a world-record red drum weighing 90 pounds from a pier at Rodanthe on Hatteras Island, North Carolina. And Hooper's redfish was no fluke. Other redfish records have been caught from piers, and each year anglers throughout the nation swarm to North Carolina's abundant piers to waylay giant migrating red drum. It is a sport that "gets in the blood," say Carolina pier anglers, no matter who the fishermen are or what type of angling background they have.

"Visiting Hatteras fishing piers is like going back to the roots of my fishing," says Vic Gaspeny, a long-time Florida Keys guide, and a man who's caught his share of "glamour fish," like marlin, sailfish, tarpon, and wahoo. "I grew up fishing for reds off the piers at Virginia Beach and Hatteras, and I love it more than any other type fishing. Pier fishing for channel bass is a microcosm. It's a social event, and I wouldn't miss it for anything."

Gaspeny has caught hundreds of redfish weighing 20 pounds or more from Carolina piers, the largest a 66-pounder. His friend Teresa Huckins once caught a 71½-pounder from Hatteras' famed Avon Pier. The fish would have been an IGFA record had she registered the fish, but she preferred to release it.

Not All Piers Are Created Equal

Red drum action is not always good at every pier, says Bob Eakes, who owns and operates Red Drum Tackle Shop in the town of Buxton, in the heart of Outer Banks pier-fishing country. Severe storms, high winds, and swift tides shift sandbars and other underwater migration routes that reds use in the surf near the piers, he explains. "A lot of people don't realize how much there is to successful pier fishing, and a lot of misinformation has been passed along about it," Eakes contends.

Timing may be the single most important factor contributing to successful pier fishing. Not only do anglers have to know – in advance – what the most productive tides are for fishing at a given pier, but to be most successful, trips must coincide with major "runs" or migrations of fish species. Experience is the best teacher in learning to time runs, just as Vic Gaspeny has found through experience when it's best to tap Carolina piers for reds. Only by asking pier-fishing regulars, reading local fishing reports, and speaking with tackle shop proprietors and pier owners will newcomers come to learn when certain fish species are most likely to be available. Such inquiries should yield information about when the Spanish mackerel run works in close enough to a given pier, or when striped bass "are in," what time of year sheepshead, kingfish, snook, pompano, etc., are around.

It helps to be observant, too. When possible, visit the piers yourself to learn what's going on. When piers are unusually crowded, there's good reason. For example, when 100 people line the end of a Texas pier in spring, it's a good bet they're not there to soak up the sun.

The best tide phases are usually moving ones, often the early stages of a flooding or ebbing tide. But this isn't always the case, and only by checking a tide table and watching which way the water "runs" will you know what the tide is doing. Wind speed and direction play an important role when it comes to tidal flow, both in terms of speed and height of the water level. By noting the wind and its relationship to tide, you're adding important input to your mental computer to duplicate fishing conditions that dictated the action at a pier during a given day. Tide phase and wind also affect water clarity. The clarity of the water is frequently paramount in the type fish caught from a pier, the location of the fish, how they'll feed, and what they'll strike. Weather is vitally important, with the best action often coming just before or immediately after violent storms.

Wind, waves, and tides slamming into a pier typically form an undulating bottom around pier pilings, as well as sloughs that usually run at a right angle to a pier and parallel to the beach. Varied bottom depths and gouged-out sloughs form underwater highways for marine fish. However, in salt water, such bottom structure is frequently shifting, which can alter the location of bait and sport fish. Pier-fishing regulars realize this, and through experience know where the best sloughs and "holes" are located during a given tide phase, at a certain time of year, for a specifically sought fish species.

While large ocean piers receive most angler traffic, small tidal river, estuary, and bay piers also offer outstanding fishing opportunities. Snook, seatrout, flounder, sheepshead, drum, and a multitude of other species are regularly caught from such piers. Marine docks and piers can be especially good, particularly at night when most people are asleep and many fish – like snook, seatrout, and striped bass – are on the prowl. Dockside fish-cleaning stations can offer superb fishing, with everything from catfish and redfish to snook and tarpon cruising the area.

Some days, for some species, the "up-tide" side of the pier may be most productive. Other days, the "down-tide" side, in, say, a deep slough, will yield the most fish. By watching where savvy pier anglers habitually fish during certain tide phases, times of day, year, etc., the neophyte angler quickly learns the ropes of where to fish a pier.

Equipment for Pier Fishing

Serious pier fishermen usually tote all their angling paraphernalia in a wagon of some type, since it's usually a long walk from a beach parking lot to the far reaches of a pier. Wooden wagons or all-plastic models are best, since they don't rust as readily as metal ones. In the wagon an angler can place his bait bucket, tackle box, rods (some anglers rig wagons with rod holders on their sides), cooler (for drinks, lunch and bait), and other needed gear. One important item all pier anglers need is a specialized "hoop net" or "pier gaff," which is used to lift good-sized fish from the water onto the pier. Even a wiggling fish of a few pounds can easily break a line or pull the hooks out if it's simply hauled up 50 or 100 feet from the water's surface.

As in all types of fishing, varied types of tackle, baits, and lures are employed for different types of fish and fishing conditions, and only by watching and asking questions of pier regulars will rookie anglers know what to use, when, and for what species. Virtually all types of tackle can be used successfully on piers, at least some of the time. Heavy 16/0 revolving-spool big-game outfits to tiny ultralight spinning gear all have their place. The heavy stuff is generally used for sharks and other large fish that run far and fight hard. Mid-size revolving-spool and spinning tackle is serviceable for kingfish, cobia, stripers, jacks, snook, and tarpon. Light-action spinning or even fly gear can provide anglers with top sport for ladyfish, pompano, bluefish, sheepshead, whiting, croakers, spots, weakfish, grunts, and others.

Many commercial fishing piers have bait and tackle shops on them or at least nearby. Usually, the right baits needed to catch the fish available can be purchased at the pier. All piers have their regional favorite lures for varied fish species, and wise is the angler who has some of them with him while "walking the boards." But a standard salt water lure selection of jigs, spoons, and plugs should serve any pier angler well.

SURF-LINE
Stripers & Salmon

By Angelo Cuanang

Expert advice on catching stripers and salmon from the Pacific shoreline.

Salmon are often thought of as open-ocean migrants that do most of their feeding offshore, gorging themselves on baitfish, squid, and krill. Striped bass, on the other hand, prefer being in close to shore in that rough-and-tumble environment of white water and rolling surf. Normally the two species rarely cross paths, except when

huge schools of anchovies push into and just beyond the surf line to feed in the plankton-rich waters. This occurs most often during summer months, but can extend into early fall. Stripers are feeding happily, putting on weight before heading back into San Francisco Bay, and the salmon are on their final feeding runs before also heading into the bay and eventually to their natal rivers to spawn. So both species feed voraciously together.

In this region, anglers will find bass and salmon feeding most actively from late June through October, with prime times being July through August. At this time, the huge dark masses of anchovies can be seen from high vantage spots overlooking the Pacific. Turnoffs and parking areas are common along Coast Highway 1, which runs along the shore.

When game fish are attacking and forcing baitfish to the surface from below, sea birds such as pelicans, seagulls, terns, and shearwaters get into the action and dive on the harried anchovies. The dark masses are pushed and broken up as the stripers and salmon force them into the surf line.

Vigilant anglers watching and waiting for such a moment rush to the scene because these so-called "runs" are often short-lived. Anglers clad in waders and armed with long surf rods will cast into the melee and hope for a strike from either a sleek, fast-moving salmon or a burly, tackle-busting striper.

Anglers who want to try this fishing

must come properly prepared to be successful. First of all, anglers should have a good pair of waders. These can be either neoprene, rubber stocking-foot, or boot-foot. Added to this is a water-resistant windbreaker. Some anglers will wear full wetsuits because of the warmth, mobility, and protection they provide against the cold Pacific waters.

In heavy surf, anglers will often have to cast long distances, 300- to 400-plus feet, to reach feeding salmon and stripers. A nine- to 11-foot surf rod is a good choice. Match this with a spinning or conventional reel loaded with 15- to 25-pound-test monofilament. The rod should be capable of handling lures from two to six ounces. When surf conditions are calmer, the fish, especially stripers, will come in close, right where the first wave curls onto the beach. In this situation, a lighter-action rod, eight to 8½ feet in length, that can cast small lures can be used with excellent results.

The Lures That Work

There is a tremendous variety of lures one can use in the surf for stripers. For surface action, pencil poppers, Striper Strikes, Creek Chub Pikies, Bomber plugs, bucktail jigs, Hopkins, Krocodile spoons, Kastmasters, and Miki jigs can draw strikes. Salmon, on the other hand, prefer lures with flash and roll, such as spoons and metal jigs. If an angler wanted to throw something both stripers and salmon would grab, a good choice would be metal lures such as chrome-finish Krocodile spoons in the two- to three-ounce size, Hopkins jigs two to four ounces, Kastmasters one to three ounces, and Miki jigs to four ounces. Also, if targeting salmon, the angler must use single-shank barbless hooks. With the lures mentioned here, I normally arm them with a single 5/0 to 6/0 single siwash hook with the barb mashed down.

Be Ever Vigilant

To be successful in the surf, the angler has to spend many days out looking at the water, watching for the right sign and looking in the right areas. While luck will always help, to be truly successful at surf fishing, particularly when chasing capricious game fish such as the striped bass and Chinook salmon, one must develop the skills of an osprey, ever vigilant and ready to strike quickly.

When you consider that some of the best fishing zones for the surf stripers and Chinook salmon can stretch from just north of the Golden Gate Bridge south to Half-moon Bay, that is a lot of intimidating property to deal with. To narrow the odds, the angler should concentrate on areas where baitfish will concentrate and where game fish can corner them. Recognizing these key feeding and brief holding zones along our coast, along with other types of physical sign, can of course narrow the search greatly for the shorebound surfcaster.

The waters north of the Golden Gate Bridge along Marin County's rugged shoreline offer a variety of topography for game fish to forage. Double Point, Stinson Beach, Muir Beach to Rodeo Beach features a combination of rocky points, small islands, coves, and sand stretches. South of the Golden Gate, Bakers Beach, Lands End, Ocean Beach, Thornton Beach, Mussel Rock, Sharp Park Beach, Mori's Point, Rockaway Beach, Linda Mar Beach, Montara Beach, Pillar Point Harbor entrance, and beaches immediately south all offer excellent opportunities. These are all key zones where salmon and stripers may push baitfish in close enough for the surfcaster to nail them. Of the two zones north and south of the Golden Gate, the southern region usually produces more fish. One of the main reasons is that access to the surf is better on the south side.

During the course of the season, salmon and stripers will use the shoreline topography to corral anchovies. They will push them up against rock points, coves, and small islands and feed voraciously, so anglers must stay sharp and watch for the signs of feeding game fish. As mentioned, one of the key indicators that stripers and salmon are pushing baitfish to the surface are diving birds. The splash of a pelican hitting the water can be seen a long way off.

Seagulls pounding the surface, terns diving, and shearwaters hitting the surface are always key indicators.

See the Bait

From a high vantage point you may also see a dark purple-colored mass changing shape and moving across the surface, similar to a cloud's shadow. This could be a massive school of anchovies being herded into a tight mass by stripers and salmon. You may also see clear holes in the purple mass. This is caused by the stripers and salmon shooting through the bait school, clearing a hole. When things are going hot and heavy, stripers will rip the surface in white-water splashes while salmon will roll and "porpoise" out of the water. At this point the angler should position himself at an intercept point that will allow him to cast over the activity. If the activity is occurring in an area where there are rocky promontories, the game fish will often herd the bait against the rocks. The angler should select the closest rock to the activity.

Watch Your Step!

When fishing these rock points, extreme care must be taken. These rocks are extremely slippery and it's easy to slip and fall. Also watch the wave action. Big ocean swells often crash onto the rocks, sweeping away everything but mussels and barnacles. In these rocky zones you have to stay sharp and watch for big waves so you don't get hurt. It's also advisable to wear a wetsuit rather than waders in these areas. In the event you get knocked down by a wave, you'll still be able to swim or crawl back up, whereas boot-foot waders can fill up with water and drag you down.

Once you get into position, cast as far as you can over the activity and allow the lure to sink. When it touches bottom, start a slow to medium retrieve so the lure works under the bait school where most of the fish are feeding. A striper's hit will feel hard and solid, while salmon strike more lightly. In either case, set the hook and keep the line tight. Stripers will normally take off on a fast, hard run. A salmon will slowly head-shake first before trying to strip line off the reel. If you plan to keep the fish, use a long bamboo or fiberglass gaff. Otherwise, a three-foot leader of 80- to 100-pound test will allow you to drag the fish up the rocks.

Head Them Off at the Pass

When striper and salmon activity is spotted slightly offshore, often they will herd the anchovies into a corner where rock meets sand or they will push the bait-fish along the outer sandbar until they hit a break or opening in the bar, where they can be pushed sometimes right into the sand. When trying to get into position for a cast, determine which way they are moving (they will often move with the current), then

position yourself on the leading edge of the activity. Cast as far as you can; on the beach a longer caster often will catch more salmon because they seem to stay a little deeper in greener water.

A fun way to catch stripers in the surf is with surface plugs. A favorite is the pencil popper. Cast it out and work it across the surface with sharp jerks of the rod tip to make that popper dance and wag across the surface. Work it all the way back to the first wave; sometimes the striper will follow it and grab in close. There is nothing more exciting than to have a big striper blast a surface plug on the crest of a wave. It's amazing how much water they can throw when they hit. Just make sure you don't try to set the hook when you see white water. Wait until the line tightens, then drive the steel home.

When water conditions are calm and the surf is small, stripers will often be in close to shore right on the drop-off where the first wave curls onto the sand. In these con-

ditions, stripers will often become finicky, preferring small lures and plugs and feeding best during early morning, late evening, and at night. The lighter eight- to 8½-foot rod matched with a light salt water spinning reel loaded with eight- to 12-pound test and a short two- to three-foot leader of 30- to 40-pound test will fill the bill here.

Cast one-ounce white bucktail jigs tipped with a white twister-tail worm, one-ounce Kastmasters, and 5½-inch Bomber Plugs, and work the pockets of deeper water in the surf. These "pockets" can be spotted by watching the wave action. The waves will break more often on the shallower areas; deeper areas, such as the drop where the first wave breaks and on the edge of bars will be a darker green and the waves will not break there as often. Cast into the pockets and also parallel to the beach along the drop-off. Allow the lure to tap along the bottom and work it all the way to the beach.

In the last few years, striper fishing in the surf has been on a tremendous upswing, with good numbers of stripers to over 30 pounds being caught in the surf and with the majority of the fish in the five- to 15-pound range. However, salmon action in the surf has not been quite as consistent. Off-shore bait schools often keep the largest schools of salmon in deeper water. Also, when salmon do move in they are in direct competition with stripers. The aggressive linesiders more often than not will nail your lure before a salmon can. But still, good salmon up to 30 pounds have been taken in the suds recently.

When conditions are just right – when the surf is calm and the anchovy schools are pushed right onto the beach – anglers have taken limits of stripers and salmon on the same day. These two species not only make a great combination on the end of a line, but also side by side on the barbecue grill.

HALIBUT
Hop to It

By Ray Dittenhoefer

RALPH DITTENHOEFER WITH A healthy flatty taken from a rip-tide hole. Remember, shiny lures work best on bright days, duller lures on overcast days.

Learn the ropes and you can take halibut almost any time along the Southern California coast.

Looking for year-round action that requires neither a boat nor specialized equipment, and is within easy driving distance of home? If you live in Southern California, consider halibut fishing in the surf with light tackle and lures.

Some fishermen think of halibut as sluggish bottom creatures, but they are actually voracious predators with teeth like barracuda and blinding speed over a short distance. They like to lie on the bottom, waiting to pounce on some unsuspecting prey that wanders by. When they're hungry, they'll strike lures and sometimes come clear out of the water while attacking baitfish in the surf.

How to Hunt Halibut

Look for beaches that have large rip-tide holes. These are best fished at peak low tides, especially around dawn. At low tide it's easier to reach the outer extremities of the holes.

Cast a lure off to the side of the hole and let the current sweep it into the hole. Retrieve just fast enough to keep your line taut until the lure swings into the hole. Then begin your regular slow retrieve, twitching the rod tip to impart as much action to the lure as possible. In cold winter waters, a slower retrieve achieves better results.

Work rip-tide holes from both sides, and if the hole is large, work it for at least half an hour. Halibut move in and out of these holes searching for baitfish during their feeding cycles, so give a large rip hole a fair shot. If nothing happens after half an hour, move on to another spot.

Stream Mouths Produce Too

Other halibut hot spots are where streams enter the surf. Streams introduce nutrients and small feed into the surf and halibut tend to congregate just offshore from these spots. These streams do not need to be substantial. The first halibut I caught in 1990 was right in front of a stream that wasn't over six inches wide, but it was the only running water for ten miles. The fish weighed eight pounds.

Often a channel forms where the stream enters the ocean and halibut tend to congregate around the sides of the channel. It is best to fish these spots at low tide. Again, reaching the channel with your lure is much easier when the tide is low. I prefer to fish the peak low tide, and then the incoming tide until I can no longer reach the channel. If low tide occurs at dawn or dusk, your chances will be best.

Streams that enter the ocean from a lagoon are ideal spots. The deeper the stream's channel, the better the fishing is likely to be. At dead low tide, get as far out toward the end of the channel as possible. As the tide begins to rise, work the inner reaches of the channel. Wade out as far as possible and cast directly into the channel where it enters deeper water. Work your lure slowly, twitching it regularly.

Bright Days, Bright Lures

On sunny days, the best lure is a 5/8-ounce Krocodile with prism tape. On darker days, or early in the morning before the sun hits the water, try Scampis, Worm Kings, and Sassy Shads. Good colors are root beer, black with metal flake, and green and silver. Color combinations that resemble smelt, anchovies, and grunion produce good results. Use four-, six-, or eight-pound test.

Halibut can turn on in the surf at almost any time, but there are a couple of situations that almost guarantee great fishing. First, check out the action during grunion runs. As these baitfish swarm the beaches at nights, a wide host of predators, including halibut, move inshore to feed on them. So try fishing at dawn after a grunion run.

When It Rains, You Score

Another excellent time is after heavy rains. The lagoons swell and the rivers entering the ocean can grow from trickles to torrents. Halibut pick up the message quickly and move in to feast on baitfish being swept into the ocean.

Be sure to fish during large tidal swings. Big low tides allow you to reach holes and pockets in the surf that you would not otherwise be able to reach with a lure. Again, big low tides at dawn and dusk are killer combinations. Incidentally, all of my biggest fish were taken during the winter, when there wasn't another fisherman on the beach.

The current legal minimum size on halibut is 22 inches. Carry a net that's capable of handling a large halibut. Small fish may come in easily, but large halibut can be very difficult to land.

San Diego Hot Spots

In San Diego, try the deep holes in front of the Mission Beach Roller Coaster. Blacks Beach is another good bet for deep rip-tide holes. The lagoons at Torrey Pines are now open and running, as is the lagoon at the Del Mar Race Track. Give these spots a try; they consistently produce legal halibut.

STRIPERS & BLUES
from the Beach

By Al Ristori

If you want to catch striped bass and bluefish in the surf, fish when they want to eat, be in a good location, and use the right gear.

"The price of a striper is eternal vigilence." I saw that statement on the hood of a beach buggy at Montauk over 30 years ago, and it's just as meaningful today as then.

Surfcasting can be one of the least expensive and most rewarding means of salt water fishing – if you're at the right place at the right time! Unfortunately, most anglers don't put enough thought or effort into the sport, and, since they rarely catch anything worthwhile, come to the conclusion that it's just not a very viable method of catching game fish.

Striped bass and bluefish are the main targets of surfcasters in the Mid-Atlantic and New England, and it's likely that no other stretch of surf in the world produces finer angling for two such high-quality game fish. After becoming a rare catch during the 1980s, the Atlantic States Marine Fisheries Commission (ASMFC) management plan has brought the striper back to almost record high levels by sharply reducing both recreational and commercial fishing mortality. At the same time, nature has provided several banner year classes, which should keep this fishery healthy for many years to come.

Bluefish populations have gone down from the historically high numbers of the 1970s and 1980s. Though they remain quite healthy, their abundance close to shore isn't nearly what it was, and bluefish blitzes are more occasional than routine. Considering the abundance of stripers, most anglers are just as happy with the current situation, since bass grow to much larger sizes, are easier to handle, better to eat, and don't destroy terminal tackle. The latter factor is tough on tackle shops, as the same plugs can be used year after year on bass while bluefish blitzes result in numerous cut-offs.

Both stripers and blues migrate up the coast each spring and back south in the fall, providing a long season. For instance, New Jersey surfcasters may start catching bass in March, and should have decent fishing by April, while the fall season extends well into December or even early January. Fishing starts a bit later and ends earlier to the north, while the season can last even longer to the south if the waters remain mild enough. Cape Hatteras, North Carolina, has a winter fishery for stripers, which are rarely seen in the surf during the warmer months.

Bluefish arrive a bit later, usually around the beginning of May, in New Jersey, and are normally south of that state by early December, if not sooner. They're primarily a summer species in New England, with few being caught after early October north of Cape Cod. Hatteras, North Carolina, used to have record blitzes of big blues around Thanksgiving during the boom years, but whatever shots surfcasters have been getting in recent years tend to be in December and then again in March or April as the schools move north.

Classic surfcasting for stripers and blues involves the use of artificials. Some purists wouldn't be caught dead using bait, though some of them will make an exception in the case of casting live eels. Fishing with lures has to be even more specifically attuned to the first rule of surfcasting outlined at the beginning of this article – being

at the right place at the right time. A bait soaking in the surf might be gobbled up by a single lazy fish if you're lucky, but success with lures usually requires a quantity of actively feeding fish.

Dawn and dusk are generally the best times to fish the surf with lures, especially if the tidal situation is right. Some beaches may be too shallow at low tide, while others are best at such tides due to deep cuts that allow game fish to safely get at concentrated baitfish that may be too hard to pin down at higher tides.

Scout It Out

The best bet when fishing a new area is to scope it out at the extreme tides. Low tide is the first priority, as the cuts, sloughs, rocks, etc., will be easier to recognize. The same place at high water may lose all distinction, especially in calm seas, but you'll then know which portions are most likely to hold fish.

In point of fact, blues and stripers could be anywhere along the beach. However, a knowledge of the beach structure will enable you to work the most likely areas hardest. A cut though the outer bar that forms a relatively deep-water slough creates an ideal low-water situation, as game fish should be concentrated within that slough or the cut. The edges on both sides next to the bar deserve special attention. That same area could be productive on higher tides, but now your effort should be directed to the white water on the bars, as long as it's deep enough to hold the size game fish you're seeking.

Roiled water is ideal for game fish that have an advantage under such circumstances in chasing down baitfish. These fish are also easier to fool with an artificial when the visibility is a little off. Crystal-clear waters may look good, but often aren't desirable when working lures. Waters that are just a bit off-color, such as a couple of days after a storm, are normally ideal.

Catch 'Em Up Close

Everyone wants to cast as far as they can, although that's not always the key to catching fish in the surf. By all means cover everything within range, but don't speed up your retrieve during the last few yards just so you can fling another cast to the horizon. For the same reason that the edges of bars are productive, the wash is often the best spot of all. Bass especially like to patrol the drop-off to pick up crabs being washed off the beach, as well as baitfish tumbled in the wash. Always retrieve your lure properly until it hits the sand (I've had stripers beach themselves as they've hit a lure in the curl of a wave) and you'll often find that the majority of your catch will be made within a few yards of the beach. In addition to the fish feeding there, any following your lure in will be forced to make a decision as they near the wash.

As previously noted, dawn and dusk are almost always your best bets for working lures in the surf, though there are lots of exceptions to that rule, especially during the spring and fall migrations. Blues are primarily daytime feeders and usually don't hit lures well at night in the surf, even if bait fishermen continue to catch them after dark. On the other hand, stripers are active nocturnal feeders and will hit lures at any time.

Use the Right Tackle

Try to match the size and shape of the bait being consumed. Small lures will catch more bass than large ones, but your tackle must be scaled down in order to fish such lures properly. Many newcomers have visions of Hatteras and Montauk Point with pros whipping lures out with 11-foot sticks, and figure that's what they need. Actually, relatively light tackle is suitable for most beach fishing with lures. Anglers along the northern Jersey shore generally prefer medium-action, two-handed seven- to eight-foot spinning rods with reels capable of holding 200 yards or so of eight- to 12-pound mono in order to cast plugs weighing an ounce or less (such as the Bomber Long-A, Gag's Grabber Mambo Minnow and Yo-Zuri Crystal Minnow), jigs from ⅜ to ¾ ounce or one- to two-ounce metal lures and popping plugs. Though surfcasters are expecting

mostly schoolies, some very large bass have been beached with such gear. Most important, the tackle doesn't wear out the angler who can cast comfortably for hours – which is often the key to being at the right place at the right time!

It's a different story if you're casting from rocks at Montauk Point or the Rhode Island breachways, but even in those areas there are nearby spots (such as Turtle Cove or Shagwong Point at Montauk) where the light tackle is appropriate and a lot more comfortable to handle. Large plugs are routinely fished by surfcasters working rocky areas known for big bass, but the effectiveness of such lures from sand beaches is usually restricted to periods when large baits such as bunkers (a.k.a. menhaden, pogies) or herring are present.

Though not always necessary, those traditional 10- to 12-foot rods with big spinning or conventional rods are a good bet for bait fishing in the surf and a must for specialized situations, such as fishing the high surf at Hatteras where big baits must be thrown well offshore. Though you'll get a lot farther with big rods, keep in mind what I said about the wash. Kids with short rods catch legal-sized stripers every summer from the surf while only casting a bait a few yards out. In the meantime, the pros with baits sitting 200 yards farther out may be doing nothing because they've ignored the most obvious potential hot spot!

Best Bait

Especially when it comes to legal-sized stripers, bait is the most consistent producer along sand beaches. Clams are hard to beat from April to December, as they are a natural bait. Stripers aren't equipped to open clams, but easterly storms throw surf clams up on the beach. Those not eaten by seagulls die and are washed back into the surf where bass get a shot at easy meals. Of course, the logical place to pick up those freebies is on the drop-off – which is why short casts are often effective.

Seaworms are better at times, especially early and late in the season, although they tend to attract mostly smaller stripers. If

Catching stripers and blues in the surf is no easy matter, but it's the most satisfying form of the sport.

you're strictly looking for a trophy striper, use cut bunker in the summer and early fall, but be prepared to wait and fight off crabs. Bunker heads may be the best choice, as they stand up to crabs longer and big bass display a particular fondness for them. Bluefish also love bunkers, but if they're present you'll have to add some wire leader in order to avoid constant cut-offs.

When large bunkers are found inside the outer bar, there will almost always be big bluefish and a few large stripers hounding them. By far the most effective means of hooking those fish is to use a snag hook to snatch a live bunker and then fish it near the school. Large popping plugs and swimmers may also do the job under such circumstances, especially with the blues, which rarely can resist the surface action of a popper.

Live eels are another popular bait, especially at night. They seem to be most effective in rocky areas, such as around jetties, at Montauk, and in many portions of the Rhode Island coast, where they often work just as well during the day if there aren't any bluefish around to chop off the expensive baits. A slow retrieve is usually best in order to keep the eel from hiding in the weeds and rocks.

Catching stripers and blues in the surf is no easy matter, but it's very satisfying and can be reasonably productive if you're will-

ing to put in the time when the fish want to feed rather than when it might be convenient to give it a try. Pounding the beaches at dawn and dusk, especially in the fall, will surely get you into fish with some regularity. The beginning of a northeaster in the fall is almost a sure thing, and action might continue all day if you can handle the building surf, wind, and rain while going to metal and larger plugs in order to get casts into the strike zone. A day or two after such storms, just as the waters start clearing a bit, is also an almost sure bet for hot fishing. Clams will produce even before the seas settle and clear. Indeed, any time you see clams on the beach is a perfect time to fish them.

Most successful surfcasters have an additional edge in terms of contacts. Get friendly with those regulars who haunt the areas you plan to fish and share information with them. That may well result in a call to "get down here right away" whenever bass or blues suddenly show up. Patronizing tackle shops that specialize in surfcasting is another good idea for getting that all-important information that others read about after the blitz is over!

Surfcasting may not be the easiest way to catch stripers and blues, but it really isn't as difficult as most newcomers imagine. Though I'm primarily a boat fishermen, I account for hundreds of surf stripers every fall by putting in a few hours a day casting lures at dawn and dusk from local North Jersey beaches – and the number of successful trips far outnumbers the shutouts, even if the vast majority of the catch consists of shorts. In this age of striper abundance, releases of ten to 40 bass a trip aren't all that unusual – if you're at the right place at the right time!

Texas Jetties for
BIG TROUT

By Robert Sloan

*Use these expert techniques
when walking the rocks
to produce some fantastic
speckled trout fishing.*

Fishing for speckled trout along the Texas jetties is some of the finest angling you'll ever experience. The options are many, and the supply of hard-fighting trout seems to be endless, especially now that commercial netting of these great sport fish has been banned for years.

You can find many jetties along the Texas Gulf Coast. The first set is on the

Texas/Louisiana border at Sabine Pass. The southernmost can be found at the end of South Padre Island on the Texas/Mexico border.

Having fished Texas jetties for the better part of three decades, I can say from vast experience that the trout fishing opportunities you'll find on the jetties ranges from casting topwater plugs for surface-feeding trout to free-lining live croakers for the most finicky specks.

One of the best days of fishing topwater plugs for trout that I can remember was at the Freeport jetties. It was in early October. A mild cold front had just passed through and its wake set the stage for calm, green, fish-rich tides to move into the jetties. A friend and I hit them just right. We tied on MirrOlure Top Dogs in red/white and silver/chartreuse, and it didn't take long to find what we were after. Big trout. And they were hungry for mullet, and our mullet-imitating plugs waddling across the water's surface were too good to pass up. It was a session of explosive action. When the action ceased we had caught 17 specks to 8½ pounds. That's about as good as it gets on the Texas Gulf Coast.

Lures or Baits?

One of the best anglers I've run across is Joe "The Jetty Man" Persohn, whose specialty is fishing artificial lures along the granite rocks that form the Sabine jetties, which stretch for three miles along the Sabine-Neches ship channel.

"One of the best all-around lures I've used at the jetties is a silver spoon," says Persohn. "The half-ounce and one-ounce SpoonDogs in silver/chartreuse or red/silver are tough to beat. But there are days when I'll tie on a slow-sinking chartreuse MirrOlure when the trout want a slower presentation."

On the flip side of fishing the jetties is Port O'Connor guide Robbie Gregory. It's a rare occasion that you'll find him fishing the rocks with lures. He's the kind of guy that lives and dies by live shrimp and croakers.

"There always seems to be a good supply of live bait at the jetties," says Gregory. "The currents that funnel through the two walls of rocks act like a vacuum and suck a variety of baitfish from the bays on outgoing tides. Or they might be coming in from the Gulf on incoming tides. I've figured out three things about fishing the jetties. First, they attract lots of trout. Second, those trout won't usually turn down a kicking shrimp or croaker. Third, the trout and baitfish are most active on strong tides."

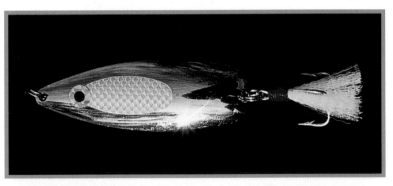

Play the Currents

Current rules at the rocks. Without current you'll rarely catch trout, or anything else, for that matter, along the jetties. Gregory keys on the various back-wash currents that occur during moving tides.

For example, one day when we were fishing at one of his best trout holes at the Port O'Connor jetties, Gregory pointed to the line of water moving with the outgoing tide. But due to a stack of rocks at the base of the jetty there was a reverse in current.

"Right there you have water going in two different directions," explained Gregory. "That sets up a location for predatory fish to ambush baitfish. The trout will stage on the down-current side of the rocks as shrimp, croakers, shad, crabs, and mullet are washed by. It sets up the classic situation to catch lots of trout."

Gregory has his best luck with a bottom rig. He uses leader material of about 40-pound test. He'll tie a loop at the top, middle, and bottom, just like a snapper rig. At the bottom loop he attaches a two- to three-ounce lead weight, depending on how strong the current is. To the middle loop he attaches a 4/0 Mustad straight-shank hook. Finally, he ties the tag end of the fishing line to the top loop of the leader and he's ready to fish.

"You want just enough weight to hold the bait in place, or maybe let it bump slowly along bottom with the current," says Gregory.

If you're not into bottom rigs, you might try fishing under a slip cork. Mike Barnes is, without a doubt, the best at fishing live shrimp under a cork while fishing any set of jetties along the Texas coast.

The Barnes slip-cork rig is simple. First you attach a bobber stopper to the line. Next thread the fishing line through one of those snow-cone-shaped six-inch-long Styrofoam corks. (It's the type that has the hollow plastic stick through the center of the cork.) Next you tie the tag end of the fishing line directly to the back side of a one-ounce trolling weight. On the opposite end of the lead weight tie on one end of an 18-inch monofilament leader of about 25-pound test. An the other end of the leader attach a No. 2 or 4 treble hook.

Neat thing about the slip-cork rig is that it allows you to fish as deep as you want. Just adjust the bobber stopper to whatever depth you want, and you're ready to fish.

"The great thing about this rig is that I can set it to fish a live shrimp eight feet deep as it floats along with the current at the rocks," says Barnes. "There are numer-ous rocks along jetties that divert the current and create an eddy. That's where trout will gang up and feed. I can set a slip cork to fish a live shrimp at exactly 12 feet so that the bait floats right over the rocks. You can cover a lot of water in a hurry with a slip cork. You just keep the reel in free-spool and feed line out as the cork moves with the current."

Timing for Jetties

Jetties come to life with trout around May 1 and the action doesn't subside till the first hard cold fronts move trout to deeper water in the bays and the Gulf of Mexico. Usually by around November 1 the jetties have played out. Peak months will be June through August for two- to three-pound jetty trout. The best month is certainly October. That's when the first cold fronts will begin pushing past Texas. As water temperatures fall in the bays, shrimp and shad begin their fall migration to the Gulf. That's when big speckled trout will stack up at the jetties and go on a feeding frenzy.

Capt. Jerry Norris with Sabine Lake Guide Service says his best days at the rocks are during October. "That's when very few people bother fishing the jetties," says Norris. "Most folks have put up their fishing gear and are hunting doves or getting ready for deer season. They're missing out on some fantastic jetty trout action."

Norris says the exodus of shad and shrimp from the bays sets the stage for some outstanding topwater action. "On outgoing tides you want to fish the channel side of the jetties," says Norris. "On incoming tides you'll do best on the outside. The way I fish the jetties is to work a

When shrimp and shad migrate, big speckled trout stack up at the jetties and go on a feeding frenzy.

mullet-imitating topwater plug anywhere from two to five feet off the rocks. That's where the heavy trout will be feeding. They will hold in the holes along the rocks and ambush shrimp, shad, and mullet."

A topwater plug such as a TopDog in chartreuse/silver or bone is tough to beat along the rocks during October. Norris says you want to work the bait as parallel to the rocks as possible with a walk-the-dog motion. I've seen his tactic in action and it will catch some giant trout.

There are times when trout will be feeding deep along the rocks, especially when it's really hot or really cold. In that situation you can jig for trout with half- to one-ounce leadhead jigs with either shad or shrimp tails. This is an excellent tactic that very few jetty fishermen use, or even know about. It's a simple way to catch trout that might be feeding from ten to 15 feet deep along the jetty wall. What you want to do is work down the jetty while bumping jigs just off the tops of the rocks. Believe me, this is a great way to catch trout and usually once you catch one you'll catch several.

The heavier jig heads are best because you can get them down to bottom and keep them in the trout's feeding zone. You can use an assortment of jig tails, such as shrimp, shad, or simply curly tail grubs. All of them will catch trout. However, you'll probably do best with shad tails during the summer months. Top colors will be shad, glow white, or red. Shrimp tails in strawberry or root beer colors are best during fall when trout are gorging on shrimp. When jigging, be sure to maintain contact with the tops of the rocks. That's where the trout will be positioned. And remember that just about every bite will occur as the jig is falling.

As you can see, there are many ways to fish the Texas jetties. And with the exception of the coldest months, the jetties will always attract speckled trout.

Understanding Texas Jetties

The jetties are built to protect shipping channels from silting up. They are all made of chunked granite. The walls of the jetties slant out about 30 feet from the top of the rocks, offering a variety of depths to fish lures or live baits.

Many of the Texas jetties can be fished by walking them. And many are user friendly, such as at Galveston and Freeport. The east Freeport jetty offers handicapped access complete with hand rails. The Galveston jetties are decked for easy walking about a quarter of the way out. Once the concrete deck ends you'll have to walk or hop from rock to rock. Both the Freeport and Galveston jetties can be accessed without a boat. So can the jetties at South Padre.

Conversely, you can only access the Sabine, Port O'Connor, and Matagorda jetties via boat. However, once you reach these jetties you can tie off to the rocks and walk them.

Caution should be used when walking the rocks. They are often very slimy and slippery and covered with jagged rocks and razor-sharp barnacles.

Also, when walking the rocks keep in mind that you'll have to carry all your gear. The most well organized rock walkers wear a Styrofoam hat full of lures and a gear belt with pockets to carry water, pliers, a stringer and rod holder, etc.

How to SURF CAST

By C. Boyd Pfeiffer

In one sense, surfcasting is no different from other types of casting. As with all casting of spinning or revolving-spool tackle, it uses the rod as a lever to power the lure or sinker/bait combination to the target.

In another sense, surfcasting is completely different, since the rods are longer and heavier, the line higher test than in most fishing, the lures and sinkers heavier, and the target farther than ever possible with lighter salt or fresh water tackle. In addition, the various fishfinder and single- and two-hook bottom rigs used for much surf fishing require casting techniques different from those used when just a lure is flipped into the suds.

Surf fishing is also sometimes a misnomer, since the basics of surf fishing are practiced from jetties, piers, breakwaters, and sometimes backcountry mud flats. Just where and how you are fishing can also dictate the tackle, even beyond the basics of spinning vs. revolving-spool tackle.

Spinning rods for surf can range from as light and short as seven-footers throwing an ounce for fishing the Gulf, to as long as 11- and 12-footers capable of throwing six-ounce pyramid sinkers and bait in the rough surf of the North Carolina Outer Banks. Length in this latter circumstance is a must, both for the additional leverage necessary with long casts as well as for added length to hold line above the breakers to prevent it from being caught and dragging the bait. The type of guides and the length of the rear grip or handle also varies widely. Some grips are continuous, while those on longer and heavier surf rods are often separated with the blank showing between the two grips.

Depending upon the fish sought and the area fished, reels will vary from spinning or casting models in the heavy fresh/light salt range (wide spool for casting), with both spinning and casting used in protected waters, some pier fishing, and in the Gulf Coast to large mills capable of holding 300 yards of 20-pound-test line (used in North Carolina and along the Atlantic). Even with the centrifugal casting control or magnetic cast control of today's casting reels, thumb stalls are best to protect your thumb against the racing reel, as are finger stalls used with spinning to prevent line cuts as the line is released under the tremendous forces used in the cast.

Casting requires that the reel, rod, and line are all matched to the weight of the lure or sinker/bait combination used. Fill the reel to within about $1/8$ inch of the spool rim. If using very heavy rigs and trying for maximum distance, tie a shock leader to the end of the line that will make a few turns on the reel spool when the lure or sinker/bait rig is hanging the proper distance from the rod tip. These shock leaders, usually about 40- to 50-pound-test line, prevent the possibility of line breakage on the cast. For optimal casting, the lure should hang down about six inches to two feet from the rod

Surf Tackle Recommendations

HEAVY SURF (such as the North Carolina Outer Banks)

Spinning — Heavy 11- to 12-foot rod, parabolic action, capable of casting up to six-ounce sinkers plus bait; large surf spinning reel with full bail or manual roller (your choice) capable of spooling 300 yards of 20-pound line.

Casting — Heavy ten- to 12-foot rod, with stiff parabolic action, capable of casting up to six or more ounces of lead plus bait; large, wide-spool specialty surf reel, with or without levelwind, and holding 250 yards of 20-pound line.

Lures and terminal tackle — Topwater plugs and medium swimming lures in mackerel and other salt water finishes, heavy spoons (like the Hopkins), and jigs in white, yellow, and black. Terminal tackle rigs as required such as fishfinder rigs, and single and two-hook bottom rigs, sinkers to six ounces, pyramid for sand, and bank for gravel and rock.

MEDIUM SURF

Spinning — Slightly fast action rod to eight or nine feet, capable of casting up to four ounces; medium heavy spinning reel with full roller capable of spooling 300 yards of 15-pound line.

Casting — Rod to eight or nine feet, slightly fast action, capable of casting four ounces; wide revolving-spool reel spooling 250 yards of 15-pound line.

Lures and terminal tackle — Topwater chuggers and medium swimming crankbaits; Hopkins-style spoons, and jigs. Standard rigs as above.

PIER & JETTY

Spinning — Rod to eight feet, parabolic action; medium heavy spinning reel holding 200 yards of 15- to 20-pound line.

Casting — Spool-rod to eight feet, parabolic action; medium revolving-spool reel, with 200 yards of 15- to 20-pound line.

Lures and terminal riggings — Appropriate-sized top water chuggers and medium swimming crankbaits, jigs, and metal casting spoons. Terminal rigs as above.

QUIET SURF (as on the Gulf Coast)

Spinning — Rod to seven- or eight-foot length, light action capable of throwing lures to two ounces; medium heavy fresh/light salt water spinning reel spooled with 200 yards of 12- to 15-pound line.

Casting — Rod to seven or eight feet, light action but capable of throwing lures to three ounces; medium-size wide-spool casting reel, levelwind, and spooled with 200 yards of 12- to 15-pound ine.

Lures and terminal tackle — Topwater lures, medium swimming crankbaits, lipless rattling crankbaits, small jigs to two ounces, soft-plastic grub tails, and metal spoons.

ACCESSORIES FOR ALL SURF FISHING

Not necessarily needed in all surf fishing, but consider sand spikes to hold a rod up in sandy surf, beach gaffs to land fish, hip boots or waders for cold-water conditions, a waterproof parka top for protection in high surf, wading shoes for wet wading in Gulf conditions, cleats for fishing from jetties, wading vest for carrying tackle while wet wading, surf bags for carrying lures in Atlantic coast fishing, fishing pliers, hook hone or file, bait knife and board, filleting knife, gloves for handling fish or cold-weather fishing, cap, polarizing sunglasses, and sunscreen.

STEP 1: Snap the lure or practice plug backward and directly overhead. The centrifugal force will spin the lure away from the rod.

STEP 2: Bring the rod back just past 45 degrees. At this position reverse the rod's direction and bring the rod sharply overhead and toward the target.

STEP 3: Release the line when the rod is approximately at 45 degrees in front of you. Follow through with the cast and gradually lower the rod, beginning the retrieve as the lure hits the water.

tip, any bait rig about the same distance from the rod tip to any swivel or snap used. Even with large tip top rings, you DO NOT want any metal snaps or swivels going through them on the cast.

If using spinning tackle with a lure, you can use several casting techniques. In all cases hold the rod with one hand on the reel seat and reel to control line release. Place two fingers on each side of the reel stem. Anglers with small hands and larger reels may need to put three fingers forward of the stem so that the index finger will be in position for easy line pickup when casting. The other hand is placed on the butt or rear end of the rod.

Position your body slightly at an angle to the direction of cast. If you're a right-handed caster, position your left foot slightly forward of the right, in the direction of your cast, as an aid in pushing the cast forward and rocking into the thrust of the cast. This leaning, rocking motion imparts more force to the cast for maximum distance. Do not position your feet and body parallel to the beach or direction of the cast. It will limit the amount of force and power you can put into the cast

In all casting with spinning tackle, the line is released at once, usually with the rod at about a 45-degree angle with the water. Releasing too early causes a high *"McDonald's arch"* type of cast that cuts distance and puts a lot of slack in the line. Too late a release causes the lure or bait to hit the water early and cuts casting distance. If you get too much of an offshore wind (from the ocean) that blows back the lure, try a hard, forceful, low-trajectory cast to get under the wind.

One simple casting method with a lure is to bring the rod back rapidly and then immediately forward to make a *"snap cast."* This is best with light lures reeled close to the rod tip, and with shorter casts when the fish are in close.

For longer casts, bring the rod back to the side and then immediately up over your head in a vertical high overhead cast into the surf in sort of a "sweep" or "lobbing" cast. This still helps to load the rod with the rearward movement of the lure, but not to the extent of the previous snap cast. One simple way to learn a "lob" cast is to extend several feet of line from the end of the rod as you would with a bait rig and lay the practice plug on the sand directly behind you. Load the rod immediately, but with gradual acceleration, bringing the rod over your head and releasing the line.

For heavy lures, bring the rod back to the rear to a nearly horizontal position. If the lure or bait rests on the sand, that's OK. Pause and then rapidly push with the reel hand while pulling with the butt cap hand to rocket the lure to the target. This places less strain on the rod, while still utilizing the rod as a flexible lever to fire the lure forward.

Casting with a sinker/bait rig requires modifications of the above. A snap cast may pull off the bait as you snap the rod forward. A better casting method is to bring the rod sideways to the rear and with the rod horizontal, pause while the bait and sinker hang straight down, and then with increasing acceleration of the rod, fire the rod forward. In short, it is a *lob cast* rather than a snap or change-of-direction cast.

The rigs used with bait also result in more line hanging down from the rod tip than with a lure, and this also requires more of a lob cast and more care on the cast. Single hook, double hook, and sliding sinker fishfinder rigs result in hooks on droppers several feet long in some cases. The method for casting these rigs is to allow the rig and bait to hang straight down from the rod tip as the rod is held angled to the rear, then bring the rod up and forward rapidly and smoothly as centrifugal force swings the sinker and bait out and then toward the target.

Another method for maximum distance uses this lobbing style of cast, while at the same time loading the rod. This is an English style of casting as popularized by John Holden. The technique is to allow enough line hanging from the rod tip (about five to seven feet) so that the distance from the tip to the sinker is about the same as the length of the rod from the reel to the tip top. Using this long length of line for leverage, turn and bring the rod to the rear while holding it vertically. Then swing the rod straight back and at an angle to push the lure or sinker away. Once the lure or sinker reaches the rearmost position, bring the rod vertical again to swing the lure back toward you and just behind your head. Then immediately swing the rod around in a counterclockwise motion (if a right-handed caster) and toward the target. This pendulum-like swing also gives this cast its alternative name, the *"pendulum cast."*

The advantage of this method is that it allows a full sweep of the loaded rod after swinging the lure back to the vertical. Timing is critical and practice essential to perfect this technique, but casts to 450 feet are possible with a practice, while

Lob Cast

STEP 1: Position the rod, line, and bait rig (practice plug shown) in the opposite direction of the target. Pause in this position. Several feet of line will hang down from the rod tip.

STEP 2: Swing the weight and bait slightly away from the casting direction and then immediately load the rod by swinging it sharply forward and toward the target.

STEP 3: Accelerate by moving the rod over your head. Release the line when the rod is about 45 degrees, pointed in the direction of your target.

Pendulum Cast

STEP 1: Point the rod, line, lure, rig, or practice plug in the opposite direction that your cast will be directed and pause.

STEP 2: Swing the lure out away from the rod by raising and then pushing it away from your body, beginning a back-and-forth motion.

STEP 3: Swing the lure back toward the side of your head. For a right-handed caster, this must be on the right side of your head as you look at the lure. Continue to swing the lure back and forth until it reaches its high point and maximum momentum.

STEP 4: Reaching a high point near but safely away from your head, swing the rod sharply to the right and angled high to load the rod and make the cast. Release the line with the lure high in the air, completing the cast.

experienced anglers regularly achieve casts in excess of 700 feet.

All the above casts can be accomplished with casting (revolving spool) tackle in addition to spinning tackle. All are practiced the same way, with one exception – the release of the cast. With spinning, the line is released off of the reel all at once. With revolving spool tackle, the line is gradually released under control as the rod comes forward from the backcast position, finally releasing the line under thumb control with the rod about 50 degrees above horizontal. Most casters of all types of casting tackle don't realize this, but in practice this is how it MUST be done to control the spool as it begins to revolve on the cast. Releasing all at once at the release position will result in a backlash or the lure hitting the water short of the target.

Surfcasting, as with all casting, does require practice. This is less true with the snap cast and most important with the English, pendulum-style cast. But in all cases, familiarity with your equipment and practice with a range of lures, lure weights, and bait/sinker rigs will make you ready for any situation that might happen on the beach, from a pier, or while perched on a jetty. Practice casting safely using plugs made from pieces of an old broom handle weighted with lead. Weight them differently for the range of lures you expect to use, usually two to six ounces.

Realize that all surf fishing uses longer rods and sometimes lob casts that are not used in other fishing. Thus, keep safety in mind at all times, and realize that with the line out from a pendulum cast and an 11-foot surf rod, you need 30 feet all around you as a safety buffer area (11 feet for the rod, nine feet for the line out, and a 10-foot safety margin). That's one reason shorter rods of seven to eight feet are often used from jetties and piers, to reduce the safety zone area needed when other anglers are fishing nearby.

Not all surf fishing requires long casts. Sometimes the blues are running bait in the suds on the Atlantic coast, while redfish and trout inhabit easily reached sloughs when Gulf coast fishing. In these cases a simple snap cast will get a lure to the fish; a light lob will present bait gently to the same area. Preserve your strength and skills for long casts for those times when the fish are off an outside bar or you need to get to breaking fish beyond the breakers, and use the right cast for the right job of presenting lures and bait in the different situations available in surf fishing.

30 Do's & Don'ts for FLY FISHING THE FLATS

By Lefty Kreh

Here are some top tips and tricks – plus some common mistakes to avoid – that'll help you hook more bonefish, permit, and other flats gamesters.

There is a special appeal to wading salt water flats. You are on your own. There is no guide to locate the fish, or to pole you closer and give you last-minute instructions. Because of this, when you finally hook and land your quarry, you feel a real sense of accomplishment.

This is close-range stuff. Most bonefish, redfish, stripers or permit are usually within 40 feet before you cast. It gives you time to intently observe the fish and its reaction. This increases your knowledge of what the fish is doing and how to react.

Most of the time it is best to wade into the current. This places stirred bottom behind you. A hat and good polarizing glasses to reduce glare are essential. You also need to know the tides. You could be stranded on a high tide or left without water to fish on a falling one. There are hard and soft flats; make sure the one you work is firm enough for good wading.

Wading is more comfortable with long pants, rather than shorts. Good footwear is just as essential as your tackle. Boots designed for flats wading are best. To prevent sand, grit, and other debris from entering the boots, place the long pants outside the boots and then slip gravel guards over the pants.

If you have to carry your wallet, fishing license, or other papers, put them in a Ziploc bag, stored in your shirt pocket.

There are some flats that fish best on an incoming tide, while others are best on a high or falling tide. Keep a logbook with these observations.

When fly fishing the shallow flats, there are a number of things you can do to catch more fish. A few are vital to success. Everything from the noise you make to the size of the line you use – even the type of clothes you wear – can make a difference.

The following is a list of simple do's and don'ts that are guaranteed to improve your performance. These tips are designed to help you spot fish more easily, approach them more carefully, cast to them more efficiently, and, of course, get more hook-ups.

DO use sharp hooks. Consistently check to make sure your hooks are sharp. It's much more important when fishing in salt water that in fresh, since most salt water species have very tough mouths.

DON'T pull off more line than you expect to cast. Surer than tomorrow, you'll be standing on it when you go to cast or when the fish makes its run. Some sharp anglers make a long indicator mark on the line with a waterproof pen, so they know exactly how much line to pull out from the reel.

DO wade with someone when possible, for safety reasons.

DON'T let the fly hit the surface when false-casting. This is especially important on the forward cast. I've seen many fish spooked because the fly struck the surface between the angler and the fish. It is one of the most important common reasons why novice anglers fail to catch bonefish.

DO strike gently when setting the hook on bonefish or permit. When one of these fish eats the fly, simply grasp the fly line and gently move the rod tip to the side, or grasp the line and slowly pull back to make a strip strike. Bonefish and permit are especially nervous, and the moment the steel is driven home they go crazy. If you strike violently at the same time the fish bolts away, the chances of breaking the tippet are magnified.

DON'T talk loudly or yell when fishing in water less than a foot deep. Loud talking doesn't seem to affect fish when you are in deeper water, but it will spook fish in the shallows.

DO wade with the sunlight to your back. Glare produced by the sun makes it extremely difficult to see fish. Try to select a portion of the flat that allows you to wade with the sun at your back or at least off to one side.

DON'T use extra-long leaders on windy days, or vice versa. It nearly impossible to present a fly properly with a long leader on a windy day. On calm days, using a short leader will result in spooked fish. The three major reasons for using a leader are that it allows the fly better movement on the retrieve; it forms a near-invisible connection to the line; and, most important, it places the splashdown of the heavy fly line far enough away from the fish to avoid spooking it. Use these criteria as guides for how long your leader should be to match the conditions on a particular day.

DON'T carry too many flies. If you fall down you may lose or ruin them. Instead, carry the necessary patterns in a floating box or impaled in a closed-cell foam block hung on a string around your neck.

DON'T work the fly with the rod tip. There are rare cases when jacks, mackerel, wahoo, or barracuda will strike if the rod is swept backward, pulling the fly at great speed away from the fish. But if we disregard those rare times, you should never use the rod to manipulate the fly. Instead, as the retrieve is begun, keep the rod low and pointed at the fish, and activate your fly by stripping in line. This keeps the line taut, which improves your chances for a hook-up if the fish strikes.

◆

DO cast only as far as you comfortably can – and take your time on the cast. Regardless of how frantically your guide or companion is gesturing toward the fish, never cast farther than you confidently can. And don't rush your cast. Trying to cast too far almost always results in a poor presentation. Rushing accomplishes the same thing, so take your time. It doesn't take that much longer to make a careful presentation.

DON'T throw your fly in the middle of a school of fish. Instead, place the fly in front of a particular fish at the head of the school. If the first fish refuses your offering, a schoolmate may pick it up.

DO kneel to lower your profile if on the retrieve the fish gets very close.

DON'T cast far above the water when throwing into the wind. This will cause the leader to fall back on the line at the end of the cast. There are very few times when you

should cast directly at the surface, but when casting into the wind you want to cast at the surface, so that the moment the leader unrolls, the fly hits the water and cannot be blown backward.

DO wait until you see the fish before you cast. Casting to an unseen fish almost always means spooking the fish with a bad cast or having to make another cast. You should see the fish clearly before you throw the fly. The best way to locate a fish your guide is trying to show you is to learn the clock method, and then move the rod to whatever time he says. For example, if he yells "Bonefish at ten o'clock!" move your rod to the ten o'clock position and sight along it. If you are not pointing at the fish, ask the guide to tell you whether you should move the rod left or right. This is by far the quickest way to locate a fish someone is trying to show you.

DON'T wade toward a white cloud. The reflection of the cloud will turn the surface pure white, making it tough to see any fish below. A good tip is to wade toward a dark shoreline. By looking at the water with the dark green shoreline in the background, you will be able to see the bottom and any fish moving over it. Working toward a dark cloud in the background will also eliminate surface glare.

DO cast above the surface when the water is calm. Any disturbance on calm water alerts the fish. A major mistake made by many novice fly fishermen is to direct the cast at the water. Driving the fly at the surface can create a lot of surface commotion, which may spook the quarry. Instead, cast at eye level. This will cause the leader to unroll above the target, and the fly will fall softly to the surface.

DON'T lift your feet when wading on tropical flats. Stingrays move onto a flat, then pound their wings on the bottom to produce a cloud of silt and sand. After dropping to the bottom, they allow the cloud to settle over them. This camouflages them so well that they are nearly impossible to see. Step on a hidden ray and it will try to drive its stinger tail into your leg. This is a very painful wound, often requiring hospital treatment. There is no danger, though, if you follow a

NEVER LIFT YOUR FEET from the bottom when wading tropical flats. If you step on a hidden stingray it may inflict a very painful wound.

simple rule: never lift your feet from the bottom. Instead shuffle or slide your feet along the sand. Stingrays are not aggressive, and if your sliding foot contacts a ray, it will flee. But step on it and it will strike back.

DON'T present the fly close to a fish that seems wary or spooky. With a cruising fish, the best method is to select a place well in front of it and toss your fly there. Try to throw the fly so it lands near an identifiable object on the bottom. This could be a sea cucumber, a piece of coral, a small patch of grass – anything you can easily identify. Watch the approaching fish. As it nears the object you cast to, begin very short retrieves. If subtle movements don't work, one or two quick strips followed by slow strips will usually entice the fish into striking.

DO vary your retrieve if the fish just follows the fly. There are almost no hard and fast rules about retrieving a fly, but here's one I live by: If the fish closely follows any fly for more than six feet and hasn't struck, I change the style of retrieve.

DO pick up and make another quick cast if the fish has moved away or obviously hasn't seen the fly. The window of opportunity in salt water fishing is small, and you must cast as quickly as you can. The instant you realize the fish either is leaving the fly or is not going to see it, pick the fly up and make another presentation.

DON'T use the same fly line for all your inshore fishing. If you are sight fishing for bonefish, you may want a line that has a short taper, which allows you to get into the action fast. But if you are searching the shallows, where a long retrieve may be more profitable, then a shooting taper is decidedly best. If the surf is rough, a sinking line, or at least a slow-sinking line, is better than one that floats. The floating line undulates with the waves, giving your fly improper action and often creating unwanted slack, while a sinking line penetrates the water and remains relatively unaffected by the waves. On windy days, switching to a slow-sinking line or even one that sinks fairly fast will let you throw a thinner line that has more weight for its mass. This will cast much better than a floating line. On very calm days, many anglers do better on spooky fish by using a lighter rod and line to reduce line impact on the water. The message here is to match your fly line to the existing conditions.

DO hold your rod low to the water while retrieving the fly. There are several reasons for doing this. If the tip is held well above surface it means a lot of sag in the line, which makes it hard for the angler to know when the fish has taken the fly. The slack must also be removed before the hook can be set. A third reason is that if the wind is blowing from the side against the line, the fly drags along the bottom, often spoiling the retrieve.

DO lift the line quietly from the water. If I were to name one of the most common faults of flats fishermen it's that they make a backcast before all the fly line has been lifted from the water. It takes a great deal of effort to lift line from the water, which steals energy from the backcast. But worse than that, to a nearby fish, ripping the line from the surface is similar to someone dragging a nail across a corrugated tin roof!

DO wade slowly. When an angler is confronted by a huge expanse of shallow water, he often feels compelled to rush forward in his search for fish. But fast wading produces noise, as well as shock waves that are easily detected by wily fish. If you see ripples moving more than a foot away from your legs when wading in knee-deep water,

you are wading too fast.

DO wade with the wind when possible. Wading into the wind means directing your cast into the breeze – always difficult.

DO keep control of the line as you shoot it to the target. Bonefish and many other species are difficult to see. When you finally make a cast and release the line, you may have taken your eyes off the fish. That brief period when you looked away often means you can't relocate the fish and make another cast.

DON'T strike upward in shallow water. If you see a fish attack your fly, and you think he has it, don't sweep the rod upward. Should the fish miss the fly, an upward sweep will remove the fly from the water and you'll have to cast again. In this case you risk spooking the fish. Instead, strike by moving the rod sideways, or make a strip strike. A strip strike is done by simply stripping the line firmly away from the fish, which will drive the hook home. With either method, the fly remains close to the fish if it misses.

DO master a number of different retrieves. This is particularly valuable when fishing for bonefish. Perhaps 80 percent of the time the fly should be presented to the fish as close as you can without alerting it. This means somewhere between six and ten feet in front of the fish. If you think the bonefish has seen the fly, make one or two long, quick strips, then let the fly drop toward the bottom. As the fish moves in, make a series of short strips, even allowing the fly to rest momentarily on the bottom. If the target is a bottom feeder (e.g., a redfish, permit, or bonefish), work the fly near or on the bottom. There are some occasions, but not many, when it is a good idea to simply throw the fly in front of a bonefish and allow it to sink to the bottom before making a retrieve. However, I would place this far down the list of preferred methods.

DO straighten or stretch your fly line before you start fishing. Many of today's fly lines have a core that when pulled from the reel will lie in tight coils. Such a line needs to have the coils removed, or you will almost certainly make a cast that ends in disaster.

FLIES *in the* SURF

By Pete Cooper, Jr.

How to avoid some common problems associated with fly fishing in the surf.

THE AUTHOR HEFTS a fine redfish he took on the oceanside beach of a barrier island. Fly fishermen have a shot at much bigger reds and specks along open beaches than in the backcountry.

For many of us, surf fishing has a very special appeal. Being in the water instead of on it, we feel more completely involved, at one with the elements. Of course, the aesthetics of the setting are one thing; another is the knowledge that great beasts lurk along the ocean rim – prizes seldom seen in protected inshore waters.

Those of us who live along the northern Gulf usually work the surf when conditions are much less extreme than those often encountered by our western and northeastern counterparts. Ideally, the sea is calm, the water temperate and clear. When this occurs, as it frequently does during the warm months, a growing number of anglers now leave their conventional gear at home and sally forth with fly rods in hand. But fly fishing in the surf presents some special problems.

I have fly fished extensively in salt water since 1966. Along the way, I've had to fight my way through most of the obstacles that plague the surf angler.

Bottom Contours

Much of the better surf fishing areas along the northern Gulf coast occur along the barrier islands. The bottom contour of their offshore, or seaward, sides is very similar: a trough against the beach, a shallow bar, another trough, a deeper bar, and then the gradual descent to deep water. As you stand at land's end, gazing seaward, you might think that you need to cast great distances to be effective. In fact, a lot of fishing time can be wasted by retrieving the fly through the normally barren water over the bars.

Although the first trough can be productive on very high tides, when it can be successfully worked with short casts while standing on the beach, the second trough is usually better. Any surf will break on the shallow bar, so you must wade just past that point to prevent the waves from wreaking havoc with your slack shooting line. I also recommend wading out to water that is about crotch deep; any deeper and it will be very difficult to shoot the line or get it back on the reel without it tangling.

Avoiding Tangles

If you are wearing a button-down shirt, keep the tails tucked into your pants. Otherwise, they'll float on the surface, where they can foul the running line. Any knives or pliers you keep in belt sheaths should be worn against your back and not at your side for the same reason. And forget those "handy" little clip-on gadgets that you pin to your shirt; keep everything you carry in fastened pockets.

The outer edge of the shallow bar is prime fish-holding structure. Cast from parallel to the bar out to about 60 degrees toward open water. Casts of 50 or 60 feet are plenty; any longer and you're inviting a tangle in the running line.

If there is any current, try to move in the same direction as the flow. That will keep the slack line in front of you. If you wade against the current, the line will pile up against your body or tangle behind you, making for headaches.

The Right Strike

On the retrieve, keep the rod tip low and pointed at the spot where you envision the fly to be. Wave action imparted on a floating or sink-tip line often causes a slight belly, but that slack is much less detrimental to your hook-setting ability than having your rod out of position. Striking by stripping in line and sharply raising the rod straight up will remove this small amount of slack very quickly and set the hook firmly.

Current, however, is an entirely different matter. If the flow is moving from your right to left, for example, follow the point where the line enters the water while keeping the rod tip low. When you feel a hit, strike with the line, but move the rod horizontally and back to your left. This quickly eliminates a large portion of the slack-line belly, giving you a more direct pull on the fly.

Clear That Slack!

Once the fish is hooked, you should immediately clear the slack running line. While a bull red or a large speck will often do this for you, some are slow to respond, and the longer that slack is in the water the more likely it is to tangle.

If you have hooked a big fish, do not attempt to grab it. This is guaranteed to cause a final burst of activity on the part of the fish, which has resulted in many lost trophies. Take the time to beach it, or carry a landing device.

If you use a stringer to secure your catch, it probably has a big foam float to keep it from sinking to the bottom and getting eaten by crabs. However, that float is one of the most efficient fly-line grabbers ever devised! I remove the float from my stringer, and have never had my catch mangled by a crab or shark – knock on wood.

Finally, when you return home from your trip, take the time to soak your reel, pliers, and knife in fresh water. Also, throw away the leader you used and resharpen the hooks on your flies. The potential for losing a trophy fish in the surf is too great to neglect these simple tasks.

Anatomy of a Tide Marsh

• Basic Blues • The Lady & the Trout • Winter Flounder 101

Inshore
FISHING

ANATOMY *of a* TIDE MARSH

By Bob McNally

All kinds of inshore game fish inhabit East Coast tide marshes, but to catch them consistently you first have to find them. Here's what to look for.

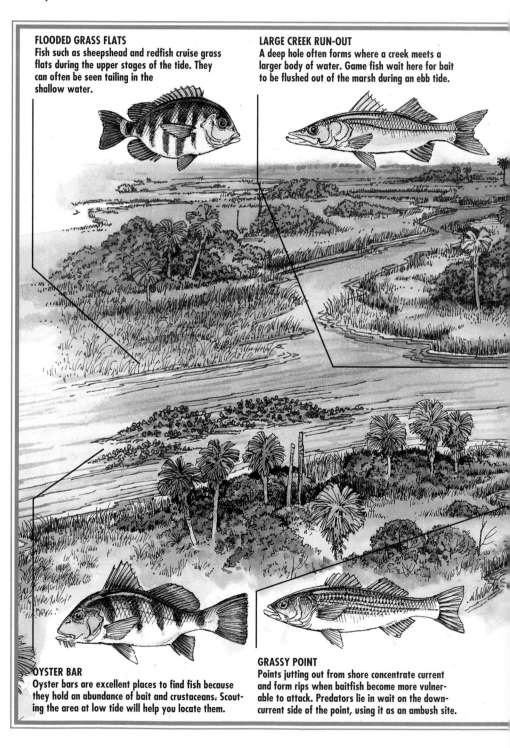

FLOODED GRASS FLATS
Fish such as sheepshead and redfish cruise grass flats during the upper stages of the tide. They can often be seen tailing in the shallow water.

LARGE CREEK RUN-OUT
A deep hole often forms where a creek meets a larger body of water. Game fish wait here for bait to be flushed out of the marsh during an ebb tide.

OYSTER BAR
Oyster bars are excellent places to find fish because they hold an abundance of bait and crustaceans. Scouting the area at low tide will help you locate them.

GRASSY POINT
Points jutting out from shore concentrate current and form rips when baitfish become more vulnerable to attack. Predators lie in wait on the down-current side of the point, using it as an ambush site.

In the complex inshore network of marine grass, muck and mire, oyster bars and barnacles that make up the coastal marsh lies the life blood of the sea, the basis for much of the world's ocean food chain. For tide marshes are vital nurseries for baitfish, shellfish, and game fish, nurturing grounds for many species big and small.

So important are tide marshes to ocean fish productivity that marine biologists have determined that nothing can be developed in a salt marsh that is more valuable to man than the marsh itself. No golf course, condominium, marina, or airport can produce more long-term economic revenue than a salt marsh!

Yet for all this productivity, tide marshes can be difficult places to fish, simply because of their large size and complexity.

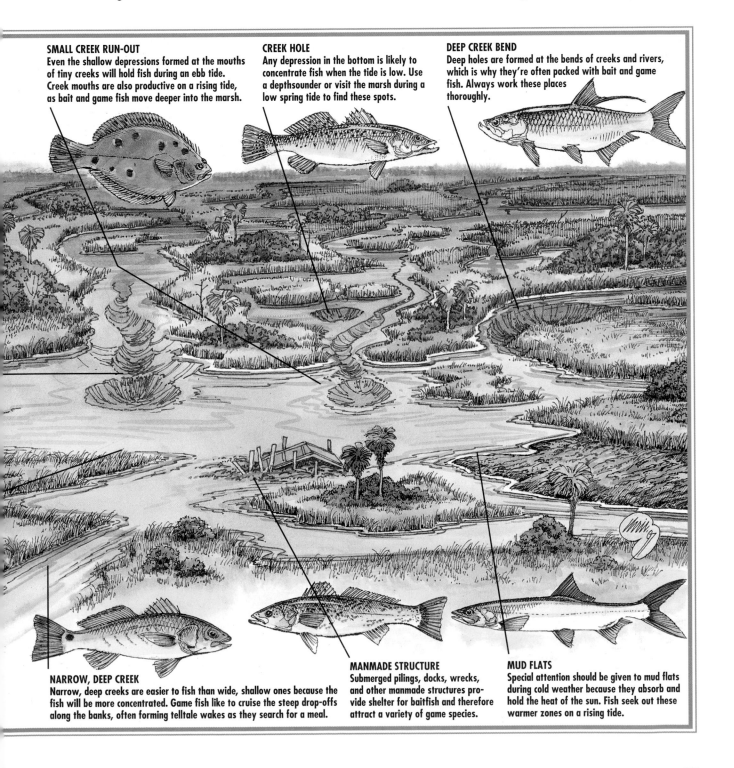

SMALL CREEK RUN-OUT
Even the shallow depressions formed at the mouths of tiny creeks will hold fish during an ebb tide. Creek mouths are also productive on a rising tide, as bait and game fish move deeper into the marsh.

CREEK HOLE
Any depression in the bottom is likely to concentrate fish when the tide is low. Use a depthsounder or visit the marsh during a low spring tide to find these spots.

DEEP CREEK BEND
Deep holes are formed at the bends of creeks and rivers, which is why they're often packed with bait and game fish. Always work these places thoroughly.

NARROW, DEEP CREEK
Narrow, deep creeks are easier to fish than wide, shallow ones because the fish will be more concentrated. Game fish like to cruise the steep drop-offs along the banks, often forming telltale wakes as they search for a meal.

MANMADE STRUCTURE
Submerged pilings, docks, wrecks, and other manmade structures provide shelter for baitfish and therefore attract a variety of game species.

MUD FLATS
Special attention should be given to mud flats during cold weather because they absorb and hold the heat of the sun. Fish seek out these warmer zones on a rising tide.

Nowhere is this more true than in the sprawling tide marshes along the South Atlantic seaboard, especially from Daytona Beach in northern Florida through North Carolina. Although this coastal region has been ravaged by man in many localized areas, there are still enormous stretches that have been spared the drag line and bulldozer. The Georgia coastline in particular offers hundreds of square miles of spartina-grass marshes.

Tide marshes in this region generally border the Intracoastal Waterway and the thousands of brackish creeks and rivers that flow into the sounds, inlets, and, ultimately, the Atlantic Ocean. The nutrient-rich mix of salt and fresh water, plus the daily rise and fall of tide, make for a rich habitat that supports a staggering variety of game fish.

The species found in a particular marsh can vary greatly according to season, bait availability, water temperature, and geographic location (i.e., snook in Florida, striped bass in North Carolina); however, the basic keys to locating fish remain much the same for tide marshes everywhere.

Think Like a Fish

It may sound silly, but one way to learn where to catch marsh-living fish is to imagine yourself as one. Think about where *you* would go to find an easy meal. For most fish, finding food is of primary concern, so look for those areas where food is plentiful and relatively easy to catch. Tide dictates much of this. When the tide floods a marsh, baitfish, shrimp, crabs, and foraging game fish scatter into areas that are dry at low tide. Conversely, when the tide ebbs and water drains into deep creeks and rivers, the fish and bait must leave the shallow areas before they're left high and dry.

Generally, the last half of a falling tide offers the most consistent, predictable fishing in marsh regions. As the tide ebbs, it carries with it hordes of minnows, crabs, and shrimp that were swept into the marsh during high tide. Many small "run-outs" funnel water and bait from the marsh into larger creeks and rivers. It is at the mouths of these run-outs that game fish gather during ebb tide, awaiting a smorgasbord of easy-to-catch forage.

Look for Holes, Drop-Offs

Often there is a "lip" or slight drop-off at the mouth of a run-out. The deeper the water and the more pronounced the lip, the bigger the fish that are likely to be holding there. A six-inch lip may hold only a single two-pound flounder, but a run-out that pours into a creek bend that's six feet deep may hold a whole school of six-pound redfish. One of the best tarpon holes I ever fished was a place where three deep marsh creeks merged. The creeks had an average depth of ten feet, but the hole where they met was 20 feet deep. During the last half of an August or September tide it wasn't unusual to jump a dozen tarpon a day in that hole. In November the tarpon were gone, but the spot was jammed with red drum. In spring, big black drum and seatrout called the place home.

Sometimes the very best marsh creeks are so shallow that they're almost impossible to navigate at low tide, even in a small boat. Such creeks, however, normally have some deep holes where fish congregate when the tide drops. Not many creek fishermen use depthsounders, but they should.

One creek I fished a few years ago near Charleston, South Carolina, almost went dry in several places when the tide dropped on a full or new moon. But there were holes as deep as 12 feet that teemed with seatrout to six pounds when that happened. It was important to check the tide charts and use a shallow-draft boat, but by fishing the creek at mid-low tide, then fishing through mid-high tide, we had banner seatrout action.

Other creek features to key on are places where an oyster bar, sand bar, or point creates a current rip or a confined area where game fish can herd or ambush bait. Such places can offer excellent fishing during early flood tides. Points are good spots to fish because game fish will lie in wait for bait to be swept past by the current.

Small creeks are often completely devoid of larger fish during low tide because the water is too shallow. Usually, game fish (and bait) move into a deeper creek, sound, or river because they fear they'll become trapped. But when the tide floods, bait and predators push back into the creeks. Again, the mouths of these creeks can offer outstanding fishing during the first of the flood tide, especially if there is a slight hole or side creek just inside the mouth. In many creeks' mouths there is a sand bar or an oyster bar that's been built up by the current, which creates a high spot or ridge between the small creek and the river or sound. Baitfish pass over this ridge on their way into the creek, and game fish are close behind.

Last spring in North Florida, some friends and I beached our skiff on a ridge near the marsh grass and had a terrific day with seatrout and redfish as they passed through the creek mouth on the flood tide. Using spoons, jigs, and streamer flies, we caught two dozen reds and trout in an hour.

High-Tide Tactics

A high flood tide can present some very difficult fishing situations, yet it sometimes yields exciting action in the grass. The problem with high tide is that the fish scatter over a wide area, making it hard to locate them.

These days, red drum are popular high-tide targets. Some anglers simply pole onto the grass flats and blind-cast with weedless spoons or flies until fish are located. A number of seasoned marsh fishermen, however, have learned that the quickest way to locate high-tide redfish is to stand on a poling platform and scan the flats with binoculars for tailing fish.

Sheepshead also move onto flooded marsh flats, where they can be sight-fished in a similar manner. While sheepshead can occasionally be caught on jigs and even flies, live crabs are best, since this is what they are feeding on, just like redfish.

During the higher stages of the tide, narrow, deep creeks will generally produce better fishing than broad, shallow ones, since the fish will be relatively concentrated. In deep creeks, you'll frequently find fish working tight to the banks as they search for bait. It's common to see redfish, tarpon, and even snook pushing a wake next to a creek bank or swirling on the surface as they feed on minnows and shrimp. These fish will readily hit lures and baits.

Scout It Out

When "learning" an unfamiliar tide marsh, it's wise to look the place over during low water so you can locate any deep holes, choice creek bends, bars, pilings, and any navigational hazards. Take special note of oyster bars and old pilings that will be covered at high tide, since they may attract schools of bait and feeding fish. One old barge I know about almost completely disappears during a full-moon high tide. When this happens it produces outstanding action with several species.

Scouting marsh creeks at low tide can also tip you off to hot spots for flounder. In muddy creeks, the scooped-out hollows of flounder lies can often be seen on the bottom when the tide ebbs. These flounder "tracks" are a good indication that the area offers hot flatty action when the tide rises.

Something else to note at low tide, especially in winter, are any mud flats that are completely exposed to bright sunlight. Black mud absorbs the sun's rays during low tide, and when the water floods, fish such as seatrout, redfish, ladyfish, and others congregate there to feed because the water is warmer and attracts forage. During warm months, key spots to note at low tide are oyster bar "humps," which can be alive with crabs and minnows during high water.

It's important to note that marsh-dwelling fish are not homebodies; they move around considerably, more than many anglers believe. On many occasions, a "hot" creek that yielded good catches of flounder, redfish, and seatrout one day may be dead the next. This is especially true if the fish are subjected to a lot of fishing pressure. In this case, I believe the fish simply move into another creek, or drop back into the sound or river to search for other suitable habitat and food.

This is why it's important to stay on the move when fishing tide marshes. If you fish a spot for 30 minutes and don't catch much, it's time to move. Try another place, tap another creek or tidal run-out. The marsh is fertile, the fish are plentiful; it's just a matter of time until you locate another school and the action heats up again.

ROCK BOTTOM

By George Poveromo

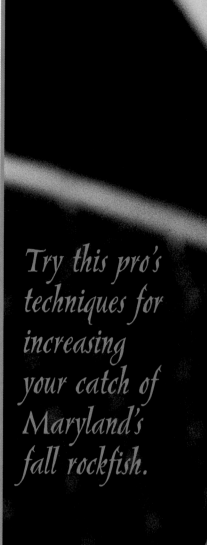

Try this pro's techniques for increasing your catch of Maryland's fall rockfish.

E d Kalb, Dale Dirks, and I were becoming less optimistic with each fishless hour, and the reports that were coming in over the VHF weren't giving us much encouragement. Had it been a pleasant fall day on the Chesapeake we wouldn't have minded so much, but slow-trolling through tumultuous seas whipped up by a persistent 25-knot wind was no picnic.

Kalb, a friend and devoted fisherman from Annapolis, Maryland, had invited me to join him for a day of catching striped bass, known on this part of the coast as rockfish. Before I arrived in town, Kalb had been enjoying some fast catch-and-release action from several schools he had located, and the possibility of a quick score was why he had us braving the elements on a day when most anglers were holed up indoors. The fishing wasn't easy, but our perseverance eventually paid off with a few fish that took time out of their fall migration to hammer our jigs.

Fall Rock Festival

When the waters of Chesapeake Bay start to cool in September and October, rockfish begin moving out of the tributaries and head toward warmer, deeper wintering grounds to the south. During this time they feed aggressively, building up fat for the winter, although they seldom stay in one place for very long.

While the upper Chesapeake features an abundance of shell lumps, the bottom around Annapolis doesn't have as much fish-attracting structure. That's why a lot of local experts like Kalb prefer trolling over live-baiting, since it allows them to cover a lot of ground in order to locate the traveling pods of stripers.

According to Kalb, spurts of fish begin passing through the local waters from about September on. The schools are largely on the move, but will often take up station for several days in a certain area if it harbors a lot of bait. That's why Kalb does a lot of pre-season catch-and-release striper fishing, which allows him to locate the whereabouts of a few schools that will make his trips more productive when the season opens.

"The most obvious signs to look for are diving birds and breaking fish," Kalb explains. "However, when there's no surface

ED KALB (left) with an Annapolis rockfish caught on a grub-tailed bucktail trolled just above the bottom in the fall.

activity I often stick with a plan that involves trolling the mouth of the Severn River, then fishing off various points and over good bottom structure, such as lumps, shell-covered bottom, and channel edges. I fish pretty hard around Tolly Point, which is the southernmost point of the Severn. It seems the stripers concentrate a lot better there, plus the rips are definitely a lot stronger.

"I'll also fish around Hackett's Point, which is on the north side of the Severn's mouth. There's a lot more ground to cover, but the average size of the fish seems bigger. Along these points I'm fishing in approximately 25 to 30 feet of water. If there's no sign of fish or if there's no current, which is crucial, I'll head out into open, deeper water to search for birds and activity on my fishfinder."

Kalb uses a back-to-basics approach when fishing around points, which include the area between Thomas and Horseshoe points, and across the Bay around Gum Thickets and Brick House Bar. Since it's often necessary to fish the lures right over the tops of lumps and ridges, and because the lures are frequently jigged, Kalb advises anglers to hold their outfits while trolling. To fish a lure deeper, the rod tip is held just above the surface. If the helmsman marks a sharp rise on the fishfinder, the rod must be raised to avoid a snag. If the fish are concentrated on the down-current side of a ridge, lump, or other piece of structure, the lures must be lowered immediately after they clear the top, so they drop right into the fish's feeding zone. Otherwise there's little chance of a strike.

Because rockfish spend most of their time on the bottom, Kalb trolls very slowly. If the lures don't bump bottom when the rod tip is lowered, they're not getting deep enough.

"It's so important to fish a lure or two right on the bottom," Kalb states, adding that it often takes a slow trolling speed to get down to the proper depth. "Sometimes there's no such thing as trolling too slowly. When I'm trolling with the current, I'll shift into neutral, let my baits sink a moment, then shift into gear. Sometimes I'll shift in and out of gear repeatedly, or slow-troll into the current, just to keep my baits in the strike zone. One-and-a-half knots is my average trolling speed."

Kalb's medium-action bottom-trolling outfits are light enough to hold most of the day. He spools his Penn 309 and 330 GTi reels with 40-pound-test braided line and trolls bucktail jigs rigged with soft-plastic grubs. A 12- to 16-foot section of monofilament leader is used between the lure and one eye of the three-way swivel, while a snap swivel tied to the end of the braided line is clipped to a second eye. A two- to three-foot section of 30-pound monofilament and a

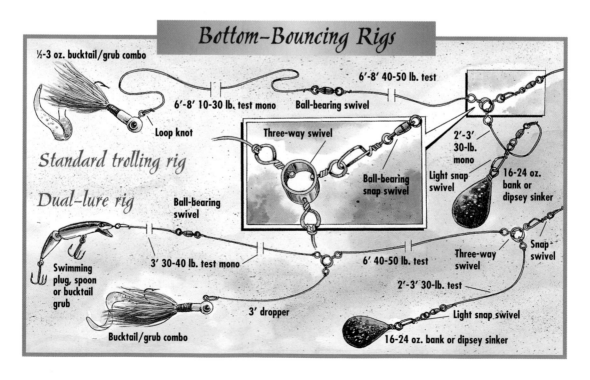

Bottom-Bouncing Rigs

½-3 oz. bucktail/grub combo

6'-8' 10-30 lb. test mono

6'-8' 40-50 lb. test

Ball-bearing swivel

Loop knot

Three-way swivel

2'-3' 30-lb. mono

Standard trolling rig

Light snap swivel

16-24 oz. bank or dipsey sinker

Ball-bearing snap swivel

Dual-lure rig

Ball-bearing swivel

Swimming plug, spoon or bucktail grub

3' 30-40 lb. test mono

6' 40-50 lb. test

Three-way swivel

Snap swivel

Bucktail/grub combo

3' dropper

2'-3' 30-lb. test

Light snap swivel

16-24 oz. bank or dipsey sinker

bank or dipsey sinker is tied to the third eye of the swivel via a light snap swivel. Should the sinker snag bottom, the lighter monofilament or snap will break and save the more expensive lure and terminal hardware.

Trick for Tough Fish

When the fishing gets tough, Kalb frequently switches to a dual-lure setup. Similar to the rig described above, a three-way swivel is used to connect the fishing line, bank sinker, and leader. However, instead of tying the lure directly to the leader, Kalb cuts the leader back to about 12 feet and ties in a second three-way swivel. Attached to one eye of the second swivel is a bucktail grub on a three-foot leader. A six-foot leader with a spoon, swimming plug, or second bucktail/grub combo is tied to the remaining eye of the swivel. Kalb believes that the additional commotion and predator-chasing-prey illusion created by this rig will often coax a wary rockfish into striking.

When his search for rockfish takes him into open water, as it did on our outing, Kalb frequently fishes six lines. This includes a pair of 5/0 to 9/0 Crippled Alewive spoons rigged with four- to six-ounce, in-line sinkers that tend to ride higher in the water column; two mid-depth lines towing larger, flashier spoons with eight- to 12-ounce in-line sinkers; and a pair of chartreuse or green jig/grub combos on the deep lines. The deep jigs are fished on the three-way swivel rigs with 16 to 24 ounces of weight.

All of Kalb's outfits are spooled with 30-pound monofilament, with the exception of the two deep lines. On those, Kalb prefers to use braided line over the commonly used Monel wire. His reasoning is that braided line cuts through the water about as well as wire, has very little stretch, and isn't prone to kinking. When fishing deeper than 40 feet, however, Kalb switches to Monel.

In open water, some Bay anglers try to locate the fish first before setting out their lines. However, Kalb deploys his trolling spread immediately in the hopes of intercepting any migrating fish. "Unless the birds are diving or there's a lot of bait, the rockfish are usually on the move," says Kalb. "The deep lines still get most of the strikes, but the mid- and upper-level lines pick off fish here and there. I feel that the sight and sound of a six-line spread help attract fish in open water."

To enhance the visual appeal of his spread and when the fish are scattered, Kalb often trolls an umbrella rig on a deep line. He arms his umbrella rigs with a large single-hook plug or spoon down the center, which imitates a predator chasing after the small, hookless tubes and triggers the rockfish's competitive instinct. The single hook also makes the rig legal in Maryland.

Low & Slow

Kalb usually trolls at around three knots when he's searching for pods of fish or bait, but otherwise he really slows down in open water, especially when working deep channels. He says that it's sometimes necessary to barely creep along in order to get the lures down near the bottom in deep water. Sometimes his average trolling speed in the channels will be around one knot.

Kalb acknowledges that trolling small lures such as 5/0 and 7/0 spoons and half- to two-ounce bucktails catches more fish, but prefers to target the larger stripers by using bigger lures. "When Maryland had a 12-inch size limit on rockfish we trolled small lures all the time," Kalb explains. "Now our minimum size limit is 18 inches. Personally, I would much rather catch a 20- or 30-inch rockfish instead of playing with a lot of small ones. That's why I now use spoons in the 7/0 and 9/0 range, and one- to three-ounce bucktails. The time between strikes is longer, but the chances of catching a big fish are greater. However, I have no reservations about scaling back to small lures and releasing a bunch of small fish on a slow day. Besides, a lot of times catching fish comes down to matching your lures to the size of the baitfish in the area."

Trolling for fall rockfish around Annapolis can be fun and productive. If you know how to read the water and keep your lures close to the bottom, Kalb's trolling strategy can really increase your score, whether you're after large numbers of small fish or looking for that lunker or two.

THIS BIG DRUM WAS CAUGHT via the sight-casting method in Ocracoke Inlet, a major Outer Banks hot spot. Drum can be taken here from March to October, but April through June is prime time to sight-cast for them.

SEEING REDS

By Joel Arrington

Try your hand at the exciting game of sight-casting to trophy red drum along North Carolina's Outer Banks.

In North Carolina, there's but one place to go for trophy red drum – the Outer Banks. While stocks have dwindled elsewhere, the barrier islands continue to produce the kind of fish that drum anglers dream about. Bait fishing has been the traditional method of catching them, but an even more challenging technique has evolved. I'm talking about sight-casting for red drum. In this sport, anglers cruise the inlets and beaches, visually searching for dark masses moving along below the surface or over the shallow lumps. Once the fish are spotted, the boat closes in and the angler fires off a cast. It's never easy, but that's what makes it special.

While October and November are the peak months for catching trophy drum in general, April through June is the best time to sight-cast for them between Cape Hatteras and Drum Inlet. In spring, the fish begin migrating into Pamlico Sound and Chesapeake Bay after wintering offshore, and gather near the Outer Banks inlets. They travel in large schools, foraging along the beaches and shoals and entering the inlets at high tide, where they wait for food to be swept through on the ebb. Most experts agree that the best time to sight-cast for drum is on the outgoing tide, so plan to arrive at the inlet near the top of the flood. That way you can enjoy four to six hours of good fishing if the conditions are right.

The drum can be spotted almost anywhere in and around the inlets, in water ranging from a few feet to over 20. In shallow water you can often see the schools as they move over the light-colored bottom, while in deeper water the fish may be seen cruising just below the surface. The sandy lumps of the inlet are prime places to cast to drum in very shallow water. While the majority of sight-fishing takes place in the inlet itself, schools can also be found foraging along the beaches north and south of the inlet, as well as on the protected sound side of the inlet. Weather plays an important role in this fishery. Obviously, you need a sunny day and clear water in order to spot the fish from a distance, which is why April, May, and June are the best months. The fish may arrive in March, but the weather at that time is still highly variable, with wind and clouds making it hard to find the drum.

Most experts agree that the best time to sight-cast for drum is on the outgoing tide.

Spotting Fish

In sight-fishing, you must train yourself to look *through* the surface of the water. Polarizing sunglasses are a must, since they reduce glare and provide greater contrast. Side-shields and a long-billed hat also help reduce distracting glare. From a distance, a school of drum will appear as a slowly moving shadow or dark patch. As you get closer, you should be able to make out individual fish, each of which may display varying color, depending on turbidity, sunlight, and their own pigmentation, which varies from dark to light. If you're new to sight-fishing you may mistake rays for a school of drum, since both are plentiful in spring and are similarly colored. If you do find rays it's a good sign, since rays and drum also inhabit the same areas.

Ideally, you want to find a "contented" school that is moving along slowly and looking for food, since these fish will be more receptive to eat a lure or fly. Look for schools that are round in shape. A spooked school will be stretched out in a line and moving fast; however, even these fish will grab a bait, lure, or fly on the run if placed in the right spot.

To give yourself an advantage in spotting fish as you idle slowly along, stand as high as possible on the boat and position yourself with the sun and wind at your back.

> *Most experts agree that the best time to sight-cast for drum is on the outgoing tide.*

Boats with towers offer a distinct advantage in fish spotting. Note that you have the best chance of seeing fish after the sun climbs 20 degrees above the horizon.

On overcast days or when the water is turbid, look for surface disturbances. Drum will push a characteristic wake and often swirl near the surface as they feed. On calm days you can sometimes see these "surface signs" from a quarter-mile away. Drum may also create an oily "slick" on the surface as they feed on crabs. The slick often emits a characteristic odor, tipping you off to feeding activity upwind. In short, any irregularity on the surface should be checked out.

Careful Approach

Once a school is spotted, maintain the same speed while maneuvering into casting position, since any change in engine sound will likely spook the fish. Try to steer the boat parallel to the school's path, staying just within casting range. Estimate the depth of the fish and their speed of travel, then cast ahead of the school, so your offering will drop to the right level by the time the fish arrive.

Two-ounce jigs and heavy metal spoons (i.e., a No. 4 Hopkins) are preferred because they can be cast far and sink rapidly. Remember that the largest fish are likely to be near the bottom of the school, so give the lure time to sink. If you use flies, try 5/0 Clouser Minnows and other weighted streamers in the five-inch range fished on sinking lines. Fast-sink shooting heads can be extremely helpful in reaching the fish. Flies should be cast farther ahead of the school than jigs so they'll have time to sink to the proper depth.

If you decide to fish a fly, exclude other tackle. Avoid the temptation to lob a jig to the school just before they come within fly-casting range – you cannot fish both types of tackle at the same time.

While sight-fishing is an exciting and

THE OUTER BANKS remain one of the few places in North Carolina where giant drum can be caught on a regular basis. To protect the big spawners, many anglers now choose to tag and release their fish.

challenging way to catch drum in the inlets, the weather and the fish don't always cooperate. In this case, there's the option of fishing bait over the shoals and inlet bars, where drum sometimes concentrate in the deep pockets. The trick is to slip in, anchor, and cast a baited, single-dropper rig with a two- to four-ounce pyramid sinker to the edge of the shoal and pull it into deeper water. For tackle, most prefer a stout, seven-foot boat rod and a revolving-spool reel spooled with 20- to 30-pound mono or braided line. Use a five-foot leader of 40- or 50-pound mono and a 7/0 hook baited with whatever fresh, oily bait is available at the local fish houses. Bluefish, croaker, and

popeye mullet all work well. The best bait fishing tends to be right at dusk and after dark, a time that may be dangerous for inexperienced boaters. Charter a captain first if you're unfamiliar with the inlets.

Now that drum are becoming scarce in other parts of the state, many sportsmen have taken to releasing the bigger, breeding-age fish. Most will no longer kill a red drum over 27 inches in length, preferring to keep just a few in the 18- to 27-inch range. In recent years, participants in the state fishing tournament have released 96 percent or more of "citation-size" fish (40 inches or 45 pounds), evidence that anglers are doing their part to conserve these wonderful fish.

INSHORE FISHING

BASIC BLUES

By Eric B. Burnley

Expert advice on targeting spring blues off Virginia and Maryland.

Even though the available scientific and statistical information indicates a severe decline in bluefish populations along the East Coast, you may have trouble convincing Paul and Kathy Herman of Tyler, Texas, that big blues are hard to find. Fishing with me aboard the *Gimli* last April 28, they caught and released 82 bluefish weighing eight to 13 pounds. We were drifting over open bottom in nine to 12 fathoms off Virginia Beach between the Chesapeake Light Tower and the *Gulf Hustler* wreck on a warm, calm day. The water temperature was 61 degrees and the blues were swirling on the surface, taking any plug or spoon that passed by their noses. We fished for six hours, drifting less than one mile from our starting point. The Tylers were into fish the entire time, catching them on medium-action baitcasting gear almost nonstop.

I have been chasing bluefish for 30 years, and in all that time I have never experienced a better day. When the blues are receptive to surface plugs, it's one of the greatest thrills in fishing.

Don't Strike Too Soon

One mistake excited anglers make is trying to set the hook when they see the splash made by the fish's initial strike. This action seldom results in a hooked bluefish, although it can create a fair amount of excitement on the boat as the plug comes sailing by like a missile. If you keep cranking and maintain steady pressure on the lure, the blue will hook itself, leaving you the job of keeping him on as he jumps all over the ocean.

I like to use a single-hook surface plug since it is easier and safer to remove from a thrashing bluefish. Most strikes are directed at the tail of the plug, so one hook in that location is more than enough. Dr. John Trant in Virginia Beach has a woodworking shop in his garage where we produce very effective poppers out of wooden dowels. Any number of commercially produced surface lures will work, but you will usually have to remove the trebles and attach a single tail hook yourself.

Spring Bluefish Hot Spots

Chesapeake	Loran Numbers
Light Tower	27103.0/41286.2
Tiger	27101.6/41188.0
Gulf Hustler	27069.7/41272.7
Ricks	27035.7/41245.2
Hanks	27048.3/41188.9
The Elevens	26963.0/41087.5
Fish Hook	27045.0/41240.0

In the spring, the blues seem to congregate near the surface where the water is warmer. You can employ shallow-running swimming plugs or large spoons to attract their attention. These lures require less work on behalf of the angler, and may work when a surface plug will not draw a strike.

Finding Them Fast

Casting can be productive after you locate a concentration of big blues, but trolling will help you find the fish sooner. Once again, use shallow-running lures since the fish are traveling in the warm surface water.

When the fish are close to the surface during the spring run, they seem to be spooked by boat noise. To overcome this, we run our lures 75 to 100 yards back. Later in the year, these same fish will come right up to your transom to take cedar plugs set for tuna, but in April and May they are boat-shy.

Rigging Tips

Rigging lures for casting or trolling can be done with 50- to 100-pound mono leader which is easier to use and handle than wire. Most of the lures are long enough to keep the blue's teeth away from the leader, so wire is not required to prevent bite-offs.

A six- to 10-foot leader will do the job if you are pulling plugs or spoons without a trolling sinker placed ahead of the lure. If a sinker is used, the leader length should be increased to 30 feet to overcome the damping effect of the weight.

Casting leaders of 12 to 18 inches should be long enough to prevent abrasion to the running line. All connections between line and leader must be made with black terminal gear; anything shiny may attract the attention of another bluefish. Ball-bearing swivels should be used when trolling, while barrel swivels will suffice for casting. An Albright knot can be used between leader and line, providing a crank-on connection that can aid in landing big fish with light casting tackle.

The Right Water

Locating big blues in the spring may take some effort, but a temperature gauge will help speed up the search. As a rule, you are wasting your time fishing in water with a surface temperature below 60 degrees. You may find some big blues in colder water, but they are usually reluctant to eat.

In April, I may run 25 to 30 miles east of Cape Henry before I find 60-degree water and begin to troll a spread of four lures. Since the blues are usually near some type of structure, I will work around and between wrecks and lumps. As an example, I may begin the day at the Fish Hook, troll over to the Ricks Wreck, work down to the Margaret Hanks Wreck, across the Southeast Lumps and over the Elevens. If I encounter a concentration of blues I will break out the casting gear and the chum bucket. If trolling proves completely unproductive I may select a wreck, set up a chum slick, and see if the fish are more interested in bait than lures.

Once you locate a wreck, it should be marked with a float before you begin to fish. When the seas are calm and the wind is light, you can prospect the structure by drifting across it and working metal jigs. Strikes are possible anywhere from the bottom to the surface, and you may improve your score by sweetening the jig with a strip of fresh-cut bait.

Jigging may produce sea bass or other small fish. As soon as you catch one, put a 7/0 live-bait hook on a six- to 10-inch wire leader through the eye sockets and put him back in the water. Allow the bait to swim free, and if there is a bluefish anywhere near the wreck it will find the bait.

Chum to Hold Them

When you find some action you may want to set up a chum slick to hold the fish close to your boat. Anchor over or just uptide from the wreck so the chum will pull the fish away from the structure. On occasion, I have held the fish at the boat while drifting, but putting the hook down is more reliable.

Ground menhaden is the most popular chum and we use it frozen in three- to five-gallon containers. The frozen chum is placed in a five-gallon bucket that has been perforated with one-inch holes. The chum bucket is tied to a stern cleat and allowed to drift in the current behind the boat. The frozen menhaden will slowly melt, releasing a slick that should act like a dinner bell for hungry bluefish.

Once we are set up on the anchor and the chum is doing its job, we begin to drop chunks or fillets of fresh cut bait back into the slick. If the current is strong a chunk cut from the back of the bait works well, while a fillet provides more action in the water when the current is slow. A bait fished directly on the bottom on a fishfinder rig can be very productive, and you may need a split shot or crimp-on sinker to get the drifted baits down to the fish.

To make a natural presentation, you should pull line from the reel at a rate that allows the bait to fall unrestricted through the water column. This rate will vary with the strength of the current, and you should try to keep the line somewhat slack as it enters the water.

When fishing with bait, you will need a wire leader ahead of the hook. We tie six inches of single-strand tobacco-colored 40-pound wire to a 7/0 long-shanked hook via a haywire twist. A loop is formed in the tag end of the wire with another haywire twist, and a black snap swivel connects the wire to the line. Make up at least a dozen rigs per angler, as big blues are hard on hooks and leaders.

Time to Experiment

Blues, like all fish, are unpredictable. On most occasions they will follow the chum to the boat and wait like hungry puppies for the bait to drift down to them. At other times the chum seems to have little effect. As an example, on the day we caught those 82 blues I put out the chum bucket and the fish seemed to avoid the slick. Their preference for a particular lure or bait may also be a bit frustrating. On one trip last year, the blues would only hit surface poppers, totally ignoring fresh bait, diamond jigs, and swimming plugs. On another day they refused to strike a topwater plug, even though you could see them splashing around on the surface.

It may be several years before bluefish population levels return to what they were in the 1970s and 1980s, but if we are willing to run a little farther, fish a little smarter, and release most of the fish we catch, we should be able to enjoy reasonbly good action until they return in force.

Release Tips for Big Blues

• Rig your lures with single, barbless hooks, both to facilitate release and to protect yourself from injury when handling a big bluefish.

• Net your fish instead of using a gaff. Nets don't injure fish and they make it easier to handle fish in the boat.

• Wrap the bluefish in a wet towel while you remove the hook. This procedure makes the fish safer to handle and prevents damage to its skin.

• Wear gloves when you handle a bluefish. I soak my gloves in sea water to prevent damage to the fish's protective slime coating.

• Use pliers or a dehooker to remove the hook.

• Release fish carefully. Hold the bluefish by the tail and lower it into the water. If the fish is tired work it back and forth until it regains its strength.

• Use appropriate tackle. Light tackle may be fun for the angler, but it is death on fish. Big blues require at least 15- to 20-pound line to get them in as quickly as possible so they can be released in prime condition.

• Never touch the gills. This rule holds true for any fish you plan to release.

• Carry a scale and ruler. Keep track of the weight and length of each fish, or, if you are trying to catch a citation-sized fish, you can cull out the small ones while they are still alive.

• Work quickly but carefully. The less time your fish spends out of the water the better its chance of survival, but always be aware of those teeth!

Captain Cathi Jones knows how to connect with big speckled trout in the waters off Destin, Florida.

THE LADY & THE TROUT

By John E. Phillips

"**D**on't jerk that rod!" my guide barked as I started to set up on a good fish. Sheepishly, I lowered the rod tip and began to reel until the line came tight, feeling the weight of a critical stare on my back. Had I detected a threatening tone in Cathi Jones's voice?

"Keep a tight line," Jones cajoled, her voice softening a bit. "Let the drag and the rod play the fish. Just don't jerk!" Like a Little League coach trying to build confidence in an eight-year-old pitcher, Jones guided me through the fight until the large speckled trout slid into the net.

Every angler who fishes with Jones gets the same treatment, regardless of how many years he or she has fished. A fourth-generation captain, Jones plies the inshore waters of Destin, Florida, 150 to 175 days a year in her *Back Bay Lady*. She's the only full-time inshore guide in Destin, and she's been doing it for 20 years. Her ancestors worked as charter captains, taking clients offshore for red snapper and grouper, but Jones gave up the tradition of sturdy boat rods, 150-pound line, and heavy lead sinkers for the challenge of catching speckled trout and redfish on light line and live bait.

ALTHOUGH JONES'S SPECIALTY IS TROUT, she also knows how to put redfish in the boat.

Go Light

"Light line is one of the keys to catching speckled trout," says Jones. "During the spring I won't fish anything heavier than six-pound test, even for really big trout. However, once the water warms up I'll use eight-pound test through the summer. After my anglers take a limit of trout I'll change to 12-pound test and try to locate a school of redfish. The light line allows the bait to get to the bottom faster and doesn't seem to inhibit its movement. It's also less visible to the fish."

Although most speck fishermen use split-shot to help get their bait down to the bottom, Jones avoids using any weight. "I don't want anything on the line that the trout can see," she says.

On the end of the line she ties a No. 6 Mustard Kahle hook, a style traditionally used by snapper fishermen. Mustad has recently introduced a special kahle-style hook called the Croaker hook (model 37160NPD) designed specifically for fishing live baits like croaker and pinfish. "I like the Kahle design because it catches the fish in the lip or jaw 95 percent of the time, which keeps the light line away from the trout's sharp teeth," explains Jones. A second reason she prefers these hooks is because they set themselves – the angler doesn't have to jerk back on the rod to drive the hook home, which can tear it out of the fish's mouth or create a large hole that the hook can fall out of during the fight. With a Kahle hook the angler should simply reel once the fish has the bait, which causes the ingenious design to catch in the fish's mouth.

"Another advantage of Kahle hooks is that they cause less damage to the fish," Jones adds. "I seldom gut-hook a fish with these hooks, which means the fish is more likely to survive after being released. Jones points out that the small treble hooks used by many inshore fishermen can get caught deep in the fish's mouth or stomach, where they will be hard, if not impossible, to remove without killing the fish.

Gator Baits

The bait Jones uses also contributes heavily to her success. "During the spring I use three- to five-inch live mullet, locally called finger mullet, which are the main forage fish at that time," she says. "I have my clients cast them into shallow bays and bayous and let the mullet swim just under the surface in three to eight feet of water. At first light and just before dark, the big trout

LIVE CROAKERS are among Jones's favorite baits for big trout. She pins them on Kahle hooks, which results in a higher percentage of lip- or jaw-hooked fish.

come out of the deep holes to feed in the shallows, where they're primarily looking for mullet."

During the rest of the year Jones prefers to use live, three-inch pinfish and croakers up to eight or ten inches long, which she catches in the shallow back bays with a castnet. "My baits are usually much bigger than those used by most trout fishermen," Jones explains. "However, I've learned that bigger baits generally produce bigger trout."

Jones also wants her baits to be as fresh as possible, so she catches them an hour before each trip. She also carries a castnet with her so she can restock her live well if the baits become sluggish or if she runs out. "You must have fresh, lively bait to catch the largest trout," Jones emphasizes. "Even if we lose an hour trying to catch bait, we can make it up by taking more fish."

Jones has found that croakers often produce the most trout during the hot months, especially when she fishes deep holes (20 to 40 feet) in the bay. "During summer, big trout often hold in deep holes right on the bottom. Golden croakers and Atlantic croakers are bottom feeders. As soon as you cast them out they swim straight to the bottom, right to where the big trout are holding. You can usually feel the line start to twitch when the croaker sees a big trout heading its way, after which you almost always feel a hit." Jones considers hook placement another key to success. "I hook the bait high in the back instead of in the lip so it can swim to the bottom faster. If the angler accidentally pulls on a bait that's hooked through the lips, he'll lift the bait off the bottom. But if the hook's in the back of the bait, pulling on the line actually makes it swim deeper.

"I also like to have only a small portion of the hook in the bait. Once the trout takes the bait it will shake its head to throw the hook.

If the bait remains attached to the hook, the added weight may help pull the hook out of the fish's mouth. With the hook placed lightly in the back, the fish may throw the bait but not the hook." Jones wants the bait to tear off for another reason: other trout in the school may attack it and cut the line. Current is another major part of Jones's strategy, and she tries to fish the holes on a strong tide, whether it's flowing into or out of the bay. "Or I'll fish the Intracoastal Waterway, where I can always find some current," she says. "The worst times to fish are during a screaming spring tide or a slack tide. You can usually take trout anytime in between. When the current is slack or very weak I'll head for a really deep bayou or bay where the fish aren't dependent on current."

Trout fishermen often catch redfish accidentally, but Jones knows how to target them through specialized methods. "When I'm fishing for redfish I prefer to use live shrimp," she explains. "I rig up by placing a small slip sinker on the line and tying on a barrel swivel. Then I tie on three feet of 12-pound-test leader to the other end of the swivel. At the end of the leader I tie on a Mustad No. 4 Kahle hook. The sinker gets the shrimp to the bottom and the barrel swivel keeps the sinker from sliding down to the bait. This setup also allows the shrimp to move freely in the current."

Tricks for Tough Times

As many experienced anglers know, the two most difficult times to catch trout and red-fish are in the dead of winter, when the fish may feed only every two or three days, and during the extreme heat of August, when hot weather also makes them sluggish. During these times a strong current is vital for success.

"In winter and August I try to schedule my trips around the tide," Jones says. "I do most of my fishing in the Intracoastal, where the current is strongest. If the fish aren't there or aren't feeding I'll move out to Choctawhatchee Bay and fish in 35 to 40 feet of water."

Why is current so important? "The reason the light-line, live-bait tactic works so well is because the current sweeps the bait into the deep holes naturally," explains Jones. "The bait swims right to where the big trout are waiting!"

After anchoring above a hole, Jones has her clients cast their croakers upcurrent and let them swim down through the hole. If the bait makes it through without getting eaten, she has them reel in and cast again. Although large trout most often hold right on the bottom, sometimes they'll hang in the mid-depths. In this case, the bait will often shift gears on its way down and come racing to the surface – with a big trout hot on its heels!

Don't Jerk!

As mentioned, it's not necessary to set the hook when using Kahle hooks, and Jones constantly has to remind her clients not to yank back on the rod the moment they feel a tug. "The best way to lose a trout or redfish is to jerk the rod tip up hard and to try and set the hook. If you're using a Kahle hook, all you have to do is reel when you feel the fish take off with the bait."

Jones also coaches her anglers to wait for the fish to eat the bait before reeling. The angler should point his rod tip at the water and allow the fish to take out several yards of line in free-spool before flipping the bail or putting the reel in gear. If there's solid weight on the end of the line, the angler should raise the rod gently and begin playing the fish.

"The real secret to landing a big trout or red is to not horse it in," says Jones. "Steady pressure and a slow retrieve result in far more fish in the boat."

In an average four-hour trip, Jones can usually put her party on ten to 15 legal-size speckled trout and possibly one or two redfish. Catching 20 keeper trout in a four-hour trip isn't unusual – *if* her anglers follow instructions. Jones admits that sometimes the fish just won't bite no matter what she tries, but adds that "even on a bad day, the trout and redfish will eat *sometime*. To catch them consistently you have to be there with live bait and light line when they start to feed."

WINTER FLOUNDER 101

By Tom Richardson

What better way to start the New England fishing season than with a little back-to-basics flounder action?

It felt strange to meet Mitch Chagnon at 9:30, almost awkward, like seeing him in a suit. Fishing with this amiable charter captain usually means setting my alarm for 3:00 A.M. and meeting him at the dock in Pt. Judith, Rhode Island, well before dawn. But this was a real treat. I actually got to eat breakfast, and didn't race out of the house leaving behind lots of important stuff. No speeding tickets *this* time!

We puttered around Mitch's garage for a while, tinkering with tackle, then stopped by a local tackle store for a few scoops of rabbit food pellets and a bucket of some very ripe mussels. By the time we launched my boat at the public ramp in nearby Galilee it was 12:30. The sun was shining, with a brisk northeast wind making it feel much colder than the thermometer's 50-degree reading. It was a typical early-spring day in southern New England, the kind that lures fishermen from their winter dens.

We headed into Pt. Judith Pond, Mitch guiding me through the twisting channels he knows so well. The water was as clear as a Florida flat, it being too early for the aquatic vegetation and plankton to have begun to grow. We weaved deep into the pond, through bays and coves, Mitch pointing out spots that would hold schoolie stripers in a month or so. The trees were bare along the banks, the brown earth hard and barren. A few ducks and geese paddled idly through the riffled water, hunched low against the wind. The water temperature was 42 degrees. I couldn't imagine anything could be living in the frigid pond, but below us creatures were stirring in the cold mud.

A Flounder Hole!

Eventually we came to a narrow channel connecting two small bays called, appropriately enough, The Narrows. After a bit of boat positioning we cut the engine and dropped anchor. Other fishermen were here, too, hardy souls huddled in their tin boats, just glad to be out on the water. Wasting no time, Mitch began scattering handfuls of rabbit pellets, which quickly sank to the bottom. Then he took some of the mussels and crushed them with an oar handle. He placed the mussels and shells in a wire chum basket, added a few handfuls of the rabbit food, and doused the contents with a liberal squirt of Berkley Power Scent gel. He fastened the lid and instructed me to drop the whole mess overboard, directly under the stern.

As the chum basket soaked on the bottom ten feet below, emitting its delicious aroma, Mitch removed some of the mussels from their shells and crammed them into a perforated film canister that he had rigged just above his sinker. He then added a few rabbit pellets and another squirt of Power Scent and popped the lid back on the canister. Finally, he took a seaworm, sliced off an inch-long piece, and placed the small bit of wriggling nematode on his hook. I followed Mitch's lead and prepared my own rig, then lowered it to the bottom. Now it was time to sit back, kick our feet up, and bask in the sun. Ahh, the simple pleasures of flounder fishing!

Soon Mitch's rod tip began to twitch, an indication that he had a customer down below. He waited for the tip to bend over and then set the hook with a slow upward stroke. In a few seconds the first flounder of the season was flopping at our feet. We measured it out at 16 inches and tossed it into the cooler. Another season was underway.

In southern New England, winter flounder, also known as "blackbacks," begin to get active in the salt ponds, estuaries, and back bays when the water temperature climbs into the low 40s, which usually happens around the end of March or early April. Even so, the fish are still pretty sluggish, so you're best off waiting for a nice warm day if the temperature is only

marginal. According to Mitch, the ideal situation is a sunny day with the high tide ocurring sometime after noon. He explained that this gives the water a chance to heat up in the shallows. As the tide drops, this warmer water flows into the deeper zones, making the flounder more active.

Mud Bottoms Best

A good flounder hole will also have a mud bottom as opposed to sand, since the darker substrate absorbs and retains heat better. Mitch prefers to fish in off-color water for the same reason, since the particles of detritus and plankton also hold heat and warm the surrounding water.

Since flounder tend to be lazy in the early season, it's best to look for places where an eddy will form, or where a depression or piece of structure offers some protection from the current. Ideally, you should be able to hold bottom with no more than a three-ounce bank sinker.

After you find a likely looking spot that meets the above requirements, it's simply a matter of dropping anchor, throwing out a chum pot, and sending a bit of seaworm to the bottom. It shouldn't take long for a hungry flounder to find your bait. In fact, if you don't get a bite in 15 minutes, either move to another part of the hole or seek out an entirely different spot.

Like the fishing itself, a flounder rig is a pretty simple affair. Take a 20-inch piece of 20- or 30-pound mono and tie a short dropper loop in the middle. Then tie a surgeon's loop in one end and the other end to a swivel. Finally, attach a snelled flounder hook to the dropper loop via a loop-to-loop connection. Or you can tie a long dropper loop, snip off one leg, and simply snell the flounder hook directly to the remaining end. The important thing is to make the dropper section long enough so the bait will rest on the bottom.

Chum Them In

Chum is a key part of successful flounder fishing, since these fish rely heavily on smell to home in on a meal. Most pros carry the prerequisite bucket of rabbit food, which can be purchased in five-pound bags at pet stores and some tackle shops. Simply scatter a few handfuls of the stuff around the boat from time to time. Also mandatory is a small mesh chum pot, which can be picked up for

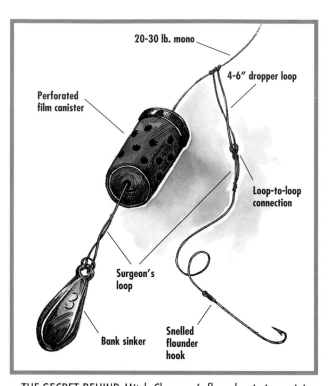

THE SECRET BEHIND Mitch Chagnon's flounder rig is a mini chum pot made from a film canister that rides above the sinker.

Labels on illustration: 20-30 lb. mono; 4-6" dropper loop; Perforated film canister; Loop-to-loop connection; Surgeon's loop; Bank sinker; Snelled flounder hook

about $10 at a tackle shop. Fill it with some rabbit food and some crushed mussels or clams and you're in business. While you're fishing, it's a good idea to raise and lower the chum pot occasionally in order to stir up the contents and bottom sediment.

To create even more scent, Mitch has come up with a clever device that he makes himself. It's a mini chum pot made from a film canister that rides directly on the leader above the sinker. He fills it with chum, replaces the lid, and sends down the whole package. The scent emanating from the little can as it's jiggled above the bottom leads flounder directly to the baited hook.

As for bait, nothing's better or easier to obtain than the good old seaworm. Since only a small bit of worm is all that's needed on the hook, a dozen or so will go a long way.

After Mitch and I had boated a few keepers, the bite dropped off, so we pulled anchor and headed to another of his secret spots. A short run brought us to a protected cove behind a small island. Mitch had me circle the area until he located the deep hole he knew was there, then we dropped over the anchor and the chum pot again. Soon flounder were coming in hand over fist, and we filled our limits of four fish apiece in about half an hour.

Good thing, too, because it was getting noticeably frosty as the sun began to sink closer to the trees along the west bank of the pond. I fired up the outboard, drew my parka a little tighter, and headed down the pond into the teeth of a stinging Northeast wind. Tears streamed down my cheeks. I was cold, but happy. Spring was not really here yet, but at least there was a reason to fish!

HALIBUT *Havens*

By Jim Hendricks

If it's big halibut you seek, forget about drifting the flats and set your sights on structure.

THIS HEFTY 15-POUND HALIBUT was caught by 14-year-old Joshua Hendricks on a soft-plastic jig hopped over a section of hard bottom off the coast of Southern California.

In the time-honored tradition of Southern California halibut fishing we had drifted for hours over the vast, sandy flats. But by mid-aftenoon we had boated only a handful of fish, all under the 22-inch limit.

It was a bust, so around 3:00 we decided to anchor up and fish a rock pile for calico bass and sand bass. What happened in the next hour, however, turned the day into one of the most memorable fishing trips of my life.

Almost as soon as we settled back on the anchor, the sand bass began biting well, and it looked like we'd be finishing off the day by catching and releasing a bunch. Then my son Grant hooked a fish that was far more powerful than even the biggest sand bass. Clearly this fish was a heavyweight. It shook its head violently and bullied its way along the bottom, peeling off line at will. Yet it never ran far. For several minutes, the fish cruised around in the shadow of the boat, hardly swimming more than ten yards in any one direction.

Grant couldn't move the fish more than a few feet, and eventually it bit through the 12-pound mono. We were all disappointed – but not for long.

Minutes later, our friend Steve Riley set the hook on another big fish. It too shook its head furiously, then burst across the bottom, pinning Steve to the gunwale. He struggled to hold onto the rod while fumbling to loosen the drag.

Down below was a truly big fish, and it wanted to stay where it was. But eventually the fish began to rise – inch by inch, a half crank at a time. When it finally emerged from the depths, its body illuminated by the afternoon sun, we couldn't believe our eyes. It was a halibut, and easily the biggest California halibut ever caught on my boat!

But it wasn't ours yet. This monster had strength in reserve, and I cautioned Steve to ease it up gently and lead it within gaffing range. Too much pressure would ignite a powerful, last-ditch run for the bottom, and that's when most big halibut are lost.

Steve did his job well, and, thankfully, so did I. The gaff hit home, and we wrestled the fish aboard. It weighed 33½ pounds!

Steve's "barndoor" and Grant's mystery fish – which I am convinced was also a big halibut – underline an important axiom among Southern California halibut experts: *For truly large halibut, focus on structure.*

For evidence, look at the larger halibut caught aboard my 22-foot boat, *Split Decision*. In the past 18 months, we've landed two fish over 30 pounds, two over 20 pounds, and a half dozen over ten pounds. All of these fish were caught while the boat was anchored up near structure, such as wrecks, rock piles, and hard-bottom areas. In fact, all but one of these fish were incidental catches. In most cases, we were actually fishing for calico and sand bass, which led me to my own axiom: *If you want to catch big halibut, go bass fishing!*

California halibut, not to be confused with their larger cousin, the Pacific halibut, gravitate to structure for the same reason all predatory fish do: to find food, such as octopus, shrimp, mackerel, topsmelt, perch, sardines, and more.

Don't Drift!

With this reasoning, the anchoring-over-structure method of halibut fishing seems pretty straightforward. Everybody should do it; however, most halibut fishermen in Southern California don't. Instead, they spend most of their time drifting over mud and sand flats. The words "halibut" and "drifting" have become almost synonymous among flatty fishermen. To be sure, you can catch a lot of halibut – including some big ones – by drifting at certain times of the year, particularly during the spring and fall spawning periods when the fish gather on the flats in large numbers. The problem is that it's hard to catch the big ones because there are so many smaller, more aggressive fish around.

For anglers who want to increase their odds of hooking a big California halibut, as well as those who want to catch these fish all year long, structure fishing is the key. Don't expect big volume, just big fish.

There is no *bad* type of structure when it comes to halibut. We've caught them while fishing over just about every conceivable type of structure: wrecks, rock piles, shale bottom, gravel bottom, scattered rocks, inshore reefs, jetties, and breakwalls.

Depth does not seem to be a critical factor, either. This may surprise the drift-fishermen, since the spawning aggregations tend to occur in a particular depth. Not so with structure halibut. Their main objective is food, and they'll swim anywhere to find it. We've caught halibut on structure as deep as 200 feet and as shallow as ten feet. Most of the spots I fish range from 25 to 75 feet deep. Different types of structure do require different techniques, however.

The Structure Factor

I divide halibut structure into two categories: high relief and low relief. High-relief structure includes wrecks, rock piles, reefs, jetties, and breakwalls. Ninety percent of the time, halibut will stake out or actively hunt near the base of high-relief structure, around the rock/sand interface zone. Occasionally we'll hook a fish right on top of a wreck, or one that's nestled atop a flat boulder in a rock pile, but that's the exception.

With this in mind, you should anchor your boat so you can fish the bottom immediately adjacent to the base of the structure. You should also work the structure itself, since a halibut may hunt within the structure zone.

Low-relief structure includes hard shale bottom, gravel bottom, and small, scattered rocks. In these areas, most halibut move right into the structure area, and you should anchor your boat so that you can present your lures and baits directly within the structure zone.

No matter what type of structure or what depth, the best method calls for anchoring slightly upwind or upcurrent from the structure. Whether you're working the base of the structure or fishing within the structure itself, keep your offering on or very near the bottom.

Current is another important factor in halibut fishing. These predators definitely feed more actively when there's a good current running, which carries baitfish and other forage around the structure. Many factors influence current, but the tide is certainly one of the strongest. Therefore, I like to fish the middle of the falling or rising tide, when water movement is at its peak.

Tackle, Baits & Rigs

To land a big halibut you need a top-quality rod and reel. The best rod is a seven-foot, conventional live-bait stick. A fast-taper rod rated for 12- to 20-pound test is perfect for twitching baits and lures for halibut, yet it also has enough power to battle a barn-door to the boat.

Halibut fishing also demands a quality reel with a smooth drag system. When fishing spots less than 75 feet deep, you don't

need a lot of line capacity, since halibut don't run that far. I prefer conventional reels with star-drag systems.

Big fish like big baits, and halibut are no exception. Some of the best include queenfish (often called "brown bait" or herring), lizardfish, sardines, squid, and even small mackerel. Live anchovies – one of the most readily available live baits in Southern California – don't seem to produce as many big halibut.

Many of our biggest halibut have also been hooked on soft-plastic lures rigged on leadhead jigs. One of my favorites is a single-tail, six-inch Kalin Mogambo. The "dorado" color has produced more big halibut for us than any other. We use lead-heads with a 5/0 hook, ranging in weight from 3/8 ounce to one ounce, depending on how much it takes to stay on the bottom.

Despite the presence of big fish, top halibut anglers recommend using the lightest line possible. Most prefer 15-pound test, and hardly any use line heavier than 20-pound. For fishing live bait, use a sliding egg sinker – held above the leader by a barrel swivel or a small split-shot – to keep the bait on the bottom.

A sharp hook is a must for halibut fishing. Bronze treble hooks are growing in popularity for live-bait halibut fishing, as they seem to produce more hook-ups. Carry a variety of sizes – from No. 4 to 2/0 – to accommodate a wide range of live baits.

Anglers who keep their baits moving around structure catch more halibut. California halibut are sight-feeders, and movement triggers the strike. This is one reason that lures produce so well. The most productive technique calls for constantly twitching the bait or lure along the bottom to attract the attention of nearby halibut. While a halibut usually lies in ambush, it will also get up and chase a good-looking meal.

CALICOS ON YOUR OWN

By Nick Curcione

The ubiquitous calico, or kelp bass, is the ideal target for the California small-boat angler.

In terms of sporting qualities and accessibility, the calico bass (also known as kelp bass) ranks high on the list of Southern California's most popular inshore game fish. Similar to fresh water bass, calicos are a structure-loving species whose favorite haunts are areas of rock and kelp. In contrast to open ocean roamers like tuna and billfish, calicos are considered an inshore species (even around the offshore islands they stay relatively close to shore), so you don't need a large boat to pursue them. In fact, smaller boats provide an advantage when fishing close to structure because of their maneuverability.

The calico's geographical distribution covers a vast area extending from central California to Magdalena Bay in Mexico. Its habitat is also wide-ranging, making it possible to fish under a variety of conditions. Calicos can even be found in the surf, but of more interest to private-boaters is the fact that jetties, breakwaters, back bays, harbors, oil platforms, rock piles, wrecks, and kelp forests are all calico country. As long as there is some type of structure, you're likely to find calicos. You can catch them in water so shallow it will barely float your boat, to depths of well over 100 feet.

Almost Anything Works

As you might expect, calicos can be caught on any kind of gear: conventional, spinning, and fly. You can cast, troll, drift, fish deep or near the surface, use many types of live and dead bait, or a variety of artificials. But the best part of all is that it's a year-round fishery.

Calicos are relatively non-selective feeders, which is why they can be taken on such a wide variety of baits and lures. In terms of the former, calicos will readily eat anchovies, sardines, "brown baits" (queenfish, herring, tomcod, and white croaker), squid, octopus, mussels, crabs, and shrimp. The lineup of artificials includes jigs, leadhead/plastic-tail combinations, and deep-running plugs.

As far as live bait is concerned, most calicos are probably caught on anchovies, simply because it's the most frequently available live bait for the party and private-boat fleet. Depending on prevailing conditions, anchovies can be fly-lined on the surface or fished in the depths with weights ranging from small split shots and rubber-core twist-ons to larger egg and torpedo sinkers. Hook sizes can range from No. 6 to No. 1, with No. 2 and No. 4 the most commonly used.

When fly-lining or using smaller weights, it's best to collar-hook the anchovy. With heavier sinkers (¾ ounce or more), it's more effective to nose-hook the bait by pushing the hook up through the lower jaw to where it penetrates the tip of the nose.

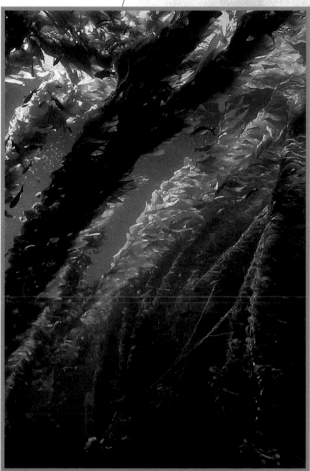

CALICO BASS LIKE TO hang around all kinds of inshore structure, including jetties, rock piles, wrecks, and kelp beds like these.

Can't Beat a Squid

Anchovies may be the most widely used bait, but squid are calico candy. They also offer a number of advantages to the small-boater. As far as procuring them, you'll save yourself considerable work by buying them from the bait receivers. And unlike anchovies, when they aren't available for sale you can at least try to catch them yourself. This is a nighttime affair and involves the use of bright lights to attract the spawning squid to the surface, where they can be brailed or caught on squid jigs. More important, once you do have them, they prove a lot more versatile than anchovies.

First off, squid tend to be hardier than anchovies, and seem to fare much better in the smaller bait tanks normally found on private boats. Secondly, the ones that don't survive can be fished whole, in strips, and even cut up for chum. Because they are able to carry such enormous quantities of bait, the party boats can afford to do a lot of chumming with live anchovies. But private-boaters usually don't have that luxury. However, at least as far as calicos are concerned, dime-size squid chunks can sometimes be more effective chum than live anchovies. Even when you can't get live baits, frozen squid (thaw it out in a bucket of sea water first) will work well in all the ways mentioned above.

When chumming with pieces of squid, the trick is to anchor upcurrent from a piece of structure so that the diced portions drift into the bass's feeding zone. Instead of simply throwing out handfuls, it's much more effective to place the chum over the side of the boat. This way it will sink faster and the birds won't have an opportunity to steal most of it.

Basic Techniques

A basic way to fish squid involves a sliding-sinker setup. The line is run through an appropriate-size egg sinker, and the hook (3/0 to 5/0) is tied directly to the end. The offering is cast out and the reel fished in free-spool. Experience is the best teacher in determining how long you should let the calico run with the bait before engaging the reel and striking. Naturally, because squid are larger than anchovies, it will usually take the bass more time to engulf the bait. But bear in mind that the longer you allow the fish to run with the bait, the greater your chances of getting cut off or fouled in the structure.

When you do hit them, and this applies regardless of the offering, you want to apply steady pressure and continue winding. Many anglers pause with the rod bent after they strike a fish. Instead, you want to short-pump the rod while simultaneously turning the reel handle to gain line. The object is to turn the fish from the structure and get it coming your way. Even when you do it right, you're still going to lose some fish, but that's part of the challenge.

Another simple way to fish squid is to hook a strip of it on a leadhead jig, with or without a soft-plastic tail. With this method, the reel is usually fished in gear and the jig left on the bottom. Bass will peck at the squid, but so will the pesky blue perch, and this can really frazzle your reflexes. In any case, you have to learn not to strike prematurely, because if it is a calico, you will end up pulling the bait away from the fish. Wait until you feel steady pressure, then strike and wind as described above.

As with bait fishing, jigs will work in shallow and deep water. When fishing structure close to the surface, cast next to it and start retrieving as soon as the jig hits the water. Strikes often occur within the first ten to 15 feet. Twenty-pound test is a good choice for casting the lighter surface iron.

Yellow/brown, yellow/green, and blue/white are popular color combinations.

Vary Your Retrieve

When fishing deeper structure in the 50- to 100-foot range, cast out and let the jig sink with the reel in free-spool. Be alert for strikes as the lure falls. The calico's feeding zones and preference for lure action vary, so you should be prepared to try a variety of retrieve techniques. The straight drop with a moderate, steady retrieve toward the surface; the yo-yo method, which involves raising and lowering the rod as you retrieve; and kicking the reel in and out of gear while winding in a few feet of line during the drop, have all proven effective at one time or another.

Another way to catch calicos is by trolling with a variety of deep-running plugs like Rapalas, Rebels, and MirrOlures. A slow troll along kelp beds and rock outcroppings can yield very good results, and it's a great way to go if you find yourself without any bait or chum.

Try these techniques and you're sure to do well with calicos – a fish that is seemingly made to order for the small-boat fisherman. Once you've experienced the fun of finding and catching calicos on your own, you'll know why so many Californians hold them in such high esteem.

Pop-Fly Reds

By Pete Cooper, Jr.

Take fly fishing for redfish to an exciting new level by tossing poppers to them in skinny water.

As a fishing writer, I get some pretty radical phone calls, like the one I received one day from Dave Ballay at the Venice Marina in Venice, Louisiana. It turns out he had just discovered a spot where redfish tails were popping out of the water everywhere he looked, and he suggested that I grab a fly rod and haul my butt down there ASAP. Now, I've known Dave long enough to realize that when he rings my phone to tell me something like that, he's not jiving. So I hied myself to his hot spot and within two hours I had taken ten fish, the largest of which appeared to be a bit over ten pounds. But the best part was that these supposed bottom feeders literally crawled all over a popper.

Actually, I've been fishing fly-rod poppers for redfish for over 30 years, beginning with my initiation on the turtle-grass flats off Traylor Island near Rockport, Texas. Five years later I was fishing for largemouth bass in a pipeline canal near Venice when a red that weighed only two ounces shy of 15 pounds slammed my popper. Admittedly, that catch was an accident of sorts, yet it reinforced the fact that these fish are quite willing and able to eat something that's swimming on the surface. Thus encouraged, I took my meager knowledge of saltwater fly fishing and directed it toward a practical application.

The particular area for my experiment was a shallow, brackish marsh, the bottom of which was covered with thick grass. Conventional lures, even topwaters, would often foul in the goop at inopportune moments, or else the fish would spook from their impact. A fly-rod popper, on the other hand, floated above the grass, and its quiet entry allowed me to cast much closer to the fish without spooking them.

Since then I've taken hundreds of redfish on poppers, but my favorite part of this approach is that it almost always involves sight-casting. There isn't much in the fishing world that beats casting a floating fly to a visible fish and watching it attack!

The Right Conditions

Still, this is not a technique for all seasons, weather, or water conditions. For example, reds won't usually rise more than three feet or so to strike a popper, so use this as your maximum depth for fishing them. Shallower is usually much better for popper fishing.

As in all sight-fishing situations, you must have good water clarity and bright sunlight to locate fish that are not showing their tails or backs. Also, the surface must be relatively calm in order for poppers to be most effective.

This brings up a point of contention that has special relevance. Many anglers have wrongly accused redfish of being somewhat nearsighted. While reds may develop a case of tunnel-vision when rooting for some hidden morsel, they can see quite well for some distance. It's just that the ones with their noses in the grass may need a little attention-grabber, which is why poppers really shine. Even so, you may need to make three or four casts right over the fish before it looks up and gives chase.

Use soft pops interspersed with brief pauses, which gets the fish's attention and gives it time to home in on the fly. A moderate retrieve with soft, steady pops has accounted for most of my fly-caught redfish. It has also spooked a lot of them if I happened to be retrieving the fly toward the fish. Apparently, reds don't like to be attacked by a popper, especially in shallow water. They also don't care for any change in the retrieve while they are following the popper. Maintaining a steady pace is usually best.

Then there are the fish that rush the popper on its splashdown, only to sit there looking at it. Or the ones that follow it

Many anglers have wrongly accused redfish of being somewhat nearsighted.

tentatively without striking. When a fish appears behind a popper and doesn't immediately strike, quickly "slide" it away: no pops, no pauses, just a steady pull for as long as it takes, or as long as you can keep it up.

Pencil It Out

There are many kinds of poppers that are suitable for reds, but the "pencil popper" isn't one of them. It's just a theory on my part, but I feel that the design of this popper places the eyes – a target for the fish – too far from the hook point, which could lead to missed strikes.

I now make my own poppers in sizes No. 6 to 1/0, with the majority of reds falling for a size No. 1 (about 2½ inches long). Color does not seem to be all that important, but green over white, yellow, or chartreuse all work well. I make the popper bodies from small cylindrical perch floats, while a friend makes his from the foam-rubber soles of worn-out beach sandals. You can also purchase commercially made pre-formed bodies, either with or without hooks. All the above materials can be easily painted with Testor's model enamel, available in hobby shops and art-supply stores.

Naturally, if you don't want to make your own, you can buy saltwater poppers through mail-order houses and fly shops – if you don't mind paying the price. Fresh water bass poppers work well too, and cost about half as much as the saltwater designs. Use a size No. 2 and remove any rubber legs. They hold up to repeated strikes well enough, and after a day of use you can simply throw them away. If you choose to keep them, be sure to rinse them well in fresh water before putting them in your fly box.

Whatever your choice, the next time you find yourself searching for reds in reasonably clear, calm, shallow water – grassy or not – tie on a popper instead of that Bendback or Clouser. Aside from catching fish, you will experience the thrill of watching reds strike on the surface. Believe me, they hold nothing back. It's neat stuff, and a major reason why I almost exclusively use poppers when fly fishing for inshore reds.

FISHING POPPERS FOR REDFISH is productive throughout the year as long as the water is calm, shallow, and reasonably clear. Here the author takes a moment to admire a popper-caught red before release.

Offshore FISHING

Blue-Water Clues: Where the Fish Are • Baits & Lures: Mix Tricks for Trolling •

Early-Season Tuna Tactics • Six Tricks for Stubborn Dolphin

BLUE-WATER CLUES:
Where the Fish Are

By Bob McNally

The key to locating offshore game fish is keeping one eye on the ocean and the other on your depthsounder.

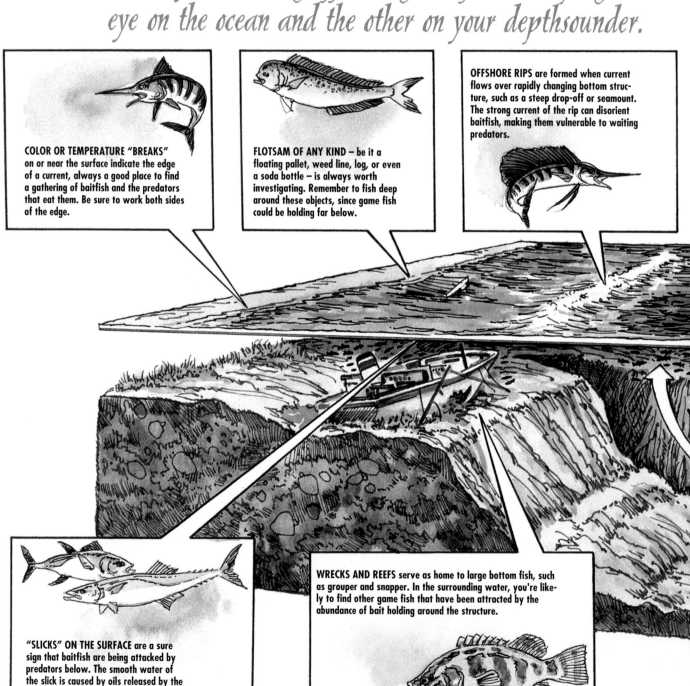

COLOR OR TEMPERATURE "BREAKS" on or near the surface indicate the edge of a current, always a good place to find a gathering of baitfish and the predators that eat them. Be sure to work both sides of the edge.

FLOTSAM OF ANY KIND – be it a floating pallet, weed line, log, or even a soda bottle – is always worth investigating. Remember to fish deep around these objects, since game fish could be holding far below.

OFFSHORE RIPS are formed when current flows over rapidly changing bottom structure, such as a steep drop-off or seamount. The strong current of the rip can disorient baitfish, making them vulnerable to waiting predators.

WRECKS AND REEFS serve as home to large bottom fish, such as grouper and snapper. In the surrounding water, you're likely to find other game fish that have been attracted by the abundance of bait holding around the structure.

"SLICKS" ON THE SURFACE are a sure sign that baitfish are being attacked by predators below. The smooth water of the slick is caused by oils released by the wounded bait.

The open ocean is a mighty big place, but not every square mile of water is jammed with hungry predators. In fact, only a very small portion of the ocean holds game fish in large quantities. Therefore, the key to successful offshore fishing is concentrating on those spots where game fish are likely to congregate, and being able to recognize the telltale signs that indicate the presence of fish.

One important rule used by veteran offshore captains throughout the world is to "watch for something different." By that they mean keeping an eye out for anything that varies from the surrounding water or bottom, since it will usually be attractive to fish. Seamounts, ledges, drop-offs, reefs, wrecks, and canyons are obvious differences in the ocean floor. Their locations are often marked on a chart, which makes them easy to find with GPS or loran and a depthsounder.

But other, less-noticeable differences are important, too. For example, a sudden variation in water color or temperature may be a significant clue to the location of fish. A lone bird far on the horizon may signal baitfish – and game fish – below. A weed line or foamy current rip on an otherwise barren ocean could point the way to a trophy.

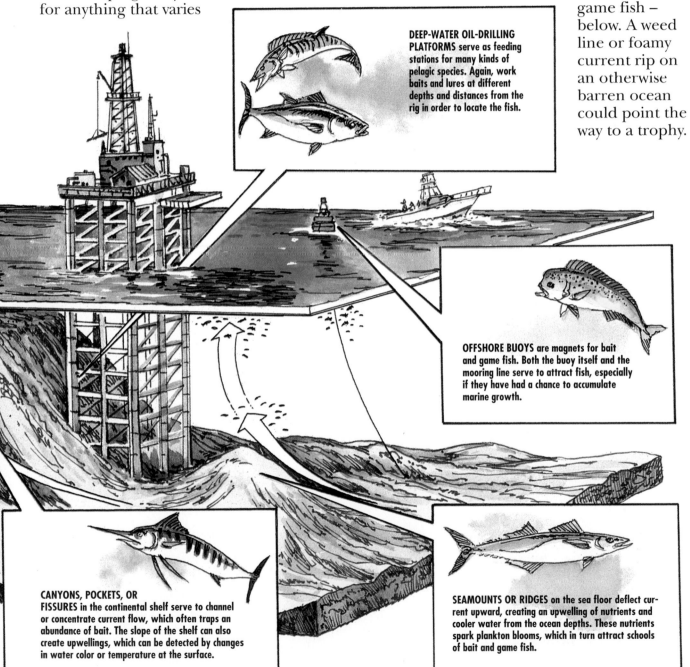

DEEP-WATER OIL-DRILLING PLATFORMS serve as feeding stations for many kinds of pelagic species. Again, work baits and lures at different depths and distances from the rig in order to locate the fish.

OFFSHORE BUOYS are magnets for bait and game fish. Both the buoy itself and the mooring line serve to attract fish, especially if they have had a chance to accumulate marine growth.

CANYONS, POCKETS, OR FISSURES in the continental shelf serve to channel or concentrate current flow, which often traps an abundance of bait. The slope of the shelf can also create upwellings, which can be detected by changes in water color or temperature at the surface.

SEAMOUNTS OR RIDGES on the sea floor deflect current upward, creating an upwelling of nutrients and cooler water from the ocean depths. These nutrients spark plankton blooms, which in turn attract schools of bait and game fish.

Flotsam Action

How such subtle anomalies can be attractive to game fish was made crystal clear to me last June while fishing a Mako Boat owner's "Funament" off Walker's Cay in the Bahamas. *Salt Water Sportsman's* George Poveromo and veteran offshore angler Barry O'Neill had trolled the better part of a day without much luck when they happened upon a small buoy trailing a broken rope and chain. Hovering around the 30-foot length of rope were small baitfish – the food-chain base for sport fish. Poveromo and O'Neill trolled around the buoy, and in a very short time caught dolphin, wahoo, and tuna. O'Neill even released a 150-pound blue marlin!

Flotsam not only attracts surface predators to baitfish on top, it also holds fish deep. I know one angler who regularly catches wahoo and kingfish while deep-jigging under flotsam. He first pulls surface lures around the floating object, catching any fish on top (usually dolphin or billfish), then he trolls big plugs deep, which sometimes produces wahoo, kingfish, and tuna. Finally, he tips a big jig with a ballyhoo and plumbs the depths. It's amazing how many fish he catches that way.

Weeds & Slicks

Weed lines and kelp paddies are other types of flotsam that hold fish. Dolphin, tuna, wahoo, marlin, sailfish, and many other species are commonly caught by trolling along weed lines or around scattered kelp paddies. Not all weed lines and paddies hold fish, however. The most productive ones are usually alive with lots of small baitfish hovering around and under them. This attracts small dolphin and football-size tuna, which in turn attract marlin, wahoo, and other large predators.

Another visual clue to good fishing is the presence of slicks created from the oily residue of bait that's been slashed to pieces below the surface. Birds sitting on the water near a slick or plucking scraps from the surface are a good sign that game fish are feeding below.

Rips & Edges

Tide rips are always prime places to concentrate on, especially those found off inlets. The bigger rips are fished so hard that many skilled fishermen head for the less noticeable rips, especially the ones in deep water. These "secondary rips" can be important hot spots in today's crowded ocean.

A secondary rip can be indicated by a color change that occurs well offshore of an inlet and moves out with the ebb tide. When the tide turns back toward the inlet, the cloud of off-color water often becomes separated and continues moving offshore. Finally, when the tide ebbs again, a new color-change edge occurs. By this time, the first color-change edge, or "break," is now a secondary one, and can sometimes be found five to ten miles offshore. As it flows along, it marks the edge of the tide current. When such a secondary rip features a well-defined color break (dirty river water on one side, clean ocean water on the other) and some flotsam, it's a prime place to fish.

Color edges don't necessarily have to involve brown water. Along the coast of Florida, the edge of the Gulf Stream is marked by a distinct line of deep blue water on one side and milky green water on the other. Sailfish, tuna, and other predators like to cruise close to this edge, sometimes waiting in the green water to get out of the current, then darting into the Stream to nab a meal.

Breaks & Birds

Another type of edge to look for is a temperature edge, usually found in conjunction with a color change. A rapid change in water temperature could indicate the edge of a current, eddy, gyre, or upwelling. Even a fluctuation of one or two degrees can be important. Baitfish and game fish usually collect along the edges of these temperature "fronts," which is why many pros rely on the aid of satellite ocean temperature charts.

Birds have long been known to indicate the presence of fish. For instance, southern fishermen always pay special attention to soaring frigate birds. These large, graceful birds often shadow schools of game fish, or even a single blue marlin, waiting for them to drive bait to the surface. In the Northeast, fishermen welcome the sight of tiny storm petrels, which often indicate the presence of giant bluefin tuna. And on the West Coast, the presence of a lone jaeger frequently means that game fish have been feeding in the area. Whenever you find bird activity offshore, it's worth investigating the area thoroughly.

Underwater Structure

Fortunately, not all prime offshore fishing spots are as small and difficult to locate as flotsam, weeds, birds, slicks, edges, and tide rips. In almost all offshore areas, there are large, often permanent objects that regularly attract and hold sport fish. Better yet, they are easy to find with navigational equipment. Such objects include reefs and wrecks, seamounts and canyons, oil rigs, buoys, and government and military structures.

Often such places are seasonal in the fishing they offer. For example, an offshore wreck may hold lots of snapper and grouper in spring and fall, only to become a home for kingfish, barracuda, and amberjack during summer. Furthermore, during the migrational periods, dolphin, wahoo, tuna, and billfish may be available. It is important to note these seasonal changes, because the type of species present may dictate fishing methods, baits, lures, rigging, etc. For instance, you don't want to be bottom fishing for grouper when the time is right for wahoo.

Look for Small Spots

Many anglers believe deep wrecks are best for holding a variety of fish. The trouble with most big wrecks is that they're often fished hard. For this reason, some savvy anglers have learned that the smaller spots, such as a tiny ledge or patch of coral hard bottom, can actually produce more and bigger fish.

Locating these small uncharted honey holes isn't that difficult. Many captains find theirs by keeping their depthsounders on as they head offshore. Anytime they mark an irregular bottom contour, hole, or hump, they hit the "quick fix" button on their loran or GPS to save the location's coordinates. When they have the time, they return to these places and check them out thoroughly.

Artificial reefs can also be popular places to fish. However, sometimes the best action can be had over small sections that have been separated from the main reef. For example, I often fish a small cluster of concrete culverts that were accidentally dropped 300 yards from the main reef site. The culverts hold tremendous numbers of fish, simply because few people know about them. Therefore, it pays to snoop around artificial reefs and wrecks

THE KEY TO FINDING offshore action like this? Always investigate anything unusual, no matter how small.

to find the smaller structures. A careful search pattern and the skillful use of a depthsounder come into play here.

Work Between the Structures

Most anglers know that king mackerel hang around reefs, ledges, and wrecks. Trouble is, many other fish like barracuda, amberjacks, and sharks do too, which can get in the way of anglers who are after just kingfish.

In many offshore areas, king mackerel are not at the top of the food chain, so other larger or more aggressive species can "push" the kings off the reef, ledge, or wreck. For this reason, schools of kings often won't be found right on a structure with bigger predators. This is when it's productive to fish slightly away from the structure. If fishing a reef network, where several small reefs surround a large central reef, try fishing in between the structures and you should get a lot of strikes from the "lesser" predators. This tactic also works over flat areas lying between natural ledges, as long as the ledges aren't too far apart (200 yards max).

Oil or gas rigs in deep water are similar to artificial reefs, and the baitfish that gather around them provide a food source that attracts offshore game fish on a seasonal basis. Frequently, the uptide side of the rig holds the most fish, but any place bait is spotted near a rig is worth fishing.

Shelves, Canyons & Seamounts

One of the best situations for offshore fishing is when the tide pulls bait from shallow

UNLIKE RIPS OR WEED LINES, manmade structures like drilling platforms and buoys are fixed fish-attractors that are easy to locate by loran or GPS day after day. They often produce different species throughout the year, depending on the season.

water to deep. "Shallow" is a relative term, since a blue-water ledge may fall from 300 to 2,000 feet, while a nearshore drop-off may fall only from 30 to 60 feet. But wherever it occurs, when current washes over a drop-off – from shallow to deep – the stage is set for a feeding frenzy that may include everything from grouper and snapper near the bottom to sharks and wahoo at midlevel to tuna and marlin near the surface.

A similar situation also occurs when current pushes water into the edge of a ledge, seamount, or canyon. This produces an upwelling of nutrients from the bottom of the water column. When the nutrients reach the sunlit surface waters, they spark blooms of phytoplankton, which in turn produce blooms of zooplankton, both of which attract vast schools of baitfish. Bait can also be driven by wind and current from deep, open water against the edge of the drop-off, where it becomes trapped by the current. Usually the most productive places are cups or fissures in the contour of a drop-off, which act as baitfish traps.

Finally, remember that there are no hard-and-fast rules when it comes to finding fish offshore. Indeed, the very best offshore captains are highly adaptable. Naturally, they have a game plan in mind when they head out, but during the run to and from their planned location they use their eyes and electronics to look for the subtle yet telltale clues that might mean fish. Signs like a color change, a lone frigate bird circling overhead, a small hump on the bottom, or a slight rip could lead the way to the best catch of the day, or a hot spot that no one else knows about.

Baits & Lures:
MIX TRICKS FOR TROLLING

By George Poveromo

Combine natural baits and lures together in your offshore trolling spread? It's not as crazy as it sounds, and you may be pleasantly surprised by the results.

When choosing an arsenal for offshore trolling, many anglers are pretty bull-headed. Chalk it up to being superstitious, true to their school, or just plain stubborn, but they mostly troll either artificials or natural baits exclusively.

Lures and natural baits each have distinct advantages, and it pays to know when to choose one over the other. For example, when there's a lot of water to cover, lures enable you to troll faster, increasing the chances of locating fish. Unless damaged or broken off, lures are easily rinsed and stowed for another outing, and that convenience eliminates a lot of time-consuming rigging chores. Conversely, it's difficult to ignore the effectiveness of natural baits when game fish are concentrated. The slower trolling speeds save fuel, while the scent and taste add another dimension to the spread. Sometimes the latter can provoke a "window shopper" into striking, and an experienced bait troller normally enjoys better hook-up percentages.

But what about combining lures and baits in a single spread? Can such a thing be done? And, if so, how can you keep every offering performing properly? Some of the best offshore skippers troll mixed spreads with consistently good results, poking holes in the common perception that you can't fish lures and baits simultaneously because of the differences in speed requirements. But mixing the two creates interesting illusions and actions, and creating a winning spread simply requires some insight, precise positioning, and a bit of experimentation.

Tuna Tricks

Capt. Dave Preble, a premier tuna and white marlin specialist out of Rhode Island, mixes lures and baits regularly.

A SELECTION OF RIGGED NATURALS AND LURES that can be effectively trolled together. The trick is to experiment with line length and boat speed until all baits are running properly.

"There's not many people mixing lures and baits around here," says Preble, "but I do it a lot. I get a kick out of skippers who see tuna on the surface and can't get a strike, claiming they're not feeding. That's a bunch of bull. Those fish are feeding on top, but on tiny bait. While a lot of anglers get locked into pulling only lures, I'm mixing and matching baits and lures in an attempt to find the combination that catches fish."

Some of Preble's top producers are skirted strip baits carved from the bellies of oceanic bonito. He makes them around seven inches long, with split tails to create a fluttering action, and generally fishes these flashy baits from the lower outrigger lines and straight off the transom. Sometimes he'll even run a small (seven-inch) bird about eight feet in front of a strip bait on a flat line to add more commotion. Traditional jet-head lures are then fished off the top outrigger lines and the center rigger.

"With this combination, I have some diversity in my spread," says Preble. "I have the straight-tracking characteristic of lures, highlighted by the slightly different action of the skirted strip baits. In addition, the skirted baits add flash and emit a scent. When the tuna are scattered, I can troll fast in order to uncover them. At a quick pace my lures track well, and because of their skirts, the strip baits run well, too. The skirts prevent the baits from washing out or running poorly when I'm trolling pretty fast. When we're into fish, I can slow down and still maintain an attractive spread. And because the top outrigger and center rigger lines are on a much sharper angle, those lures will also perform well at slower speeds.

"Yellowfins seem to love that combination, and those strip baits are the ticket. That's just one way I combine naturals and artificials for yellowfins. One of the keys in creating an effective combination spread, in my opinion, is to match the size of the lures and baits to what the fish are feeding on, and then arrange every bait and lure so they're acting like they're supposed to, either at slow or fast trolling speeds."

Create a Feeding Frenzy

In the Gulf of Mexico, Capt. Mike Frenette of Venice, Louisiana, combines lures and natural baits for more "splash and dash." Frenette's aggressive trolling style accounts for impressive numbers of big yellowfin, dolphin, marlin, and wahoo each season. One of his favorite arrangements is a seven-line spread made up of lures, horse ballyhoo, mackerel, and mullet.

"I mostly troll around 5½ knots and rarely over seven," says Frenette. "Therefore, I use baits and flat-headed lures, which perform best in that range. The only exception is a heavy, jethead lure I run straight back on the center rigger, which tracks under the surface."

Frenette says a lot of factors determine the exact positioning of his baits and lures. However, his main objective is to create an illusion of "anxiety and competition." For example, his port-side spread might consist of a horse ballyhoo off the long outrigger line, with an eight-inch, flathead lure positioned roughly ten feet in front of the ballyhoo and fished off the short outrigger line. A swimming mullet is fished off the transom flat line in the clean water behind the prop wash. The starboard arrangement includes a horse ballyhoo off the long outrigger, approximately 15 feet behind a splashing mackerel fished off the short outrigger line. The closest flat line tows another eight-inch, flat-head lure, right where

A WAHOO MIGHT FIRST BE attracted to the smell of natural bait emitted by a combo spread, then use color and action to home in on a single target.

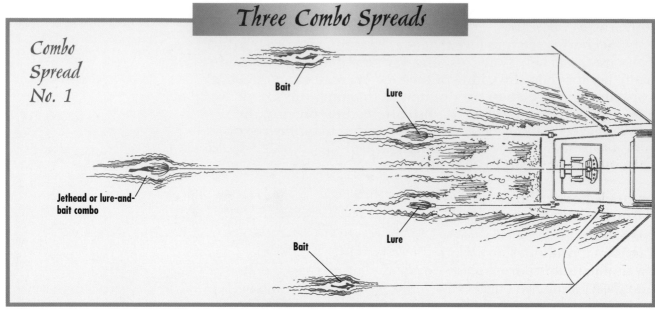

Combo Spread No. 1

Bait

Lure

Lure

Jethead or lure-and-bait combo

Bait

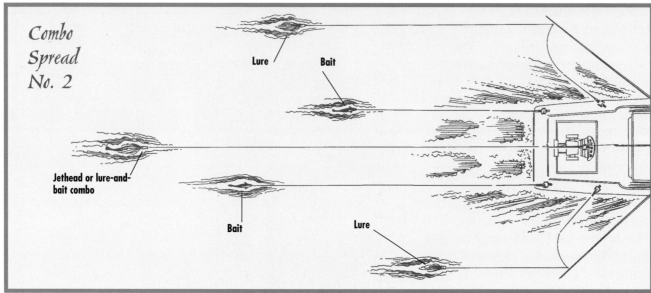

Combo Spread No. 2

Lure

Bait

Jethead or lure-and-bait combo

Bait

Lure

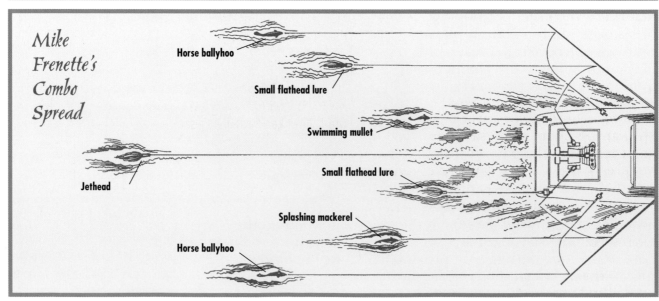

Mike Frenette's Combo Spread

Horse ballyhoo

Small flathead lure

Swimming mullet

Small flathead lure

Jethead

Splashing mackerel

Horse ballyhoo

the prop wash fades into clean water. The jethead lure rounds out the spread, and is fished at least 30 feet behind the longest outrigger bait.

"Between the splashing mackerel and ballyhoo, smoking lures, swimming mullet, and subsurface jethead, there's a lot of dissimilar action in my spread. And I believe it really stands out," says Frenette. "Between some of the smaller lures smoking in front of the larger baits, and those lures riding well behind them, there's an illusion of a feeding frenzy. I think that game fish might view the horse ballyhoo, mackerel, and swimming mullet as predators chasing down bait, which are imitated by the smaller lures. Sometimes this illusion elicits a response from a game fish, triggered by the sense of competition. In other words, a fish doesn't have to be hungry to enter my spread, just greedy.

Fine-Tune Your Combo Spread

Capt. Skip Smith has spent decades trolling for trophy game fish throughout the mid and southern Atlantic, Gulf of Mexico, Caribbean, and Pacific. An innovative offshore authority, Smith regularly combines artificials and natural baits to catch marlin, sailfish, tuna, wahoo, dolphin, and even king mackerel.

Smith believes the different actions liven up a bait spread. Although he prefers blunt-nosed lures in a mixed spread, he says getting all types of lures to run properly at slower speeds is achieved by altering their running angles.

"You can get any spread of lures and baits to work well together through a few simple adjustments," says Smith. "I usually run natural baits such as ballyhoo, splashing mackerel, or mullet off the outriggers, with my lures directly off the transom on flat lines. Regardless of whether I'm running flat-head or streamlined lures, they'll track amazingly well when they're kept close to the boat. That's because the angle of the line coming off the rod tip is more pronounced, forcing the lures to track at a slightly upward angle. You're making the lures perform at their peak, without picking up speed and jeopardizing the action and durability of the natural baits. The lures will track straight and smoke right behind the transom. They're sort of like teasers with hooks in them."

Smith is also a firm believer in combination baits. "Adding a small lure in front of a ballyhoo, mullet, strip bait or even a mackerel can increase your odds of catching fish," he says. "For starters, there's more smoking action created by these baits. Plus the lures prevent the baits from washing out at fast trolling speeds, enabling more ocean to be covered when fishing's tough. I've found that lures with a slightly slanted head perform better with a natural bait. Sometimes the flat-head lures want to run one way, while the bait tracks another. That can make for an awkward arrangement.

"Then there's the flash appeal from the natural bait fluttering behind the lure. Add a hint of scent and taste, and you can understand why combination baits are top producers. I've often said a lure/ballyhoo combination is the ultimate marlin and tuna bait. And billfish eat them like candy during the free-spool mode. If a fish misses the hook on the strike, you can drop back and let the lure and remaining bait flutter down, or begin jigging it. Many times the fish will come back for the remains."

While a lot of anglers refuse to buck tradition by mixing lures and baits, they could be missing out on a lot of fish. The next time you're offshore, try building a combination spread. As long as each bait and lure is swimming properly, you just might discover a killer combination!

Early-Season TUNA TACTICS

By Capt. Mitch Chagnon

In the North-east, getting early-summer yellowfin and bluefin tuna to eat trolled baits and lures requires some special tricks.

WHEN TUNA FIRST ARRIVE in the Northeast, they're still in "migration mode," meaning that they tend to be very picky about what they choose to eat. To get them to strike, you need to approach them carefully and appeal to their sense of competition.

don't know what's worse: spending all day offshore and catching nothing or spending all day surrounded by tuna that turn up their noses at everything you show them. As many Northeast anglers know, the latter scenario is common in the early part of the season, when schools of yellowfin and bluefin tuna first show up along the 30-fathom line south of Block Island, Rhode Island. However, there are several tactics that often get them to eat when nothing else seems to work.

Beginning in late June and early July, tuna invade the inshore banks of south Cape Cod. Tagging and telemetry studies have shown that tuna use the north-flowing Gulf Stream current as a migration route. When eddies of warm water break off from

the Gulf Stream and move inshore, they bring the tuna with them. Cold water off the coast of Cape Cod, brought by influences from the Labrador Current, pushes the tuna in a westerly direction along the banks. The combination of warm Gulf Stream water, rapidly warming inshore waters, and upwellings along the banks creates massive blooms of phyto-plankton, the basis of a rich food chain. As the summer progresses, the tuna rest and feed in this warm, bait-filled environment.

Why Won't They Eat?

So why are these fish so hard to catch when they first get here? After discussing the matter with several marine biologists, I discovered the reason.

Tuna have three sources of energy within their bodies. The most readily available source is found in the bloodstream in the form of glucose, or blood sugar. The energy drawn from glucose is responsible for those initial runs that burn out drag washers and spool reels. A second source of energy is stored as glycogen in the liver.

If additional energy is needed, fat stored within the muscle tissues is converted to energy. Animal physiologists compare this last process to the "second wind" experienced by long-distance runners. These fat sources provide tuna with the energy needed for their long migrations.

Since tuna rely on fat reserves while migrating, they feed only periodically and their stomach cavities shrink. The result is that they do not feed as often as tuna that have settled in an area. Because their bodies have been drastically depleted of available energy, they have to be very selective about when and what they eat. They need to receive the maximum energy return for the energy they use to catch their prey. In other words, they will be extremely reluctant to waste energy on anything that might not be food.

Spreader-Bar Solution

To catch fish under these conditions, there are two things you should do: appeal to tuna's competitive instincts, and concentrate on the prime feeding periods of early morning and dusk, when the light is also in your favor.

On my boat, the *Sakarak,* we've found that multiple spreader bars fished close together will work on early-season tuna. We try to be on the grounds by first light so we can fish during the early-morning hours, when the light is low and the tuna can't see the lines, hooks, bars, and other terminal gear easily.

Although every boat is different, I've found that a speed of 4.5 to 6 knots is best for trolling spreader bars. Set your outrigger baits as far back as possible, and adjust the line so the closest baits on the spreader bar are barely in the water, with the leader riding out of the water as much as possible. Try to achieve this with all the baits in your spread.

A Winning Spread

My spread consists of one spreader bar 60 feet back on the center rigger, two spreader bars off the long riggers at 50 feet, two more bars off the short riggers at 40 feet, and two daisy chains on the flat lines at 30 feet (roughly on the third wave). The last bait on the main line (the one with the hook in it) is spaced farther apart than the others on the bar or chain to make it look weak or injured. I use AFTCO Roller Troller clips on all my outrigger halyards to facilitate retrieval and resetting of the spreader bars.

The size of bait I use on my bars depends on the condition of the seas. On calm days I prefer six-inch squids rigged on 80-pound coffee-colored wire, and use the lightest spreader bars available. On rough days or during low-light conditions I fish larger 12-inch squids. As for hooks, I use 6/0 Mustad stainless big-game hooks on the six-inch squids and 9/0s on the larger squids. Last but not least, I always make sure the hooks are razor sharp by honing them with a diamond file on the way to the grounds.

Mackerel can also be used on the spreaders and daisy chains. I prefer small mackerel; however, these can be hard to

Spreader bar — 50'

40' — *Spreader bar*

30'

Daisy chains

60'

40'

Spreader bar — *Spreader bar*

50'

Spreader bar

find early in the year, so I freeze a supply of tinker mackerel when they're abundant in the fall. I brine them in a cooler of sea salt and ice immediately after they are caught. I also add a little formaldehyde to preserve the color and help toughen the bellies.

Making Them Strike

Approach and presentation are the real keys to early-season success. Once you locate a school on the surface, approach it at a 40-degree angle, pulling one of the long spreader bars in front of the fish (see diagram on pg. 134). If the fish make a move toward the baits, leave the rod in its holder and pull the spreader bar away by reeling in the line. If you don't hook up, set the spreader bar back and repeat the process. Sometimes it's necessary to tease the school a couple of times before competition between individual fish gets one to commit to a strike.

On sunny days, always note the position of the sun and your angle of approach, since the shadow of your boat falling over the school could put the fish down. If conditions prevent an angled approach, get far ahead of

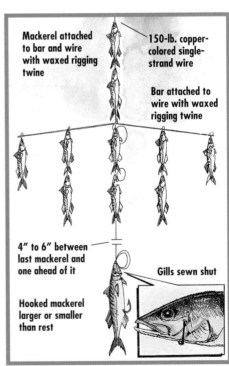

Mackerel attached to bar and wire with waxed rigging twine

150-lb. copper-colored single-strand wire

Bar attached to wire with waxed rigging twine

4" to 6" between last mackerel and one ahead of it

Gills sewn shut

Hooked mackerel larger or smaller than rest

BRINED-MACKEREL SPREADER BAR

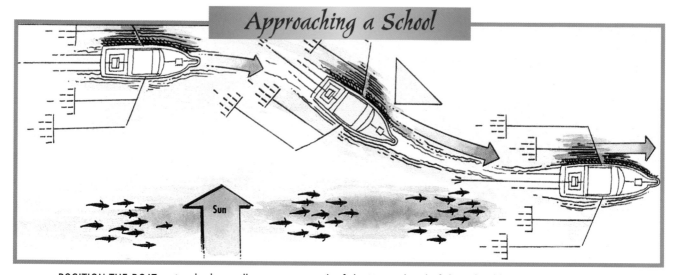

POSITION THE BOAT so its shadow will not pass over the fish. Move ahead of the school by running parallel to it, then slowly angle in so the inside rigger baits swing in front of the lead fish. When all the lines reach the head of the school, straighten out and run in front of the fish, slowing down if necessary to allow them to overtake the baits.

the school, slow down, and wait for the fish to come to you. Then make a turn to either side to position one of the long rigger bars in front of the school. Once the fish turn to investigate, use the teasing technique and pull the baits away from them.

Many times the fish will follow a particular bait and suddenly hit one of the others. Multiple strikes are common, especially with schools of 40- to 50-pound fish. If you get a fish to follow a bait, watch the other lines carefully. If possible, have a crewman on every rod, ready to pull the offering away from the fish as soon as he sees a follow.

The Jig Trick

Even after tuna have settled down in their summer feeding grounds, they can still be fussy, leisurely cruising around and pushing bait. You'll often see this on blue-bird days, when bright sun and calm waters give tuna the edge. Their keen vision can detect the faintest irregularity in your baits and turn them off immediately, creating unbelievable frustration for the fisherman.

But while lots of fish are visible on the surface, there are more underneath where the light is reduced. Those are the fish I target. Capt. Dick Lema clued me in on a technique for dealing with fussy tuna on bright days. He learned it from Montauk captain Carl Darenberg, who was known for producing fish in tough conditions.

Lema chooses a jig that matches the size of the bait the fish are chasing. He casts it into the school and allows it to sink 50 or 60 feet, where there is less light. The lure is then retrieved as quickly as possible with a quick jigging action. This imitates a wounded baitfish struggling to return to its school – an easy meal for tuna!

The first days of the offshore season and the first schools of tuna will get anyone's adrenaline pumping, but try to stay cool and take your time. If you see someone working a school, give them room, and if *you* hook up, leave the school and let the next guy have a shot at them. Proper etiquette and a little patience and courtesy will not only make your day more enjoyable, you won't be as likely to spook the fish.

Six Tricks for STUBBORN DOLPHIN

By George Poveromo

When dolphin turn off and refuse to eat, the following techniques can get them feeding again.

I wouldn't have bet the boat on it, but I could have sworn I saw a blue silhouette appear for an instant behind the long outrigger bait. I kept quiet as we started to retrieve the last pair of lines, idling along while we prepared for the run home. Still, I couldn't help wondering if something was back there.

I was about to chalk up my hallucination to eyestrain when a big dolphin suddenly materialized behind the bait I was reeling in. I repeatedly jigged the ballyhoo, now only 20 feet behind the boat, but the dolphin wouldn't eat. I tried free-spooling the bait 30 feet back, then quickly reeling it to the surface, but the dolphin would only follow. Then we pitched over a fresh, whole ballyhoo along with several chunks. Still no interest. It was time for something drastic.

I grabbed a 12-pound-test spinning outfit rigged with a yellow plastic grub and made a cast beyond the fish. As I reeled in steadily, the dolphin lit up like a neon sign, raced over and ate the grub. It turned out to be the largest fish of the trip.

When the dolphin bite is on, it seems you can catch them on anything, but it's not always that way. We've all experienced days when the fish just won't cooperate. Popular explanations range from "they've already been hammered by other boats" to "the full moon has them off their feed." However, a little creativity can usually turn an "off" day into a memorable one. Below are six tricks that consistently work for me when the fish develop lockjaw.

Try Something Different

As illustrated by the above incident, it sometimes pays to try a lure or bait that is totally different than the ones you were originally using. My friends and I always keep a couple of swimtail grubs rigged on spinning tackle, in addition to the usual assortment of small jigs. If a dolphin school has been worked over by other boats, the fish may not respond to trolled baits or the standard jigs everyone pitches at them. A yellow plastic grub with a pulsating tail mimics the pufferfish that hang around weed lines, a true dolphin delicacy. We'll even troll one far back in our spread if we suspect dolphin are around but not feeding.

Switching baits or lures also works on school fish. When we first get into schoolies, everyone on the boat fishes with the same color jigs. Once the fish grow tired of one color we'll switch to another, which often turns them back on. When they wise up to that color we'll switch to bait chunks and finally to live bait. When the bite slows, we'll try lures again. Switching to something different awakens the dolphin's curiosity and gets them feeding again.

SOMETIMES ALL IT TAKES to get dolphin feeding again is to show them something different. If they turn off on jigs, try chunk or live bait. If they get tired of bait, try jigs again.

Sink & Swim

Offshore trollers know how difficult it can be to catch fish when there's a lot of competition. Locating an unfished stretch of water or weed line on a calm weekend is hard enough, never mind trying to catch fish that have seen literally hundreds of trolled baits and buckets of chum. Under these conditions, try the sink-and-swim approach.

If you fail to raise a fish after making several passes by a weed line or floating object, troll up to your target, shift into neutral and let the baits sink. As the baits flutter down and flash in the sunlight, they appear as if they're stunned, creating an illusion that's different from any trolling spread the dolphin have seen that day. Stay in neutral for a couple of minutes, making sure your lines don't tangle, then shift into gear and resume trolling. The sudden movement of the baits racing to the surface creates the illusion that they've been noticed by the dolphin and are fleeing in fear. It drives the dolphin mad.

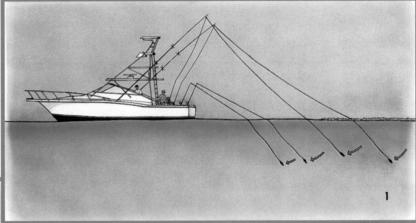

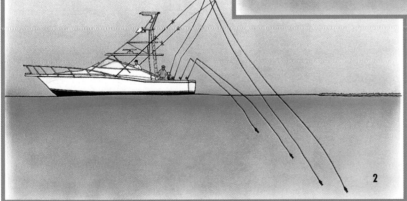

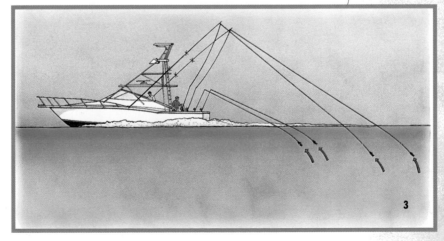

WHEN DOLPHIN HAVE BEEN FISHED HARD or if they're simply not in a feeding mood, try the sink-and-swim trick. Troll up to a weed line or floating object and shift into neutral (1), allowing the baits to sink and flash in the water (2). After a few minutes, shift into gear and throttle forward, (3) causing the baits to rocket toward the surface. The sudden and unusual movement of the baits may trigger the dolphin's feeding instincts.

DOLPHIN HANG AROUND WEED LINES and floating objects to feed on the tiny fish that live around them (top).

IF YOU SUSPECT DOLPHIN ARE HOLDING DEEP, send down a "chum bomb" made of wet sand and bait particles.

Bombs Away!

When dolphin appear to be holding deep, whether due to angling pressure or water temperature, and you can't catch them by trolling or jigging – bomb them! To create a dolphin chum bomb, simply mix some sand and water in a five-gallon bucket and sift in a few boxes of thawed glass minnows, silversides, or diced ballyhoo. Form several baseball-size chum bombs and place them in another bucket. If you suspect the fish are hanging deep around a piece of flotsam or weed line, shift into neutral and drop a bomb. As the chum bomb descends it will break apart and create a cloudy trail of sand and bait particles. The sandy cloud and the flash and smell of the bait pieces quickly draw attention. Two or three bombs may be enough to arouse the dolphin's curiosity and lead them to your boat. Chum bombs are great for school fish, too.

On–Site Live Bait

Dolphin are suckers for live bait such as pilchards, herring, menhaden, hardtails, ballyhoo, mullet, and shrimp. That's why run-and-gun dolphin anglers who chum and bait with livies usually have an edge over those who troll lures and dead baits. However, there are days when even live baits fail, such as when other anglers have already worked the school with them, instilling suspicion among the remaining fish. The fish may have also gorged themselves on local forage, and are therefore unwilling to chase down and eat a frisky live bait.

The best way to score under these circumstances is to do away with the "imported" baits. Dolphin hang around weed lines and floating objects to feed on the tiny fish that live around them. Juvenile pufferfish, banded rudderfish, bar jacks,

INSTEAD OF USING "FOREIGN" BAITS such as ballyhoo and pilchards, show the dolphin something they're used to seeing. Juvenile puffer fish, banded rudderfish, bar jacks, and triggerfish can be easily gathered by jigging gold-hook bait quills around weeds and flotsam.

triggerfish and a host of other species are a big part of a dolphin's natural diet, unlike the baits we bring offshore.

You can easily catch native live baits on site by slowly jigging gold-hook bait quills around the edges of weeds and floating debris. Then you can add them to your live well or a five-gallon bucket of sea water and continue your search for dolphin.

If you run across an uncooperative school or a larger solitary fish, impale one of these baits on a small hook (try a 1/0 or 2/0) and cast it out. You may think that most of these baits are far too tiny to fish with, but I guarantee you'll be amazed by how effective they can be when all else fails.

Create a Racket

Dolphin like noise. You simply can't scare them, no matter how hard you drop a tackle box, shout in excitement, or jump around on deck. So why not use sound to your advantage?

If a school of dolphin begins leaving your boat, or if you want to renew the interest of fish that seem to be growing cautious, shift the engine(s) into neutral and rev them up, fluctuating between idle and 4000 rpm for about a minute. This creates a loud, irregular sound, complete with air bubbles from the exhaust. As strange as it seems, the commotion generally brings the dolphin back. Splashing the water with a rod tip or working a hookless chugger also sparks their interest.

Keeping a hooked fish in the water is one of the cardinal rules of dolphin fishing, but I've also discovered that a raw-water washdown system does a terrific job of attracting fish and keeping them near the boat. When you're into a school, drape the washdown hose over the gunwale and turn on the system. The sound of the water splashing on the surface really seems to attract the fish.

Lighten Up

Sometimes a simple tackle adjustment is all you need to score with wary dolphin. A typical dolphin setup for casting or live-baiting is a 20-pound-test spinning outfit rigged with a 20-foot wind-on leader of 40- or 50-pound mono. This arrangement allows the leader to be wound onto the spool until you can lead the fish to gaff or flip it into a cooler. It also makes it possible to tie on a new hook without having to replace the entire leader.

If the fish are fussy, however, you may have to scale down to lighter line. Instead of 20-pound gear and 50-pound leaders, break out the 12-pound spinning rods rigged with 30-pound leaders. If that doesn't work, try 20-pound leaders or tie the hook directly to the main line. With school fish, don't be afraid to try eight-pound line without a leader when you can't buy a bite. You may lose a fish or two, but you're apt to get bites you wouldn't have had otherwise.

It's the same principle with hooks. Drop down to sizes between 1/0 and 4/0 and conceal them as best as possible. Try hiding them completely in a bait chunk or matching the hook color to that of the bait you're using (e.g., a bronze-colored hook with bar jacks and rudderfish, or a silver hook with ballyhoo and pilchards).

WORKMAN AND DRY fish with only two pounds of drag to keep from tearing or straightening out the hooks. If a big fish threatens to spool the reel, the angler transfers to the bow while the helmsman motors after it.

Winning Ways for
BIG KINGS

By George Poveromo

Tournament pros Dave Workman and Jeff Dry reveal some of their secrets for putting smoker kingfish in the boat day after day.

Catching a king mackerel over 50 pounds is a feat most anglers won't accomplish in their entire lives. Some believe that a mackerel that size is the salt water equivalent of a 12-pound largemouth bass. Therefore, it doesn't require a Las Vegas bookie to calculate the odds of catching two 50-plus-pound mackerel in two consecutive days of fishing, along with a couple of 40-pound-class fish thrown in for good measure. Yet that's exactly what Dave Workman and Jeff Dry did this past August during two red-hot days of fishing off Orange Beach, Alabama.

Workman and Dry are no strangers to big kings. Campaigning their 31-foot Fountain on the rigorous tournament circuit from North Carolina to Alabama, they've racked up a lot of impressive catches. Their determination also netted them two consecutive Southern Kingfish Association (SKA) Angler-of-the-Year titles. Knowing how and where to take trophy king mackerel in their own backyard is one thing, but being able to do it in unfamiliar territory is a totally different proposition. Here's how these two guys consistently get the big ones.

THE WINNING TEAM of Dave Workman, right, and Jeff Dry show off a 53-pound king mackerel caught off Alabama.

Communication & Good Bottom

Whether they're fishing locally or out of town, communication is essential. Workman talks with commercial fish houses and tackle shops to get information on fish in the area. For instance, if there are several schools of kings around he'll try to determine the average size of the fish making up each school. That's because the chances of catching a big king are much greater in schools of 18- to 20-pounders than in a school of eight- to ten-pound "snakes."

"Stop at a tackle shop and buy a good local chart," advises Workman. "Talk with the people there about the areas that hold big kings. They're not going to reveal their top secret spots, but information on where these fish are historically taken is usually easy to get.

"Study the chart and look at the natural bottom. Jeff and I are interested in bottom contours or breaks, which typically hold bait and king mackercel. A productive rise or drop can be as little as several feet. As long as the bait's there, they can be great spots for slow-trolling.

"Locating contours applies to all the regions we fish, be it along the outer edges of the reefs off South Florida or the natural curves and slopes along the shelf in the Gulf and Atlantic. Hard-bottom spots are just as important, especially in the Gulf. Discover bottom formations that hold bait in a mostly sandy environment and you have a big advantage."

Water temperature is also important. Before every tournament, Workman receives a water temperature analysis from the Miami-based Roffer's Ocean Fishing Forecasting Service. This highly detailed information alerts him to any changes in the thermocline depth, cold-water upwellings that can push fish out of an area, and the locations of temperature gradients likely to concentrate bait.

"All this information paints a clearer picture of our options," says Workman. "Everyone knows a lot of big kings are caught in inlets and passes as they follow the bait in with high tide and then out with the falling tide. But many times the fishing's slow, or there are 50 boats around you. In both cases we'll head to a more desolate spot. Knowing the whereabouts of some prime real estate, along with the current water and fishing conditions, helps us determine where our best opportunities may be."

Big Baits for Big Fish

There's nothing more enticing to a huge king than a big, frisky bait. Workman loads up with the biggest baits he can find, which means running the beach to find the larger "turbo" pogies (menhaden). In the Gulf and southern Florida, hardtails (blue runners) between two and four pounds are prime offerings. Workman claims that you'll see far less action with really big baits, but the fish that do strike are usually brutes.

"When you use smaller baits, such as

THE C&H TEAM fishes big baits to target big kings and to keep smaller fish from destroying the spread.

one-pound runners or small to medium pogies, the smaller snakes can drive you nuts," says Workman. "They'll blitz the baits and you'll waste a lot of time re-rigging. Sometimes the smaller fish are quicker and more aggressive, and will beat the big fish to the baits. That kind of action is great only if size isn't a concern.

"Big baits prevent small kings from muscling in on your spread. The little guys don't eat them as often and the baits stay active much longer. That gives a big king ample time to feed. Big kings devour huge baits all the time. I believe they're more likely to expend their energy chasing down something substantial that's really going to satisfy their appetite. Yes, big kings eat small baits, too, but we want to significantly improve our odds. We'd much rather troll all day for a shot at a 40-pound king than catch a dozen 15-pounders." Workman also contends that big baits enable him to troll a little faster and cover more ground, plus they stay friskier longer.

The C & H team also recommends using the type of bait that's prominent in the area you're fishing. If Spanish mackerel are abundant, Workman will catch and slow-troll one that's larger than the minimum legal size, and will replace his ribbonfish with dead mackerel rigged for trolling. "Big kings eat Spanish mackerel," states Workman. "When the Spanish are schooling, we'll tow one or two of them around the fringes of a school."

Stealthy Hardware

Small hooks and light drags are the norm among serious king mackerel anglers. Workman's dual treble-hook rigs (for single baits) begin with 22 inches of No. 3 wire. Each individual package of wire is thoroughly inspected, and he'll use only the dark-colored kind. He reasons that dark wire won't reflect light, which can spook a big king. Workman feels that glare, no matter how insignificant, can spook a big king mackerel.

Both the lead and stinger hooks are No. 6 trebles, with No. 4s getting the nod on big baits. The stinger hook is connected to the eye of the lead hook with No. 4 wire. Most rigs are enhanced with a C & H King Buster skirt and are finished off with a No. 10 (30-pound-test) swivel that won't snag weeds and debris. Workman's skirt strategy involves using light colors such as pearl and silver on bright days and in clear water, and loud colors like chartreuse, pink, and red in dirty water and on overcast days. To reduce the amount of time spent re-rigging offshore, Workman carries a specially prepared terminal-gear kit containing premeasured leaders (including stingers), swivels, hooks and skirts. If he has to, he can make a new rig in less than a minute.

Workman fishes Penn's new 555 and 545 Graphite Series reels exclusively, which feature a star drag for quick and easy adjustments during a fight and fast retrieve ratios of 5.3:1 (555) and 6:1 (545) that allow the angler to gain line quickly with a light drag. The reels are spooled with 15-pound mono. Workman's rods feature very light tips to lessen the pressure that could tear the small hooks out of a king's mouth.

Create an Illusion

Workman and Dry fish a six-line spread, striving to create the illusion of anxious baitfish. While they often modify their spread to compensate for different baits and sea conditions, they've had the most success with the following arrangement. The farthest bait, a skirted single pogy rig, is fished approximately 100 yards astern from a rod placed in the center T-top holder. Workman says that this far bait often works when the kings aren't aggressive. Because of

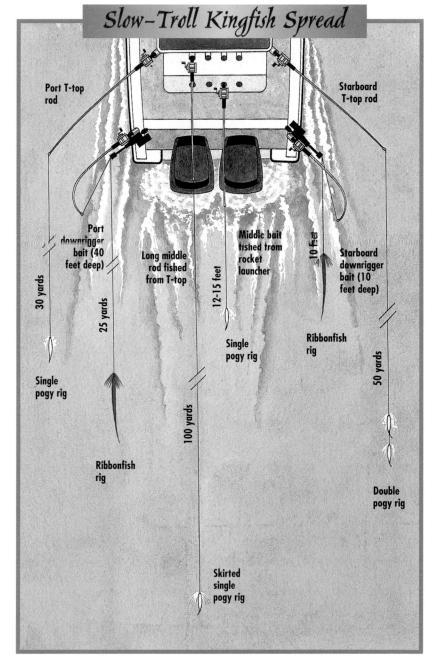

Slow-Troll Kingfish Spread

Port T-top rod

Starboard T-top rod

Port downrigger bait (40 feet deep)

Long middle rod fished from T-top

Middle bait fished from rocket launcher

Starboard downrigger bait (10 feet deep)

30 yards

25 yards

12-15 feet

10 feet

50 yards

Single pogy rig

Single pogy rig

Ribbonfish rig

Ribbonfish rig

100 yards

Double pogy rig

Skirted single pogy rig

Ribbonfish Rig

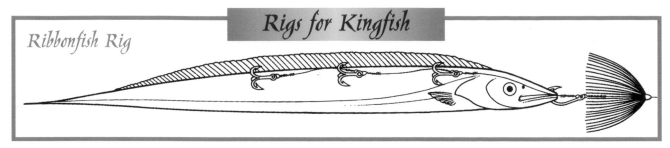

RIBBONFISH ARE RIGGED with a King Buster skirt, a No. 1/0 or 2/0 single hook through the nose, and three No. 6 or 4 silver treble hooks along the body. Bronze-colored No. 3 wire is used between the lead hook and the main-line snap, while the treble hooks are connected with No. 4 silver wire to blend in with the ribbonfish's skin.

Double Pogy Rig

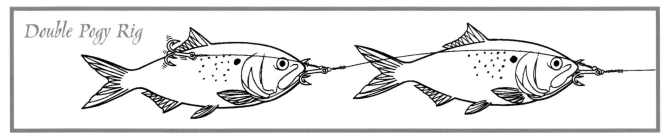

THE DOUBLE-POGY RIG (for bigger baits) uses No. 6 or 4 bronze trebles. The first treble is connected to the main-line snap with No. 3 bronze-colored wire, while the trailing hooks are connected with No. 4 wire. The third treble (stinger hook) can be pinned in the pogy's back or left to swing freely.

its distance from the boat, plus the rod's height, the bait has a tendency to swim deeper during a turn, enhancing its appeal. The starboard T-top rod tows a double pogy rig 50 yards back, while a single bait rides 30 yards back off the portside T-top rod.

To create a predator-chasing-prey illusion, which seems to put the fear of God in the portside pogy and makes the kings more aggressive, a ribbonfish is free-spooled 25 yards behind the boat and then deployed 40 feet down on the portside downrigger. Given the slight angle of the downrigger cable at that depth, the ribbonfish will be fluttering away underneath, and just behind, the pogy. A second ribbonfish is fished on the starboard downrigger, this one ten feet back and ten feet below the surface. Workman prefers this bait to swim near the fringe of the prop wash, where the white water could be misconstrued by kings as a feeding frenzy. He claims that this bait doesn't see a lot of action, but the fish it attracts tend to be big. The middle bait, fished 15 feet back from the rocket launcher, is either a single or double pogy rig.

Go Heavy on Chum

Workman doesn't use menhaden oil, claiming it can't compete with fresh ground chum. Armed with a 12-volt grinder and buckets of fresh-caught bait, Workman and Dry grind their bait onboard, pack it in a chum bag, and hang it over the side to spice up their trolling spread. If seas are rough they'll fill the boat's splashwell with chum, letting the seawash distribute the concoction. When the bag or splashwell is empty, it's repacked.

"We're putting out a continuous trail of chum," says Workman. "The ground-up chum sinks and brings in all sorts of fish, even Spanish mackerel, bluefish, and bonito. With all the bait, commotion, and scent around, it helps put kings in a feeding mood.

"We also cut the chum bait into chunks. When we first arrive in an area, or when we mark bait on the fishfinder, we'll dole out a few handfuls of both chum and chunks to get things going. We want a continuous stream of chum, something that really draws attention and masks any possible scent of oil and gasoline from the boat's exhaust.

"Another one of our tricks is to slip a frozen block of glass minnows into the chum bag. The flash of the minnows descending through the water creates a strong visual effect. A handy tip if you're fishing a tournament is to catch all the bait you'll need for chum in advance. Grind it up at the dock and ice it down in five-gallon buckets. It'll give you a head start the next morning when it's time to fish."

Workman and Dry are an enviable team. They get along well, and each one knows exactly how to deploy the baits, maintain a chum slick, and fight a big fish. As mentioned, one of their objectives is to scale down their terminal gear to draw more strikes. With the tiny trebles, pressuring a fish too much can rip a hook free or even straighten it out, so Workman fishes with approximately two pounds of drag and keeps the clicker engaged. On the strike, the angler lifts the rod from its holder, turns off the clicker, and lets the fish make its initial run before setting up.

If a big fish continues taking out line, the angler moves to the bow as the helmsman gives chase. Boat speed should be just fast enough to regain line. When it's time to work the fish in, Workman advances the star drag by a few pounds, cautiously lifts the rod, and reels on the down stroke. When the fish begins running he'll back off the drag. The goal is to let the king wear itself down, not horse it in.

"I see a lot of people take all their lines out of the water when they hook a decent king," says Workman. "We prefer to leave at least one bait out at all times. There's no telling what might happen. You may think that the 20- or 30-pound fish you're fighting is really special, but if all the baits are out of the water, how would you know that there isn't a bigger one lurking nearby? That's another one of our little secrets!"

Double-Hook Kingfish Rig

King mackerel are the rage along most of the Gulf and South Atlantic coasts, and now there's a new way to take them. It involves the time-proven method of drifting with Spanish sardines; however, the use of light gear and a special hook work together to fool even the wariest king.

I first learned about the rig at the famed Fishing Headquarters in Jupiter, Florida, where proprietors Tom and Pete eat,

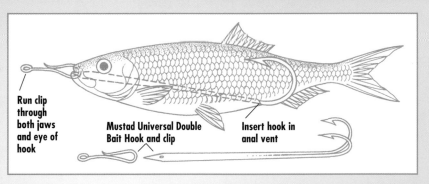

Run clip through both jaws and eye of hook

Mustad Universal Double Bait Hook and clip

Insert hook in anal vent

sleep, and breath kingfishing. The heart of the rig is a Mustad #9418 Universal Double Bait Hook, traditionally used on fresh water muskellunge and sturgeon. The pointed "eye" of the hook is inserted into the bait's anal vent and is then pushed forward and out its mouth so that the two bronzed hook points are positioned near the tail. In order to camouflage the hook and make the bait weedproof, the points are turned upward so that they are flush against the bait's body. More importantly, this arrangement makes it virtually impossible for a king to clip off the bait without getting hooked. For the best results, the reel should be fished in gear, since there's no need to let the fish run with the bait after the strike.

The fact that these hooks aren't made of heavy forged steel necessitates the use of light line. Most drift-fishing experts admit that light line fools more kings anyway, even though it's prone to tangles.

To rig the bait, hold the sardine upside down in the palm of your hand and push the pointed eye into its vent. Carefully thread the hook through the body cavity until the eye protrudes from the bait's mouth.

Now turn the hook points over so that they're positioned alongside the sardine's body.

Force the clip that accompanies each hook through the bait's top and bottom jaws, making sure it passes through the eye of the hook.

Wrap a No. 5 or No. 7 dark-wire leader to the other end of the clip and you're ready to fish. When you need to change baits simply unsnap the clip and attach another pre-rigged bait.   *By Steve Kantner*

OFFSHORE FISHING

All-Star COBIA CAST

By Capt. Frank Bolin

Several years of anticipation had made us so anxious to fish the fabled waters off Ponce Inlet that we left at daybreak. Scott and Sue Cosby were joining my wife Linda and me on this first expedition. We ran south, past New Smyrna and on to the Turtle Mound. Twelve miles south of the inlet, the "mound" (actually an ancient Indian trash heap) is a landmark easily spotted from offshore.

As the sun rose higher, we stumbled upon a temperature break. The gauge had read a consistent 69 to 70 from Daytona past New Smyrna, but when we reached the mound it jumped up to 72. That kind of change normally means fish.

First Cast a Charm

Staying on the warmer side of the break, I began a zigzag search pattern, from 20 feet out to 55 and back again. On the third pass we spotted our first manta ray in 40 feet of water, and it was loaded with cobia! Sue quickly cast a shadtail jig past the ray, reeled it up over its back, and was immediately hooked up. Every fish on the ray tried to inhale the bait. Scott then laid a perfect cast to one of the trailing fish. Doubleheader!

As I maneuvered the boat between the two fish to keep them separated, Scott's cobia turned and swam straight toward the boat. Seizing the opportunity, Linda gaffed the fish and slammed it into the fishbox. Sue's cobia had other ideas, however, and took another 30 minutes to land.

After a short breather, we resumed our stations, all eyes searching for more manta rays.

I believe that sight fishing for cobia is the most fun and exciting sport that Northeast Florida has to offer. These fish offer a great challenge on light tackle. Plus, you don't need a big boat and don't have to make a long run to the fishing grounds. Cobia move through the inshore waters, close to the beach every spring, which makes it possible for small-boat anglers to get in on the action. However, larger boats with towers are best for sight fishing, since their added height allows you to spot the manta rays and cobia from farther away.

Spring's the time to play the sight-casting game with the migrating cobia of Florida's Ponce Inlet.

Stealthy Stalking

Approach is critical in this game. Never run up on a manta ray at a full throttle or it will spook. It is better to cruise up to it slowly from the side at a slow, steady speed. Rays will often stay on the surface if the engine rpm is constant. This method also gives you time to study the situation and make a better cast.

Polarizing glasses are essential when hunting cobia. A quality pair can make all the difference. Every spring I see fishermen attempting to chase cobia without polarizing glasses. Many of them run right past the fish.

Lens color is also important. I have experimented with different shades and prefer amber lenses for early morning or late afternoon. Dark brown or vermillion lenses work better during midday hours.

Fight 'Em Light

Cobia are perfect targets for the light-tackle enthusiast. My favorite combo is a seven-foot, 12- to 15-pound-class, medium-action spinning rod matched with a medium-sized reel. I keep two outfits rigged and ready, one with 12-pound test and the other with 20-pound. This allows me to choose the appropriate rig for the size of the fish.

Keep your terminal rigs simple. I use 18 to 24 inches of 40- to 60-pound mono for my leader. I connect the line and leader with a three-wrap surgeon's knot. This knot will pass smoothly through the guides and is strong enough to hold up under pressure. I tie my lure or hook onto the leader with a tarpon (two-wrap hangman) knot.

When you're talking cobia, one question always pops up: Do you use lures or live bait? I prefer lures for several reasons. First, I like the challenge of fooling a fish with an artificial lure. Second, I do not have to take my eyes off the ray or fish to bait my hook.

I use three types of lures, depending on the depth of the ray. My favorite is a 4½-

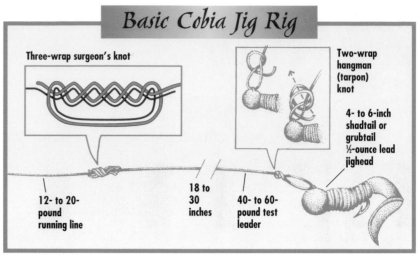

Basic Cobia Jig Rig

Three-wrap surgeon's knot

12- to 20-pound running line

18 to 30 inches

40- to 60-pound test leader

Two-wrap hangman (tarpon) knot

4- to 6-inch shadtail or grubtail ½-ounce lead jighead

to 6½-inch shadtail or grubtail rigged on a ½-ounce leadhead jig. This lure is highly visible and can be worked on top, alongside, or under the ray. I also keep a one- or two-ounce bucktail on hand. I use this when the fish are holding deep, under the ray. The weight makes it easier to fish lower in the water column without hooking the ray. The third type of lure is one I recently began experimenting with, a topwater chugger. The chugger is perfect if you're looking for a spectacular surface strike. I remove the front treble hook and replace the rear hooks with either a Mustad 8/0 #7731 or Eagle Claw 7/0 #1308 barbless hook on a stainless split ring. This makes handling and unhooking the fish at boatside easier and safer.

Check Size & Bag Limits

There is a size and bag limit on cobia in Florida; check the regulations before taking any fish home for the table. More and more anglers are practicing catch and release. Last year we had several days when we caught and released 35 fish! Smaller cobia can be boated with a landing net before release, but it is best to use a tailer on bigger fish. If you must bring them into the boat to remove the hook, cover their eyes with a towel to calm them down.

This season, if you're tempted by reports filtering through the "cobia hotline," make a trip to Ponce Inlet and check out the fabulous fishing for yourself. I'll see you out there!

TIPS FOR 'TAILS

By W.A. Roecker

Where will they show? What will they eat? Here's a guide to help you score with Southern California's unpredictable spring run of yellowtail.

The spring arrival of yellowtail off Southern California used to be almost as predictable as the swallows of Capistrano. Every April, yellows would boil up at the Coronados, eager to inhale whole mackerel fished by winter-weary anglers. But no more. Those days, it appears, are over, and now it's anyone's guess as to where and when the yellowtail will first show. Then there's the problem of how to catch them. Will they only want anchovies and sardines or will they prefer iron jigs fished on the bottom? It's fair to say that no fish is more perplexing to SoCal anglers than the capricious 'tail.

However, there are some places where you're more likely to find early-season yellowtail. Let's take a look at several spring hot spots and some time-proven methods for taking yellowtail at each one. Keep in mind that in *all* the following locations the first three hours after dawn and the last three hours before dusk are usually when yellowtail bite best. However, spring yellowtail may bite for several hours, and they can also be caught at night.

Catalina & San Clemente Islands

Live or fresh-dead squid is tops for spring yellows at these two islands, which are home to large resident fish, as well as roving schools of 12- to 25-pounders. The latter will often fight to get at the squid, which is fine unless you're trying to catch white seabass.

Whole squid should be fished on 15- to 25-pound line and a six- or seven-foot rod.

Rig the squid on a 4/0 hook tied directly to the main line and use a one- or two-ounce slip sinker to get the bait down. Cast the squid out or drop it straight to the bottom, and be prepared for a strike on the way down. Keep the reel in free-spool, using thumb pressure to prevent an overrun. When a fish picks up the bait and starts peeling off line, count to seven and flick the reel in gear. During a slack current or in cold, dirty water, even live squid may not entice yellowtail; however, you can still enjoy action with calico bass and barracuda in the lee of the islands.

Coronados Islands & La Jolla

Iron jigs often work best at these two spots, and the technique is simple. Free-spool a two- to seven-ounce iron to the bottom and reel it back up – *fast*. Again, always be ready to flip the reel in gear if a fish grabs the jig on the way down. If you're using a reel with a 4:1 gear ratio, you need to crank as fast as you can. With a 5:1 or 6:1 reel you may want to slow the retrieve occasionally.

The first three hours after dawn and the last three hours before dusk are usually when yellowtail bite best.

"BREEZING" 'TAILS can be taken on metal jigs ripped across the surface. Cast ahead of and beyond the school and retrieve the jig just fast enough to keep the lure wobbling along.

Nearly all jig strikes occur in the lower two-thirds of the water column. To coax finicky feeders, give the iron a few hard jerks as you're reeling in and let it flutter down to a stop before reeling again.

The best jig patterns have proven to be blue/white, yellow/brown, all chrome, blue/chrome, green/yellow and all white, although other colors and patterns will work, too. However, the hands-down top fish-catcher is a four-ounce blue/white jig. To add a bit of scent some anglers hang a bit of fish flesh or squid on the hooks.

Casting jigs to surface schools can be especially effective in the spring, and many anglers use nine- or ten-foot rods to increase their casting distance. San Diego dayboat skippers like Buzz Brizendine (*Prowler*), Nick Cates (*New Lo-An*), Ray Sobieck (*Producer*), and Joel Ralston (*Legend*) are experts at spotting "breezing" schools of yellows. These pros use light but large jigs, often with a silver or mackerel pattern. Blue/white or all white jigs work well, too. Brizendine recommends casting ahead of and beyond the school so the jig can be retrieved in front of the fish without alarming them. The retrieve speed should be just fast enough to keep the lure wobbling along.

Oceanside & Newport

Bottom fishing with bait is the way to go here. The favored method is to use a heavy torpedo sinker on the end of a dropper rig to get the bait down to the rugged bottom structure the fish prefer. If the fish are holding in the mid-depths, use a light slip sinker on the end of the line.

To fish bottom, attach the torpedo sinker to the end of the line with a Baja Loop. Then tie a dropper loop in the line about 18 to 24 inches above the weight and attach a hook. Lastly, run the hook through the nose of a live mackerel or sardine and send it down. To reduce snags, crank the rig off the bottom a few turns.

LA's Horseshoe Kelp & Rocky Point

The preferred method of fishing spring yellows off Southern California's kelp beds, islands, reefs, oil rigs, points and other structure is fly-lining (no weight) squid, mackerel, sardines, or large anchovies. For this type of fishing, use 25- to 50-pound line spooled on a 3/0 or 4/0 reel attached to a six- or seven-foot, moderately stiff rod. The boat should be positioned so the baits will drift toward the shore, kelp, or structure where the yellowtail will be holding. Yellowtail will often run with the bait before swallowing it, so count to seven before setting the hook.

Quick Tackle Tips

Southland yellowtail pros usually take two or three rod-and-reel outfits with them so they're ready to handle fish, baits, and lures of different sizes. Light outfits with 12- to 20-pound line on six- to eight-foot rods are good for taking smaller yellows on anchovies and small sardines. Fifteen- to 40-pound line will cover everything from fly-lining anchovies to chucking iron. Reel speeds of 3:1 to 6:1 are best. Slower reels are better for playing big fish, while faster reels are better for retrieving lures.

'Tails for the Table

If you intend to eat your catch, bleed the yellowtail right after it has been landed. The fish freezes well if kept from air and moisture. A tasty but easy way to prepare yellowtail is to soak the fillets in Italian dressing or marinade for 20 minutes before grilling. Take it off the heat when the meat flakes easily.

ACCORDING TO CAPT. BILLY VERBANAS, the blue and tiger sharks that inhabit Delaware's offshore canyons from May through October have a tendency to run bigger than in most areas. Verbanas is so confident in getting results on every trip that he offers a money-back guarantee.

OFFSHORE FISHING

The Sure-Fire
SHARKER

By Al Ristori

Delaware's Billy Verbanas probably catches more big sharks than any skipper on the East Coast. Here are some of his secrets.

When it comes to sharking, nobody does it better – or bigger – than Delaware charter captain Billy Verbanas. In recent years, Verbanas has learned where and how to take some of the biggest blue sharks in the country, and he does it on a daily basis all season long. On some trips he's also able to put his anglers on giant makos and tiger sharks, then tops things off with a little tuna action thrown in for good measure. His sharking prowess has earned him the admiration, and sometimes envy, of fishermen all along the Mid-Atlantic coast.

Being an avid sharker myself, I knew I had to learn more about Verbanas's methods. To my surprise, I found he was quite willing to share his secrets with me, and even went so far as to invite me on a two-day trip aboard his boat, the *Reel-istic*.

We left Indian River in the evening so we could be fishing in Poorman's Canyon by first light. During the 90-mile run, Verbanas told us how he had been fishing in 1600 fathoms over the past week, but had noticed an inshore movement on his last trip and figured we could find the fish in 1200 fathoms.

It was still dark when Verbanas cut the engines and mate Billy Gephart began setting up the chum slick. As is normal in sharking, the action was slow in coming, and it was 1½ hours before the first blue hit. The fishing improved steadily as the sun rose, and by late morning a steady stream of blues were swimming through the slick.

It didn't take long to see that these deep-water blues weren't like the common "tube sharks" that dominate the spring migratory run that takes place over the shallower continental shelf during May and June. Most of those blues weigh under 100 pounds and aren't much of a challenge except on light tackle. A few bigger blues may be encountered, particularly from Montauk east, but most of the larger fish are caught

Why So Many Blues?

During recent years it seems there's been nothing but bad news for those who enjoy the sport of sharking. Increased pressure from longliners has cut deeply into the stocks, as sharks have become more accepted as food fish and the price of shark fins in the Orient has increased. Blue sharks are the only exception in the Atlantic because they rate very low as eating fish and their fins aren't as prized as those of other sharks, such as sandbars (browns), duskies, and blacktips.

The National Marine Fisheries Service (NMFS) Shark Management Plan has unintentionally prevented the exploitation of blue sharks, since they are included in the total quota for oceanic sharks. Commercial fishermen are reluctant to catch the low-value blues, since it would quickly close the quota on all oceanic sharks, including the valuable makos and porbeagles. At least one fish dealer has been trying to get blues placed in a separate category so that they could be sold without depleting the oceanic quota, even though the meat would fetch just pennies a pound.

during late summer and fall in the deep waters of the canyons. Verbanas has found what appears to be an entirely separate population of blue sharks, one that resides much farther south and in far warmer waters. Incredibly, one of his tagged blues was recovered 900 miles northwest of Spain and 3300 miles away from the tagging site.

One distinctive characteristic of these offshore sharks is their size. All of the blues we saw on our trip were over 200 pounds, and some exceeded 300. Verbanas estimated the largest at 330 pounds. Although blues aren't the greatest fighters, any fish that size will do some serious pulling.

Verbanas has developed specialized stand-up gear for these sharks. His outfits consist of 80-pound-class reels filled with 130-pound Dacron and rods fitted with short AFTCO bent-butts. The angler is strapped into a belt and kidney harness, while another crew member is assigned to hang onto the harness to prevent the angler from being pulled off his feet by the 40-pound drag. While this may sound risky, the system works like a charm, not only for the big blues, but also for the much larger makos, which are the prime targets of these two-day trips.

If wrestling big offshore sharks for two days sounds intimidating, consider what one of the anglers on our trip had to overcome. Pete Zarba of Long Beach, New York, is confined to a wheelchair, but he was able to fight five big sharks to boatside for release, as well as a 100-pound bluefin tuna after we moved closer to shore. His brother Chris helped move the chair from side to side, and Pete had to reel with the rod in a rod holder. It was hard work, but he never

A TUNA CARCASS isn't pretty to look at, but big tiger sharks sure find them attractive.

gave up on a fish.

By the end of the first day our crew was all sharked out, having released 40 blues in 13 hours! Even so, we were tempted to stick it out in hopes of attracting one of the 600-pound-plus makos that Verbanas has encountered offshore on past trips. A 631-pound shortfin mako had been caught the previous month, and last summer Verbanas caught a 658-pound longfin mako (a rare deep-water species). Verbanas averages 20 to 60 makos a year, but there hadn't been much since the spring run, so we opted to try inshore.

After anchoring in the Fingers, about 40 miles southeast of Indian River, we managed to take a couple of yellowfins and a dolphin on chunk baits before dark. And later a tiger shark in the 600-pound range took a tuna head fished just off bottom before parting the 130-pound Dacron on its first run.

Monster Tigers!

The night had been clear and calm, but failed to produce any action until 8:00 the next morning when the shark rod went off. The fish missed the hooks initially, but struck again as angler Ron Schmitz was bringing the bait in. Schmitz soon found out that this shark wasn't about to be beaten quickly on stand-up tackle, and Verbanas dropped off the anchor ball to follow it. After an hour, mate Billy Gephart was able to grab the leader. The shark turned out to be a tiger in the 800-pound range, which we released after taking several photographs.

By the time we returned to the ball, other boats were fighting tuna. We tied on lighter leaders and were soon into a mix of yellowfins from 35 to 50 pounds and bluefins from 60 to 100 pounds. It was old-fashioned tuna action, with fish racing through the slick and hitting chunks with abandon.

We left the grounds at noon and were soon back at the dock flying two riggers full of flags. Verbanas didn't have enough to account for all the fish.

There are no great secrets as to how Verbanas fishes. The key to his success is simply "going where the fish are" and putting in the time and effort needed to attract them. He carries a huge fishbox full of ice, frozen chum, and mackerel, plus butterfish if tuna are a possibility. He also brings whatever fish heads and carcasses he can salvage from the dock to use as tiger shark bait. However, the large amount of bait and chum he brings is due to the length of the trip more than anything else.

A single can of chum provides all the shark-attracting scent required, and Verbanas usually doesn't add chunks to the slick. However, on a flat-calm day he may drag the chum bucket for two miles and throw in some chunks for good measure. Verbanas never breaks his slick after setting up a drift. Sometimes it takes quite a while for the sharks to arrive, but they invariably show up.

Since Verbanas never knows what kind of shark will show up, he rigs for big makos rather than blues. His leaders consist of 24 feet of cable ending in three feet of No. 19 wire, and the hooks are expensive 12/0 Mustad 7731 models, which Verbanas is usually able to retrieve with a homemade de-hooker. To prevent the shark from swallowing the bait, Verbanas instructs his anglers to set up immediately after the shark picks up the bait.

If his anglers desire, Verbanas will break out spinning tackle for the smaller sharks. In that case, he uses 130-pound mono leader, plus No. 7 to 12 wire and a treble hook with a chunk. When the shark is alongside, a yank on the leader straightens the hook for a quick release. Virtually all of the sharks caught are released, except for makos, or unless the angler decides to keep a blue or one of the more edible inshore sharks.

Tournament Terror

Verbanas has been so successful at sharking that he caused the Mid-Atlantic $500,000 Tournament in Cape May, New Jersey, to drop their shark division last year. That's because Verbanas kept walking away with the prize money year after year. In a tournament situation, Verbanas makes the long run to the canyons and usually catches the few big blue sharks he needs to sweep a contest within a few hours. He usually does the same thing every year at the Ocean City, Maryland, White Marlin Open, but was pushed back to third place last year when two other fishermen caught huge tiger sharks around the tuna fleets. Those inshore tigers are also a specialty on the *Reel-istic*, and the 800-pounder Schmitz released was average for Verbanas, who owns all the Delaware shark records, including one he set with a 942-pound mako.

Verbanas got his initiation into sharking by catching snaggle-toothed sand tigers in Delaware Bay, and still catches them close to Indian River Inlet when it's too rough to head offshore. That had happened to us a couple of weeks before our offshore trip, and we ended up anchoring near a wreck only six miles offshore while hoping for a change of forecast. A couple of small sandbar sharks were caught at night, and I hooked the lone sand tiger, a 100-pounder, shortly after daylight.

Verbanas is so confident in his ability to produce sharks on extended trips that he offers a series of guarantees. For instance, he guarantees at least one 200-pound shark per 20-hour trip, and at least one 200-pounder per person on the 30-hour trips. On the 44-hour trips Verbanas guarantees two 200-pound blue sharks per person, or a single 500-pounder on a two-day inshore trip for tigers. He prefers the longer excursions, since it increases the chances of hooking an outsized mako. In September and October, tuna are also guaranteed, in addition to at least one 200-pound shark per person.

Unlike some charter captains, Verbanas makes an effort to put groups and individuals together for long-range trips in order to reduce the cost per person. As was the case on our trip, there's usually more than enough action to satisfy everyone.

South Florida sailfishing guru Nick Smith reveals the tactics that keep him in the winner's circle.

Nick Smith's TOP TEN SAILFISH TIPS

By Scott Boyan

Catching six, eight or ten sailfish in a single day is a feat most South Florida anglers won't accomplish in their entire lives. Yet that's exactly what expert angler Nick Smith of Palm Beach, Florida, does routinely.

Smith is no stranger to double-digit sailfishing days. Fishing from his custom 36 Knowles and 25 Contender, both named *Old Reliable,* he's won just about every sailfishing award in existence. Knowing how and where to take sailfish in his own backyard is one thing, but being able to do it in the challenging waters off Miami or the vast waters north of Stuart and Ft. Pierce is a whole different ballgame. Here's how Smith consistently lands in the winner's circle.

1. The Sailfish Network

Whether Smith is fishing off Palm Beach or Miami, communication is essential to his game. He's constantly talking with a host of fishermen up and down the South Florida coast, either a few days before or the night before a trip, to get the most updated information on that area.

"Develop reliable sources of information, where you know if the guy tells you to fish in 110 feet of water, it's 110 feet, and rely on that information just like you'd rely upon it if it were your own. It's imperative that you develop reliable sources and be prepared to respond to it accordingly," says Smith.

Communication shouldn't stop there, however. Even though Smith adheres to a strict game plan, he constantly has an ear to the ground when offshore. "I try to get my ear tuned into the right conversations on the VHF," he says. Sharing duty with the VHF, Smith will spend half his time communicating on a cellular phone with other boats that are out of radio range. He constantly wants to be informed in case other areas are producing action or have the conditions he's looking for.

2. Go Fly a Kite

Smith often sounds like a coach when describing his kite-fishing tactics, using terms like Shadow Effect, Optimum Efficiency and Area of Influence. "Shadow Effect is primarily a factor during strong north-wind conditions where you've got fish tailing down-sea from north to south. When this happens, the boat's shadow is going to have a certain influence. I've watched tailing fish swim down-sea, and as they approach the boat they'll sink deeper in the water or veer off the bow or off the stern." Smith states that once these fish eventually pop back up to the surface he wants his kite baits farther away from

the boat so the fish can intercept them.

Another aspect of Smith's game plan that is often overlooked is his ability to do more with less. He calls it Optimum Efficiency. "You need to know what you can handle. Don't try to throw a dozen lines in at one time. That can be counterproductive. When I'm fishing by myself, three baits are a workable number. If I have appropriate conditions I'll get two kites out with one bait on each to get the spread. The bigger the area you cover – I call it an Area of Influence – the more bites you're ultimately going to get."

Smith also has strong opinions about the size of baits he uses. "I like bigger baits for my kites, mainly because they stay in the water better. If my long clip is 200 to 250 feet away from the boat and is 100 feet above the water, that means I could have as much as 300 to 350 feet of 20-pound line being blown around by the wind. The wind can actually have such an influence that a belly will form in the line and lift a bait out of the water. "The other reason for bigger baits is that kite fishing often takes place when seas are rougher. My theory is that the more white water there is, the harder it is for a game fish to see a baitfish swimming on the surface. Thus, I want my biggest, most visible baits on the kites."

3. Freshness Pays

Unlike some sailfishermen who head directly offshore, Smith dedicates at least one hour each morning to catching his own bait. He explains why: "Catching your own bait has a couple of benefits. For instance, I like to bring a variety of bait offshore. What might be the best kite bait might not be the best flat-line bait. I've often seen fish show a preference for one bait over another. If I only have one type of bait out there, and it's not the one they're showing a preference for, I'm probably not going to catch as many fish."

According to Smith, another advantage is the fact that you'll obviously have very fresh bait, and all things being equal, fresh bait will be more productive than a bait that's been in a pen overnight or in a live well for 12 hours. "Only good things happen when you catch your own bait," explains Smith. However, he still leaves the inlet with goggle-eyes that he purchases, in case he's unable to find the bait schools that morning.

4. Flat-Line Considerations

Unlike kite baits, Smith prefers his flat-line baits to be on the small side. He is convinced that pilchards, sardines, and greenies are superior flat-line baits to goggle-eyes. "I love small, energetic baits that can be inhaled quickly," he says. "Since we can't see what's happening 20 feet beneath the surface, I don't want a bait that's hard for the fish to eat. I want him to be able to come up, open his mouth, and get that bait inside as quickly as possible. And we've proven that we get a higher catch ratio fishing that way."

5. The Early/Late Show

"One thing that helps me be successful, that I may do a little different from other people, is that I get out there earlier and I stay later. If all things are equal, and I get an extra hour on the water, ultimately, I'm going to catch more fish then the same guy who's just as good as I am," says Smith. And he's not exaggerating, either.

As I found out last winter, fishing from 5:00 A.M. to 7:00 P.M. is the norm on *Old Reliable*. As is the case with many game fish, the sailfish action off Palm Beach is generally considered best during the hours of dawn and dusk. The fishing generally slackens during the midday hours when the sun is highest in the sky. Come 5:00 or 6:00 P.M.,

many anglers opt to call it a day just when the sailfishing is getting hot again. It's during those times that Smith finds some of his best fishing, which often allows him to turn a mediocre day into a pretty good one.

Is staying late a big advantage? During one of my days of fishing with him, in the fading light of sunset, we successfully released a triple-header from a pod of sailfish that was balling bait off Jupiter Inlet. On the ride home he told me stories of catching sailfish in the dark when all that could be heard was the splash of the leaping sailfish tethered to the end of his line. An advantage? He sold me.

6. Rigging & Preparation

Like many sailfishermen, Smith fishes with Penn 8500SS spinning reels spooled with 20-pound mono. More often than not, he'll rotate among six 20-pound outfits during the day. When fishing a three-line spread, there will always be three extra rods ready to go.

Small, short-shank live-bait hooks and 50-pound wind-on leaders are the norm among serious sailfishermen. All of Smith's 20-pound spinning outfits are rigged with 15-foot mono leaders attached to a 30-inch section of double line with a No-Name knot. "I'll retie the leader after almost every sailfish," he says. "With this system I can retie eight or ten leaders to the same double line before it gets too short. I start out with 15-foot leaders, but if I get some toothy bite-offs I'll discard the leader and start fresh if I get much shorter than 12 feet."

On the kite rods, Smith spools up with 90-pound Spectra, a small-diameter, low-stretch braided line that makes flying each kite a breeze. To help lighten the load even more, he uses only the lightest possible snaps and swivels. When he flies two kites, he'll add No. 7, No. 5, or No. 4 split shot to each kite's top outside corner for maximum veer. However, if the winds are blowing less than seven mph, he'll attach a helium balloon to his kite.

Unlike some kite fishermen, Smith dislikes the use of popping corks as kite markers. Instead, he uses red survey tape. "The survey tape gives me flexibility. I can put six rods in the boat and they're all adaptable to either a flat line or kite line within seconds.

"I also like the fact that the survey tape stays firmly affixed at the top of the leader. Unlike popping corks, I can watch the survey tape disappear into the water down to about five or six feet beneath the surface, which is a good indicator of what the fish is doing. When the popping cork hits the water, it sits there and the main line runs through the middle of the cork. The fish might be doing something completely different and all you're doing is watching the popping cork sit there on the surface."

7. Fish the Change

"There are very few absolute hard-and-fast rules when it comes to finding sailfish," says Smith. "The one solid rule that always applies is 'Fish the Change!' In the entire area of ocean that I may be searching on a given day, change of some kind, any kind, is the area where I want to be. What I'm looking for is some type of change or some combination of factors that give sailfish a reason to be there."

According to Smith, there is a long list of factors involved in locating sailfish. They include depth, water temperature, current, tide, water color and clarity, surface appearance, bait, scent, birds, the presence of other sea life, oxygen, salinity, and sub-surface temperatures. Sailfish are sensitive to the slightest changes, so be prepared to seek them out.

8. Create a Game Plan

"When I leave the dock I always have a game plan," says Smith. "That way I don't have to run out and listen to the fleet on the VHF for two hours to find out I should have been off Stuart in 200 feet of water. Now certainly I'm going to have the flexibility to change my game plan, because as someone said a long time ago, fish do have tails. They may not be where they were yesterday."

For those who are new to the sport, Smith feels the easiest way to learn is to follow the fleet. "You will make no mistake finding where the sailfish fleet is off Palm Beach in the wintertime. If you see 75 tuna

towers out there in one place, it's probably a good spot to put your baits in. Also, when you're just starting out, don't try to out-smart 75 good sailfishermen. Once you've got some feel for it, some experience, and you've developed some of the cause-and-effect relationships that happen, then develop your own thinking."

However, as Smith will tell you, following the fleet can have its disadvantages, too. "I've seen the fleet get brain-lock and just sit there for days without any fish being caught." Smith contends it's during those times that newcomers should explore new territory.

Despite all these tips, Smith believes that first-time sailfishermen should first think about the safety of their boat and crew before heading offshore into Palm Beach's rough, wintertime conditions. "There's nothing more important than your own safety. Know your own abilities. Know your boat. Don't push your luck. There are people in their grave right now because they thought they or their boat could do more than they were capable of doing in a given set of circumstances. If there's a question, it's best to be conservative."

9. Opportunity Knocks

According to Smith, more often than not there are usually more than one or two sailfish traveling around together off Palm Beach in the wintertime. It's during those times that sailfishermen should leave their baits in during hookups to take advantage of possible double- or triple-headers. "If your tackle is appropriate – in other words, if you're fishing with 20-pound outfits – it would make sense to leave your baits in the water to the fullest extent you can."

As I witnessed firsthand this winter, *Old Reliable's* configuration allows Smith to continue to hook up with fish, unlike many larger, sportfishing boats that have to back down, thus killing any chances for double- or triple-headers. The walkaround design makes multiple hookups a breeze, allowing one angler to fight his fish off the bow, while the rest of the crew continues to monitor the kite baits or fight additional fish off the stern. No removing lines, no severe backing down.

The Ultimate Sailfish Boat

It's almost impossible to discuss Nick Smith without discussing his boat, *Old Reliable*. It only takes one look to discover why it's one of the most acclaimed boats in South Florida. Custom-built by Bill Knowles of Knowles Boat Co. in Stuart,

Florida, *Old Reliable* is a 36-foot walkaround day-boat specifically designed for single-handed sailfishing. However, as Smith's long-time friend Angelo Durante once said, "when the action gets hot, it's more a runaround than a walkaround."

"From the very first line that was drawn on a piece of paper, this boat was built to do one thing, nothing else, and that's to catch sailfish," explained Smith. However, in truth, this boat would fish exceptionally well anywhere. *Old Reliable* is 35' 8" in length, sports a 12' 6" beam, weighs approximately 14,000 pounds, draws 40 inches, and with its 3208 TA 375-hp Caterpillar engines, cruises around 30 knots and tops out at 40 mph.

Sleek and functional, *Old Reliable* is a 100-percent fish boat with few creature comforts. Even the cabin is designed to be washed down. (The cabin sole is scuppered into the bilge.) And as you might expect, *Old Reliable* is designed specifically for live-bait fishing. You'll find no tower or outriggers here. Smith opted instead for a boat that would drift perfectly beam to sea to enhance his live-bait efficiency. *Old Reliable* sports a 55-gallon live well at the base of the cockpit rocket launcher with circulation provided by two Rule 500 pumps, which may be used individually or together.

Smith and Knowles, however, weren't alone in developing this highly acclaimed sailfish boat. Upon closer inspection, *Old Reliable* is full of small, ingenious designs that help make it as efficient as possible. One of the most obvious is the sleek half tower. Custom built by Bob Birdsall of West Palm's Birdsall Marine Design, the top sports a flush canvas top — the first of its kind. Another of Birdsall's designs can be viewed just to the left of the helm. There, a custom leader and survey tape (used as kite markers) dispenser lets Smith access more of both without any trips to a tackle box. "It's just one more thing to make everything there convenient and as simple as possible to support your fishing efforts."

Not too far away is another neat design. There, on the underside of the half tower, an overhead rod rack built by custom boat rigger Fred Herman of Miami, can be found. If you look closely you can see small notches that lock the spinning outfits in place to keep them from swinging and banging during travel.

Turning to the cockpit, another slick arrangement can be found below *Old Reliable's* stern hawse pipes where gimbals have been installed. Smith first saw this application on Murray Brother's *Cookie Too* several years ago and liked it. The design allows the hawse pipe to accept either a dock line or a rod butt if need be. Smith often uses the hawse pipe rod holder when he needs to spread the flat lines as far forward and as far aft as possible.

Other added features on *Old Reliable* include pop-up cleats to accentuate the boat's clean, sleek appearance, as well as to make it free of any potential hazards to Smith's fishing line.

It's the ultimate sailfish boat, and it's truly one of a kind.

10. Fighting Tactics & Release Tips

According to Smith, water pressure often plays a crucial role when battling sailfish on tackle lighter than 20-pound. "Too many people don't follow the belly of the line through the water when they're hooked up. The lighter the tackle the more you've got to follow the line and not the fish. The water acts like a pulley and you can't pull it through without high risk of breaking it."

Smith believes in giving the fish a fighting chance to survive. "I love these fish. I respect them immensely and it breaks my heart if one ever dies." To avoid long, stressful battles, Smith makes it a point to release his fish as quickly as possible. However, he's released fish that he doubted would ever survive. Only years later did he learn that one particular tagged sailfish had survived to be caught again. As Smith and his long-time friend Angelo Durante once told me, "whatever condition the fish is in, it has a better chance of survival in the water than on the dock."

Spoken like a true sportsman. Smith hopes others will take the reins to protect and monitor this great game fish in the generations to come. But for now, he hopes to continue participating in the sport he loves so much. Sailfishing since 1955, does he see himself getting tired of it?

"I can't imagine not doing it. It certainly has been exciting for me and I guess as long as it continues to be, I'm going to be out there doing it."

RED SNAPPER
Round-Up

By Robert Sloan

Spring is the best time to find big Texas snapper stacked up over structure. Here's how to catch them.

Catches of giant red snapper along the upper Texas coast continue to be nothing short of phenomenal. Consider the trip made by Dale Fontenot last April. While fishing live and dead baits over some rocks and wrecks off Galveston, Fontenot brought home a two-day limit of ten snapper. His four heaviest fish weighed a total of 99 pounds, and the biggest tipped the scales at a whopping 32 pounds!

When it comes to big Gulf Coast snapper, there's no question that March and April are the prime months. This is when the big "sows" stack up over underwater structure, such as wrecks, reefs, and rigs. But there are hundreds of such spots in the Gulf. Which ones are best?

Key on Water Depth

Dr. Curtis Thorpe of Sabine Pass has the prescription for trophy snapper. "Water depth is just as important as good structure," says Thorpe. "Two of my top spots off the Sabine Bank are located in about 75 feet of water. One is a rock and the other is a sunken fishing boat. Both are located between 55 and 60 miles off Sabine Pass.

"Out of Sabine Pass you have to travel a long way to hit 100 feet of water, so you're better off fishing the rocks, wrecks, and rigs 50 miles or so offshore. On the Sabine Bank you'll find the big spring sows between 55 and 75 feet."

Depth is the big difference between fishing off Sabine Pass and Galveston, where fishermen look for deeper water. For example, the giant snappers Fontenot caught last spring were taken from rocks in 112 to 124 feet of water. John Blackwell, another Galveston snapper pro, fishes 45 to 65 miles out in water that's 90 to 120 feet deep.

Thorpe, who feels he's wasting his time if he's not battling 15-pound-plus snappers, prefers to target fish that are suspended above the bottom structure. "More often than not you're likely to find a zillion snappers on your favorite rock or wreck," says Thorpe. "But simply dropping a baited rig to the bottom will result in lots of 'rats' weighing under five pounds. Nine times out of ten, the heaviest snapper will be suspended.

"To catch these sows I use a one-ounce SpoonDog lure tipped with a cigar minnow or pogy (menhaden). The SpoonDog sinks slowly with the current to where the fish are holding. I cast it upcurrent so that the bait will be about mid-way through the water column by the time it reaches the structure. The flash of the spoon and the smell of the dead bait are a winning combo for big snapper."

Another top lure for suspended snapper is a one- to three-ounce yellow or white jig. Tip the jig with a cigar minnow, pogy, or large squid and let it settle in the current.

Thorpe fishes his SpoonDogs on a four- to six-foot, 80-pound mono leader attached to 50-pound main line via a 3/0 barrel swivel. While some anglers use leaders as heavy as 125-pound test, Thorpe claims the 80-pound mono allows for more movement and flash. The size of hook can vary from 7/0 to as large as 16/0.

Bottom Baiting

Although Fontenot agrees that big fish often hold in the mid-depths above structure, he's found that this isn't always the case. "Free-lining baits through the mid-depths will produce large snapper," he says, "but there are times when the current is too strong to free-line. That was the situation when I caught those four giants, so I went to the bottom." His tactic was to fish a double-dropper rig with live or dead baits, 16/0 circle hooks, and an 18-ounce weight. A little trick he uses is to slide a piece of hot-pink or chartreuse tubing over the shank of the hook for added attraction. For live baits he uses eight-inch vermillion snapper; however, his 32-pounder took a strip of belly meat from a fresh-caught bluefish.

If you're going after giant snapper, you better bring tackle that's up to the task. Use a stout rod that's around 6 ½ feet long and built to handle 50-pound line, and make sure it has enough backbone to keep a 20-pound-plus snapper from diving into the structure. A roller tip is a good idea to prevent fraying.

The weather can be a factor at this time of year, and it helps if you're ready to head offshore when conditions are right. The best time to make a run is two to three days after a cold front has passed. The Gulf will have calmed and the water will be a bit clearer. Don't take a chance if the seas are rough or if a front is approaching – three Sabine Pass fishermen once lost their lives that way. As long as you play it safe and use the advice of the above experts, you can enjoy some of the best fishing for big red snapper anywhere on the Gulf Coast.

Valley of the GIANTS

By Michael A. Rivlin

I remember fishing Georges Bank when you could catch cod and pollock until your arms gave out. Today these famous fishing grounds, once considered the richest in the world, have been heavily depleted, largely due to overfishing. However, there are still some spots where anglers can tangle with huge cod, hake, and pollock.

Long-range party boat trips from New York and New England ports allow fishermen to experience some of the best bottom fishing in the North Atlantic. The action primarily takes place over deep-water wrecks on Georges, Nantucket Shoals, and in the surrounding waters. These wrecks serve as oases for groundfish, holding baitfish and providing a sanctuary from strong currents and commercial nets. Because of this, the fish grow large. Forty-pound cod are taken on almost every trip, and 50-pounders are common. And you can always dream about catching a monster like the 70-plus-pound cod landed on the *Viking Starship* a couple of years ago!

Hunting wreck fish in the Northeast is different from most types of sport fishing. If sight-casting to tarpon and bonefish on the flats is at one end of the spectrum, then deep-water wreck fishing is surely at the other. The latter takes place on large, rugged boats that sail in rough seas, through waters that have seen a lot of history. Fishing success is measured primarily in pounds caught, and any thoughts of catch and release, except for undersized fish, are best left on shore.

A handful of large party boats fish the Northeast wrecks, including the *Viking Starship* out of Montauk, New York; the *Frances* fleet out of Point Judith, Rhode Island; the *Helen H* out of Hyannis, Massachusetts; and the *Yankee Capts.* out of Gloucester, Massachusetts. Each boat has a unique personality that makes for a distinctly different fishing experience.

A Cast of Characters

Besides the aggressive nature of Capt. Steven Forsberg when it comes to finding fish, one thing that makes fishing on the *Starship* so pleasurable is its size. Like the cod it targets, the boat is huge, and all space in its 140-foot-long hull is put to good use. There's plenty of room in the cabin for tackle and food coolers, and on deck for fishermen and their huge portable fishboxes that hold the catch. Below, spacing of the bunks allows you to climb into your sleeping bag without having to step over, or on, fellow anglers. In addition, large, comfortable reclining seats in the cabin make the long trip to and from the fishing grounds easier to take.

Much of the boat's character comes from the characters who fill it, typically a mix of the New York metro area's municipal work force, including police, fire, sanitation, and transit workers. Most are expert fishermen, and many own their own boats. And there is always an assortment of well-known fishermen, captains, and a handful of mates from other charter boats aboard, not to mention the occasional basketball player or jazz musician. But for the most part, these guys are all diamonds in the rough, with unpolished exteriors and gentle hearts.

If the *Starship*'s rough-and-tumble environment is at all off-putting, you may find the regimented atmosphere of Glouces-ter's *Yankee Capts.* more to your liking. Here, mates roam the decks like tackle police, making sure you're rigged to their satis-faction. If you get bored with your assigned fishing position or partner, too bad; on this boat, anglers stick to their assigned spots like striped bass to structure.

There isn't as much room on the *Yankee Capts.* as on the *Starship*. The cabin is smaller, the seats aren't quite as comfortable, and bunks can be in short supply. All this aside, if you're new to deep-water wreck fishing, the *Yankee Capts.* is the boat of choice.

You can still catch monster cod and pollock on two- and three-day deep-water wreck trips to Georges Bank and Nantucket Shoals.

THE DEEP-WATER WRECKS are one of the few places where Northeast anglers stand a good chance of catching dependable numbers of big bottom fish, like this nice cod (left). Since commercial draggers are unable to work nets over the structure, and party boat captains limit the number of trips they make to each site, the wrecks act as an oasis where resident fish can grow to large sizes. Many deep-water wrecks hold good numbers of white hake like this (middle). A Georges Bank wreck yielded a big pollock (right) for this fisherman aboard the *Yankee Capts.* Since pollock often hold higher in the water column than cod, jigs should be fished above the wrecks.

Pollock Jigging Rig

Jigging rigs start with a three-foot, 60-pound leader with a quality barrel swivel at the top, one or two dropper loops to hold teasers, and a strong snap swivel at the bottom to hold the jig. For getting to the bottom quickly in a strong current, I prefer diamond jigs, which have a slim profile and offer little water resistance. Jig weight is a matter of fishing ability, current, and personal taste. If you're able to cast out against the drift and get at least 30 feet away from the boat, you can get away with a 14-ounce jig. If you drop straight down, 16 ounces is the minimum. And there are times when the current is running so hard that a 21-, 22-, or 24-ounce jig is called for.

They may call it jigging, but less catching is done on the jigs than on the teasers attached to the dropper loops. Teasers are not optional accessories. My standard teaser is a 6½-inch curlytail jelly worm in fluorescent pink, purple, and chartreuse. Artificial shrimp or eels, and pink, green, or white bucktails also work well at times.

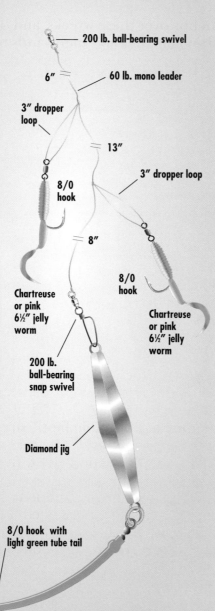

200 lb. ball-bearing swivel

6"

60 lb. mono leader

3" dropper loop

13"

3" dropper loop

8/0 hook

8"

8/0 hook

Chartreuse or pink 6½" jelly worm

Chartreuse or pink 6½" jelly worm

200 lb. ball-bearing snap swivel

Diamond jig

8/0 hook with light green tube tail

The clientele is a bit more polished and polite, and novices will find the *Yankee* mates friendlier, more attentive, more obliging.

Nighttime Journey

Weather permitting, Capt. Greg Mercurio's targets of choice for the *Yankee Capts.*'s Nantucket Shoals trips are the nine or so wrecks lying in or near the Great South Channel in 180 to 240 feet of water. This was the destination he had in mind when we left historic Gloucester one night in early spring. However, en route, Mercurio determined that strong tides would make the channel wrecks unfishable, so we steamed all the way to the southeast part of Georges, 180 miles east-southeast of Nantucket, where he knew of some other productive spots.

We started fishing at 8:30, the weather warm and foggy. Our first stop was a small wreck whose numbers Mercuno had been given by a commercial fisherman just a few days earlier. But a tricky wind and strong currents conspired against us, making proper anchoring difficult. Mercurio repeatedly tried to set us over the wreck, but met with little success.

When he finally sounded the whistle, the signal to start fishing, we sent our skimmer clams hurtling toward bottom with 20 ounces of lead. After an hour, with only a couple of dogfish to show for our effort, we gave up.

The next wreck we fished lifted everyone's spirits. The first few minutes you start fishing a wreck give you a good indication of what's to come, and this one telegraphed good news right away. It immediately produced a flurry of action with some very large fish, most of them hake. By early afternoon, when the pace slowed, everyone was smiling, especially the guy with the 40-pounder!

Plenty of Pollock!

Other than increased fishing time, the two-day wreck trips offer a kind of insurance in case of bad weather: If one day is lousy, there's hope that the next will be better. However, it doesn't always work out that way.

We awoke the following morning to a hard rain, followed by hard-luck fishing and more rain. Currents were so strong that no one could keep a bait on the bottom.

Finally, the weather let up, and one wreck in 225 feet of water had a terrific surprise for us. Mercurio had first fished it the previous summer and found lots of cod there. However, this time the wreck was stacked deep with "family-sized" pollock. I ran around the boat photographing fishermen with their catch, and when I finally started fishing, the pollock were still biting.

If you want to catch pollock, rig up with a jig and chartreuse or green teasers, for which pollock show an overwhelming preference. While cod generally hold close to the bottom, pollock swim throughout the lower half of the water column, and they'll follow a jig or teaser almost for the surface. As you're dropping down, stay alert for a bump, which often means a pollock has taken the offering. Immediately throw the reel into gear, wind in all the stretch, and set the hook. If you don't get hit on the drop, let your jig fall to the bottom, then start a moderately fast retrieve. Reel in 10 or 15 turns, pause, jig once or twice, let the jig fall slowly down, then repeat until you're at least one-third of the way back up. Then let the jig down to the bottom and try again.

Hooking my first 25-pound pollock of the day was a kick. As I lifted my rod to move the jig off the bottom, it suddenly came to a dead stop. At first I thought I'd hooked the wreck, but then something pulled back with surprising force. At the end of an eight-foot rod, in 200 feet of water, a big pollock puts up a tough fight, sort of like that of a large bluefish. I found myself moving along the rail as the fish tried to put some distance between itself and the boat. Finally, I was able to turn its head and bring it to the surface. Next to the boat, the pollock came to life again, struggling hard to get back down to safety. I was relieved when the mate managed to sink his gaff into the fish and haul it over the rail.

Whale Cod, Viking-Style

The *Viking Starship* makes a couple of Nantucket wreck trips each spring, then targets the extreme deep-water wrecks a good 14 hours out of Montauk. These so-called "whale cod" wrecks are in a class by themselves. On my last whale cod trip we began by fishing a wreck in 450 feet of water, 40 miles northeast of Georges Bank. I had fished this wreck before, and it yielded the largest cod I've ever seen, including a number in the 50- to 60-pound category.

Deep water makes it impossible to anchor over these wrecks, and on this day a strong current and high winds made things even worse. Still, Forsberg tried a few drifts, the boat swinging round in the wind. After a few minutes, he stuck his head out the pilothouse window.

"Time to tighten the hat band another notch," he called down to the fishermen lining the rails. As the wind blew him back inside I glanced at the radar screen and noticed several rain squalls bearing down on us. "That will finish most of them off," he muttered, and signalled for everyone to reel in their lines so he could begin another drift.

This was easier said than done. Bringing up 1,200 feet of line with a 20-ounce sinker in a 12-knot current, with the wind gusting up to 35 knots, is hard labor!

On my way into the cabin, I passed cook and tackle consultant Linda Rezac, who was working on a baked ham dinner for 50 in her tiny galley. "This is whale-codding at its lovable best!" she joked.

The scene inside the cabin proved Forsberg's prediction right. By the time he'd started the drift, more than half the fishermen had come inside to lick their wounds. The inexperienced ones were grumbling mutinously; they'd read in a local fishing magazine about a recent trip where huge numbers of cod were caught. "I can't wait to read about how many fish were caught on *this* trip," grumbled one disillusioned angler, implying the report was a phony.

It wasn't. On the trip he'd read about, 22 passengers caught over 1,800 cod, and

Basic Cod Rig

The standard bait on these trips is skimmer clam, and the technique is straightforward. Bait up, make sure you have enough weight to hold bottom, cast out a bit, and let your line go straight to the bottom. Try to keep your bait on the bottom by raising or lowering your rod to counter the pitching of the boat. You can also try slight, infrequent lifts of the rod, which sometimes draw a strike.

If you feel a bite, wait for the second or third solid tug before setting the hook. Raise your rod as high as possible, then reel in quickly as you lower the rod and take up any slack. Then continue a slow, steady retrieve to bring the fish to the surface. Cod have extremely tender flesh around their mouths, and it's easy to pull a hook loose.

If you're having trouble scoring, try bottled scent. Douse the clams and bait skirt with bunker oil or any attractant flavored with shrimp, mackerel, or squid. Braid Neon, originally formulated to attract big game, works surprisingly well. You might also try bringing some alternative natural bait with you. Scout your bait shop or fish store for fresh herring, whiting, or other small, whole fish.

The simplest bait rig is a single 6/0 to 8/0 hook tied to a heavy-duty, 150-pound, three-way swivel, with as much lead as you need to hold bottom hanging one to 1½ feet below. I prefer a rig with two extra-long dropper loops, one close to the bottom, a second 1½ feet above it. I use a loosely tied sinker snap to attach the lead. That way, if it gets hung up on bottom, I can pry it loose without sacrificing the entire rig.

Bait skirts placed above the hooks can dramatically improve your catch. The most effective one I've ever found is a green Hi-Seas Shaker glow skirt. I crimp an 8/0 baitholder hook to a short piece of leader and thread it through the skirt's acrylic body; a swivel crimped at the other end is attached to the dropper loop.

Rig labels: 200 lb. ball-bearing swivel · 6" · 5" dropper loop · Red squid skirt (optional) · 8/0 stainless steel hook · Clam chunk · 18" · 60 lb. mono leader · 5" dropper loop · 1/0 swivel · Crimp · 8/0 stainless steel hook · 5" · Clam chunk · Hi-Seas Shaker glow skirt · Sinker snap · Bank sinker

---

some of those steaks and fillets had made their way into my cooler! Long-range wreck trips are unpredictable. When they are bad, they are very, very bad. But when they are good, they're outrageous.

Tackle Tips

The standard bait-fishing outfit on these trips consists of a 3/0 revolving-spool reel with 30-pound test (too light in my opinion) or a 4/0 filled with 50-pound test. The Penn Senator 113H with an aluminum spool and power handle, midsized Newells, Shimano TLDs, or Daiwa Sealines are some of the outfits you'll commonly see along the rail. For a rod you'll need a seven- to eight-footer that's sensitive enough to detect bites, but which also has enough backbone to set a hook in 300 feet of water. It's a good idea to have a couple of standby outfits rigged and ready to fish. That way, if there's a good bite on and your reel jams, you can quickly switch to another and not miss any action.

There are regular wrecks and there are whale cod wrecks. The first time the *Starship* crew scouted them, they had to revise their tackle selection. Because of the size of the fish, it's common to see guys fishing with rigs normally reserved for school tuna: 6/0 reels and 5½- or six-foot stand-up rods with roller guides.

You'll also want to bring at least one jigging outfit with you. Even if you fish wrecks exclusively, there will almost always be times when jigging is called for, especially if there's a pile of pollock sitting on the structure, or if you need to drift-fish. (See sidebars for more on tackle and rigging.)

Conserving the Resource

As Georges Bank – sometimes called the "Valley of the Giants" – runs out of fish, the *Viking* fleet has visited the wrecks with increasing frequency. Even on the deep-water whale cod wrecks, fishing pressure from the *Starship* alone may be overwhelming those stocks. As a result, Capt. Forsberg plans fewer whale cod trips in the future so that wreck populations can rebuild.

Depending on how you look at it, these offshore wrecks are either refuges or feedlots.

Overfishing is a problem the *Yankee Capts.* has always taken steps to avoid. According to Capt. Mercurio, these wrecks have remained productive season after season, in part because of his deliberate management policy. From May to September, the *Yankee Capts.* visits each wreck just once a month. But even with this policy, the best trips are the ones earlier in the year, after the wrecks have had a chance to "recharge" over the winter.

Not entirely. During daylight hours, the wrecks are normally dominated by the far more aggressive cod and pollock. In the past, hake were commonly caught starting at dusk and through the night, when the cod and pollock were resting. But on one *Yankee Capts.* trip, hake dominated the daylight catch. Observed one veteran codfisherman, "When you start to see hake come up, you know it's petering out."

Depending on how you look at it, these offshore wrecks are either refuges or feedlots. Largely protected from commercial nets, fish gather, eat, grow, and get harvested by hook and line. I confess that at times fishing them feels like shooting fish in the proverbial barrel. On the *Yankee Capts.*, an older fisherman observed wryly, "It hurts me whenever I see a big cow come up. Everyone gets all excited to see a 50-pound fish. But all I think of are those thousands of eggs that the big cow won't get a chance to produce."

What's ahead for wreck fishing on Georges Bank? Back in the mid-1990s, the National Marine Fisheries Service (NMFS) issued a report stating that Georges Bank cod stocks were seriously depleted (mostly due to commercial exploitation) and that steps should be taken to reduce catches significantly. As a result, NMFS quickly implemented a package of emergency regulations that included closure of three important fishing areas on Georges, including what is known as the "Nantucket Lightship Closed Area," in which many of the best wrecks, including the *Andrea Doria,* are found. However, intense pressure on NMFS and federal managers by members of the party boat sector to reopen this particular area to rod-and-reel sport fishing has proved successful, so most scheduled trips to this area will continue as they have in the past.

The distant future, however, is uncertain. The New England Fishery Management Council (NEFMC) continues to work on long-range, comprehensive plans to rebuild stocks of cod, haddock, and flounder off New England, and just how party boat and recreational fishing fit into the picture remains to be seen. Statistics show that sport fishermen take just a fraction of these important species annually, and many anglers are of the opinion that the recreational fishery should be allowed to continue at some reasonable level, even if the commercial sector becomes tightly restricted.

Chances are good, though, that Northeast party boats will continue to offer these exciting trips to some of the best wrecks on Georges Bank and the surrounding waters. There's no thrill quite like the surge of an outsized cod, pollock, or hake as it grabs a jig and heads for cover, straining the muscles and stout tackle of the lucky angler hundreds of feet above. For bottom fishermen in the Northeast, it doesn't get any better than that!

DAVID LINKIEWICZ, left , AND CAPT. GENE VANDER HOEK of the Kona charter boat *Sea Genie II* hold a fly-caught striped marlin.

HAWAII FLY-O

By Jim Rizzuto

The bait-and-switch routine for taking bill-fish on fly is catching on big-time in Hawaii. Boat 'im, Danno!

With all the great fishing opportunities Hawaii has to offer, it's somewhat surprising that so few fly fishermen have ever waved a rod there. Dave Linkiewicz did, and in a week of fishing off Kona hooked five different species on a fly, including striped marlin, spearfish, yellowfin tuna, rainbow runner, and mahimahi. Two of those fish – a 37-pound spearfish on 20-pound tippet and a three-pound yellowfin tuna on six-pound tippet – have earned him IGFA fly rod records. In fact, Dave's spearfish may be only the second one ever caught on a fly.

"Kona already has fly fishing records for skipjack, bigeye, yellowfin, spearfish, and bluefin trevally, but the potential is really unlimited," says Capt. Gene Vander Hoek, skipper of the *Sea Genie II*. Vander Hoek hosted Linkiewicz during his record hunt in March, 1995, and is one of several Kona skippers eager to see more fly fishermen on their decks. "Conditions here are perfect for fly fishing," says Vander Hoek. "Most of the year, winds are light and seas calm, so you can see the fish and present a fly effectively."

And Kona definitely has the fish. Within a dozen miles of Honokohau Harbor you might have a shot at blue marlin, striped marlin, spearfish, mahimahi, wahoo, skipjack tuna, bigeye tuna, yellowfin tuna, rainbow runner, and maybe even amberjack, barracuda, kawakawa, and trevally. Meanwhile, fly casters around the world have been perfecting ways of drawing open-ocean fish into casting range and getting them to attack a fly. Always an innovative bunch, Kona skippers have borrowed and adapted three different methods that have produced records and record claims.

Billfish were once thought to be impossible to catch on a fly, at least when it came to IGFA regulations, which dictate that the boat must be out of gear before the fly is cast to the fish (the IGFA won't recognize a fish caught on a trolled fly). But the arrival of the "bait and switch," a technique used with great success in other parts of the world, has changed all that.

Tease, Switch & Frankenbait

Capt. Vander Hoek has used the method to set six new IGFA records. "We find and raise fish by trolling hookless lures – the same models that have taken marlin, tuna, and other game fish all along, only unarmed," he says. "These teasers are trolled in a pattern off one side of the boat to allow a fly caster to set up on the other side. This also lets the crew do its job without stepping all over the caster's line or bumping into his tackle.

"The caster strips out his fly line so it will reach a predetermined spot, usually about the third wave. Casting farther than 40 or 50 feet is seldom necessary. Then he strips the line back into the boat, either coiling it on the deck or in a casting basket or bucket, depending on his preference. He lays his fly on the fighting chair or the transom and sets his fly rod down in a secure and handy spot."

After the fish is spotted in the teasers, the angler moves into casting position with his rod in one hand and the fly in the other. The crew brings in all of the teasers except the one the fish is following. Once the other lines have been cleared, the fish is led toward the casting spot.

Teasing Techniques

"When the fish is at, say, the fourth wave, the teaser is yanked out of the way while the fish's momentum carries it into position at the third wave," says Vander Hoek. "That's when the skipper yells 'Now!' and shifts to neutral."

As the boat is taken out of gear, the angler throws his fly

LOOSE RUNNING LINE is coiled in a bucket by the transom while the heavy shooting head and fly are left on deck. This arrangement allows the angler to fire off a 30-foot cast in a matter of seconds once the fish is spotted behind the boat.

into the air to backcast and then shoots it forward toward the fish. All of this must be done quickly, because the fish won't stay around very long if it doesn't see food.

If the cast is on target, a hot fish will usually grab the fly as soon as it sees it. "Dave [Linkiewicz] caught a stripey [striped marlin] and a spearfish with me, and for both it was two pops and the fish was on," said Vander Hoek.

Not all fish cooperate, but Vander Hoek has a secret weapon to deal with them. "Sometimes you wait too long and the fish is too close to the boat. To attract its attention and get it back into position, we keep a spinning rod handy with a sewed-up ballyhoo. We call it the 'Frankenbait.' Even if the fish peels off to the right instead of the left, or gets past the boat, the deckhand can cast the Frankenbait to it, get the confused fish excited again, and lead it back into fly casting range."

A HOOKLESS "FRANKENBAIT" TEASER is used to lure fish back into casting range if they swim past the spread.

The Frankenbait can often turn a fish on that shows no interest in the first place. "One time we found a big mahimahi at one of the FADs [fish aggregating devices], but it rejected every fly I threw it for 20 minutes," said Linkiewicz. "It would race to the fly and turn away at the last second. Then we tossed it the ballyhoo. It grabbed it, and we pulled it away again and again. Then, when I cast the fly, I had time for one strip before the mahimahi was on it."

FADs & Flotsam

Hawaii's FADs offer other kinds of opportunities, too. "A FAD buoy is where we caught Dave's tuna record and missed a sure record on rainbow runner," said Vander Hoek. "We came up to the FAD, saw a pair of rainbow runners swimming nearby, and checked the record book to see what was open," Vander Hoek said. "The two-pound tippet was vacant, so Dave tried the fish with a two-pound rig. Unfortunately, the rod was too stiff for the tippet – it was better suited for six or eight – and he ended up breaking both fish off.

"To get the tuna, Dave used a sinking head, made a legal cast near a FAD, and then we just drifted to let the fly sink as far as the line would let it. Then Dave stripped the line back in to work the fly. Each of the three times we hooked up, the line was about halfway in."

The length of the fly line is a practical limit on how far down the fly can sink. "If you go past the fly line and strip the backing onto the deck, when a fish hits the backing will come up in a tangle. Or worse yet, the thin backing can slice through your finger."

When the big yellowfins are feeding with porpoise, Vander Hoek hopes to try for records on heavier tippets. "We think we might be able to get in front of the school early in the morning, cast out a sinking line, and strip it in the same way. Of course, surviving a 100-pound yellowfin run may be something else."

Chum for Tuna

Capt. Kevin Nakamaru, also of Kona, targets tuna a third way. He chums schools of yellowfin and bigeye within range, and then fly casts to them with a modified fly line system. "A standard fly line creates so much drag in the water that it can keep you from ever catching a light-tackle tuna record on two-pound tippet," says Nakamaru. "No matter what you do, the resistance of the thick line on a high-speed run will exceed the breaking strength of the tippet."

Instead, Nakamaru uses a quick-cast

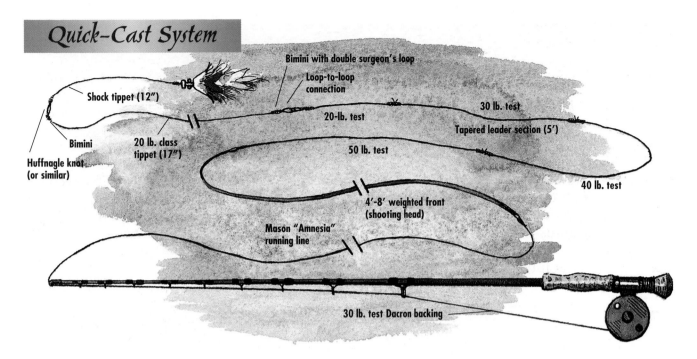

Bimini with double surgeon's loop

Loop-to-loop connection

Shock tippet (12")

30 lb. test

20-lb. test

Tapered leader section (5')

Bimini

20 lb. class tippet (17")

50 lb. test

Huffnagle knot (or similar)

40 lb. test

4'-8' weighted front (shooting head)

Mason "Amnesia" running line

30 lb. test Dacron backing

system he learned from veteran salt water fly caster Terry Baird. The momentum of the cast is generated by a four- to eight-foot (depending on tippet size) section that Nakamaru calls a "weighted front." The leader, including class and shock tippets, is connected to the weighted front, or shooting head, which is connected to the shooting line. The shooting line is a stiff type of monofilament designed to minimize tangling. Nakamaru says he prefers Mason's Amnesia mono for his shooting line, since it has little memory. "Although it does tangle at times, it clears very well on an oval cast because of its stiffness," Nakamaru says.

Baird introduced Nakamaru to the oval cast. "You backcast the fly with an oval motion of the rod and then shoot the weighted front forward – snapping it with a motion similar to a double haul," Nakamaru says. "This throws the heavy line forward and carries the shooting line with it for a distance premeasured by the caster."

Ferocious Fish

Distance really isn't a problem in the waters Nakamaru fishes. "The tuna are pretty ferocious at the seamounts and the weather buoys," he says. "It usually doesn't take a long cast to hook up – but it's another matter to keep them hooked without breaking them

off on light tippets."

Nakamaru broke off 15 yellowfins in a row using two-pound tippet before finally boating a three-pound, eight-ounce fish, which he submitted for the record. As of this writing, he has caught bigeye tuna, yellowfin tuna, and rainbow runner big enough to challenge fly rod records.

Nakamaru uses the same teaser system Vander Hoek uses for baiting and switching, but prefers to let the caster decide when the fish is within range. "As the skipper sees the angler make his backcast, he takes the boat out of gear. This way, the angler is never surprised by the captain telling him when to present his fly to the fish. However, he should be aware of his distances by making numerous practice stops and casting to imaginary fish beforehand."

Chumming tuna schools within reach of a fly is not a new method, even for Kona fishermen. Back in 1989, Michael Schwartz caught a 15-pound, eight-ounce skipjack on 16-pound tippet to fill that IGFA slot. "It's an exciting technique with a lot of luck involved," says Vander Hoek, who fished with Schwartz the day after he caught his record. "You chase down an *aku* [skipjack] school, get into position, toss a handful of anchovies, make a cast, and hope you hook one before they can breeze underneath you. There are a lot of big *aku* out here well over 20 pounds, and the 20-pound-tippet category is wide open."

Tactics & Tackle

Skippers and crews accustomed to fighting fish on trolling gear are learning an important difference when it comes to fly fishing. "You can't really go after a fish with the boat," says Vander Hoek. "Most fly reels crank at a one-to-one ratio, which won't pick up line quickly. You can't chase the fish faster than the angler can reel. About all you can do is ease back on the fish to prevent a tippet-breaking surge."

An active fish can be a special problem for fly tackle. The jumps can jerk the line and pop the fragile tippet, but even a deep-swimming fish can slap the leader with its tail and snap it. Dave Linkiewicz's spearfish only jumped once, but his 30-pound striped marlin jumped 20 or more times and body-wrapped the 16-pound tippet in the process. "On an eight-pound tippet, that stripey would have been the record," said Vander Hoek, "but on eight-pound, we might not have boated it.

"All the skipper can do is stay with the fish until the angler can get it within reach of an eight-foot gaff. That's when your deckhand has to contain himself. He may be used to grabbing a 400-pound-test leader and wrestling the fish to gaff, but there is no leader, only a tippet that will break if you touch it. Fly regulations allow you no more than 12 inches of shock tippet, then a minimum of 15 inches of class tippet. After that, you can have as much butt section as you want back to the actual fly line."

When fishing Kona, or other areas now being opened to fly casters, expect to bring your own rods, reels, lines, and flies. Be sure to include standard baitfish patterns like blue-and-white feathered streamers. If you tie your own flies, go with a tandem rig tied on two stainless hooks in sizes 4/0 or 5/0. "If you are looking for solid hook-ups, stainless steel is really beneficial for light-tackle fishing," says Vander Hoek. "It holds a good point and slides in easily for good penetration. Also, the metal doesn't rust and stain your fly. On the other hand, stainless steel might not be your choice for blue marlin, which could crush or break the hook in its jaw hinge."

What Size Rod?

The size of the rod will depend on the species you want to catch. "If you are after a blue marlin, you might go as heavy as a 13- to 15-weight," says Vander Hoek. "For a fish the size of a spearfish or striped marlin, you might prefer a 12-weight because it's more versatile and forgiving. But you also have to match the resistance of the rod to the strength of the tippet."

"Salt water fly rods usually come with extension butts to keep the reel away from your body when you do battle, but any butt longer than two inches gets in the way," says Linkiewicz. "You want the reel close to your body but not touching it. Longer butts tend to catch the fly line when casting or trying to clear line off the deck after the strike."

Linkiewicz prefers rods with large guides and an oversized tip-top. "Small guides will create problems when you try to clear line after the strike, and sometimes during the fight."

The reel must be able to stand up to salt water, and it must have adequate line capacity and a smooth drag. The drag doesn't require the heavy-duty engineering of a big-game reel, especially when you are fishing with two-pound, four-pound, or eight-pound tippets, but it can't be erratic or you'll pop off fish if the drag seizes. Many salt water fly casters prefer to set their drags much lighter than the tippet can handle and then add tension by palming the outer edge of the reel spool.

Before setting off in pursuit of a record, be sure to talk with the skipper to make your intentions clear and to agree on the methods and procedures you want to use. Catching big game on flies is difficult enough, even when skipper, angler, and crew are working well together.

Author Biographies

Joel Arrington, a prize-winning photographer, stays busy contributing to books and magazines. Arrington has fished widely in the Americas and Australia, but is best known as an authority on mid-Atlantic fishing.

Captain Frank Bolin is a freelance writer whose articles and columns have appeared in many national and regional newspapers and magazines. He is also a fishing club lecturer, conservation speaker and charter captain.

Scott Boyan is Associate Editor at *Salt Water Sportsman* magazine. He writes several of the columns and contributes many articles and photographs to *SWS*. He has fished throughout the U.S., Mexico, the Bahamas and the Azores.

Dick Brown, author of *Fly Fishing for Bonefish* and *Bonefish Fly Patterns*, has also contributed to many other salt water fly fishing titles. He writes regularly for many major national magazines including *Salt Water Sportsman, Fly Fishing in Saltwaters* and *Saltwater Fly Fishing*.

Eric B. Burnley has been an outdoor writer for 25 years with articles and photos appearing in many national and regional publications. He is the author of *Surf Fishing the Atlantic Coast*. He also operates a guide service and manages a tackle shop in Norfold, Virginia.

Mitch Chagnon, a native of Rhode Island, has plied the waters of New England for over 40 years. He is a well-respected charter captain who possesses an intimate knowledge of both offshore and inshore grounds, and works closely with various conservation and sport fishing groups. In addition to his chartering work, Chagnon lectures at many sporting shows and is a field representative for the Berkley Outdoors Technology Group.

Peter Cooper, Jr. has fished in salt water extensively for over 40 years and is recognized as a pioneer of salt water fly fishing in Louisiana. He has been that state's regional staffer for *Salt Water Sportsman* magazine since 1990 and a full-time freelance outdoor writer since 1989.

Angelo Cuanang, a freelance writer, photographer and a regional editor for *Salt Water Sportsman* has had his articles and photos appear in many sportfishing magazines. He has also appeared in or hosted several TV shows and videos. Angelo has written two books, *Sturgeon* and *San Francisco Bay Striper*.

Nick Curcione is an outdoor writer, photographer, lecturer and instructor with more than 30 years of angling experience. Nick's writing credits are extensive and include numerous articles in local, national and international publications. He has also written four books.

Ray Dittenhoefer, a former National Freediving and Spearfishing champion, has learned a great deal about fish behavior through diving. He has been sportfishing for over 30 years. Ray began writing for *Salt Water Sportsman* in 1989 and has written for many publications since.

Barry Gibson is the Editor of *Salt Water Sportsman* magazine and has been a charter boat captain in Boothbay Harbor, Maine, since 1971. He has served as a government fishery manager, has fished extensively in North and South America, and contributes to a variety of outdoor publications.

Jim Hendricks, a native of southern California, has fished the local waters his entire life. His specialty is inshore fishing. He is a frequent contributor to numerous sportfishing publications including *Salt Water Sportsman* and *South Coast Sportfishing* and is Editor of *Trailer Boats* magazine.

Lefty Kreh has been an active outdoor writer and photographer for more than 40 years and has written for *Salt Water Sportsman* for 34 years. He has written for almost every major magazine in this country and abroad. Lefty has starred in many fly fishing videos and television shows, and is the author of several books, including *Salt Water Fly Fishing* and *Salt Water Fly Patterns*.

Bob McNally is a full-time outdoor writer living near Jacksonville, Florida. He has written over 4,500 magazine articles for every important outdoor publication, and is the author of 11 outdoor books. He travels in excess of 50,000 miles annually pursuing fish for his writing/photography/broadcast work.

Boyd Pfeiffer is a nationally known writer/photographer known for his skills with and knowledge of fresh and salt water tackle. He has worked for *The Washington Post*, written for 50 outdoor magazines, received over 60 awards for his writing and photography and written 14 books, including *The Compleat Surfcaster*.

John E. Phillips has written and sold 19 books, thousands of newspaper columns, magazines articles and photos. John is the Outdoor Writer for the *Birmingham Post-Herald* newspaper and other regional publications. His work also appears in national publications like *Salt Water Sportsman* and *Outdoor Life*.

George Poveromo, a Senior Editor with *Salt Water Sportsman* magazine since 1983, is a nationally recognized sportfishing expert who has fished many places through out the world. He writes the monthly Tactics & Tackle column for *Salt Water Sportsman*, in addition to numerous fishing features. George is also the producer and host of the *Salt Water Sportsman* National Seminar Series, and the High Hook line of how-to sportfishing videos.

Tom Richardson is Managing Editor of *Salt Water Sportsman* magazine. In addition to his photo and article contributions to *SWS*, Richardson is a freelance photographer and writer, as well as a masthead contributor to the internet fishing magazine *Reel-Time*. In 1994 he won first prize in the Salt Water Magazine category of the Outdoor Writers' Association of America's writing contest.

Allan J. (Al) Ristori has been fishing for over a half century. Ristori has written thousands of magazine articles and has long served as a regional editor for *Salt Water Sportsman*, where his first national article was published in 1965. Ristori is also the author of *North American Saltwater Fishing; The Saltwater Fish Identifier;* and *Fishing for Bluefish*. He's fished over much of the world, holds several world records and is a Coast Guard licensed charter boat captain.

Michael A. Rivlin is an environmental journalist with a special interest in marine and estuarine conservation issues. He is former Field Editor of *National Fisherman*, and Editor of *Estuarian*, a newsletter about habitat conservation in the Hudson-Raritan. Rivlin lives, works and fishes on the shores of Sandy Hook Bay, NJ.

Jim Rizzuto is author of five books and over 2,000 articles; he has written about fishing in Hawaii for 35 years for publications in the U.S., New Zealand, Australia, Japan, England, Italy and South Africa.

Bill Roecker was born in Madison, WI and began fishing at the age of four. Raised in Eugene, OR, he has been a logger, poet, hang glider pilot and a university professor, and is currently a writer and videomaker in Oceanside, CA.

Ray Rychonovksy, an award-winning writer and photographer, has been fishing most of his life. He has written for many of the major outdoor magazines, and he is Past President of the Outdoor Writers' Association of California. He is the author of *The Troller's Handbook*.

Robert Sloan has worked as a photojournalist for 17 years, with articles in national magazines such as *Field & Stream* and *Salt Water Sportsman*. He has been the Outdoors Editor of the *Beaumont Enterprise* newspaper for nine years. He specializes in salt water angling and has had stories published from around the world.

Mark Sosin is an award-winning writer, photographer and TV producer. More than 3,000 of his articles have appeared in major magazines, and he has authored 24 books on the outdoors. He has been Senior Editor at *Salt Water Sportsman* since 1991. Mark is also the producer and host of "*Mark Sosin's Saltwater Journal,*" director of the *Billfish Foundation* and Past President of the Outdoor Writers' Association of America.

Photo & Illustration Credits

PHOTOGRAPHERS

(Note: T=Top, C=Center, B=Bottom, L=Left, R=Right, I=Inset)

Andy Anderson
Mountain Home, ID
© Andy Anderson: cover background, pp. 3TC, 4C, 42-43, 58-59

Joel Arrington
Raleigh, NC
© Joel Arrington: pp. 94, 97

Chip Bates
Old Lyme, CT
© Chip Bates: p. 98

Scott Boyan
Nahant, MA
© Scott Boyan: pp. 157, 160

William Boyce
Saugus, CA
© William Boyce: pp. 5TL, 41, 130-131

Dick Brown
Harvard, MA
© Dick Brown: pp. 30-31 all

Hanson Carroll
Islamorada, FL
© Hanson Carroll: pp. 4T, 18, 28, 79

Bruce Coleman, Inc.
New York, NY
© Tony Arruza: pp. 3B, 118-119
© S. L. Craig, Jr.: pp. 5T, 54

Pete Cooper, Jr.
Buras, LA
© Pete Cooper, Jr.: pp. 82, 117

Angelo Cuanang
South San Francisco, CA
© Angelo Cuanang: pp. 61, 149, 150

Ray Dittenhoefer
Beaufort, SC
© Ray Dittenhoefer: p. 62

Richard Gibson
Pompano Beach, FL
© Richard Gibson/Hi-Seas Photography, Inc.: pp. 123, 156

Jim Hendricks
Downey, CA
© Jim Hendricks: pp. 4B, 109, 112

Kenneth J. Howard
San Anselmo, CA
© Kenneth J. Howard: back cover BC

Scott Kerrigan
Wilton Manors, FL
© Scott Kerrigan: pp. 9, 127

Gary Kramer
Willows, CA
© Gary Kramer: cover BR, back cover BR

Lefty Kreh
Hunt Valley, MD
© Lefty Kreh: p. 80

Bill Lindner
Minneapolis, MN
© Bill Lindner: cover BL, pp. 23, 36-37

David Linkiewicz
Chandler, AZ
© David Linkiewicz: pp. 170, 172

Bob McNally
Jacksonville, FL
© Bob McNally: p. 124

Ron McPeak
Battle Ground, WA
© Ron McPeak: p. 113

Brian O'Keefe
Bend, OR
© Brian O'Keefe: pp. 12-13

Bob O'Shaughnessy
Boston, MA
© Bob O'Shaughnessy: pp. 24, 38

C. Boyd Pfeiffer
Phoenix, MD
© C. Boyd Pfeiffer: pp. 4TR, 72, 74-76 all

John E. Phillips
Fairfield, AL
© John E. Phillips: back cover BL, pp. 5B, 102, 103, 104, 146, 161, 163

George Poveromo
Parkland, FL
© George Poveromo: pp. 5C, 90-91, 91I, 126, 136, 138 all, 140, 141, 142

Tom Richardson
Brookline, MA
© Tom Richardson: pp. 8, 107

Al Ristori
Manasquan Park, NJ
© Al Ristori: cover BC, pp. 50, 64, 152 both, 154

Michael A. Rivlin
Highlands, NJ
© Michael A. Rivlin: p. 165 all

Jim Rizzuto
Kamuela, HI
© Jim Rizzuto: p. 171

David J. Sams/Texas Inprint
Dallas, TX
© David J. Sams/Texas Inprint: p. 68

Dave Shepherd
Quincy, MA
© Dave Shepherd: pp. 33-34 all, 166, 168

Robert Sloan
Beaumont, TX
© Robert Sloan: back cover TL, pp. 3BC, 69 both, 71 both, 84-85

Sam Talarico
Mohnton, PA
© Sam Talarico: back cover TC, TR, pp. 3T, 6-7, 49

Earl & Deborah Waters
Homosassa, FL
© Earl & Deborah Waters: p. 39

ILLUSTRATORS

Chris Armstrong
Jacksonville, FL
© Chris Armstrong: pp. 21, 44-45, 86-87, 92, 108, 120-121, 129, 133-134 all

Dan Daly
Camden, ME
© Dan Daly: p. 173

John Carroll Doyle
Charleston, SC
© John Carroll Doyle: cover painting

John Dyess
Glendale, MO
© John Dyess: p. 137 all

Peter Goadby
Pymble, Australia
© HarperCollins Publishers: Endpaper illustrations

Steve T. Goione
Toms River, NJ
© Steve T. Goione: p. 148

David McHose
West Palm Beach, FL
© David McHose: pp. 16-17 all, 143, 144 both, 145

Salt Water Sportsman
Boston, MA
© *Salt Water Sportsman*: p. 164

Dave Shepherd
Quincy, MA
© Dave Shepherd: pp. 33-34 all, 166, 168